HOW DO WE LOOK?

A CAMERA OBSCURA BOOK

HOW DO WE LOOK?

Resisting Visual Biopolitics

FATIMAH TOBING RONY

DUKE UNIVERSITY PRESS   DURHAM AND LONDON   2022

Printed in the United States of America on acid-free paper ∞
Project editor: Annie Lubinsky
Designed by Aimee C. Harrison
Typeset in Arno Pro by Westchester Publishing Services

Library of Congress Cataloging-in-Publication Data
Names: Rony, Fatimah Tobing, author.
Title: How do we look? : resisting visual biopolitics / Fatimah Tobing Rony.
Other titles: Camera obscura book (Duke University Press)
Description: Durham : Duke University Press, 2021. | Series: A camera obscura
book | Includes bibliographical references and index.
Identifiers: LCCN 2021012166 (print) | LCCN 2021012167 (ebook)
ISBN 9781478013679 (hardcover)
ISBN 9781478014607 (paperback)
ISBN 9781478021902 (ebook)
Subjects: LCSH: Women in popular culture—Indonesia. | Women—
Indonesia—Social conditions. | Women in mass media. | Mass media—
Political aspects—Indonesia. | Biopolitics—Indonesia. | Ethnographic films—
Social aspects—United States. | Documentary films—Social aspects—United
States. | BISAC: SOCIAL SCIENCE / Feminism & Feminist Theory | PERFORMING
ARTS / Film / History & Criticism
Classification: LCC HQ1752 .R66 2021 (print) | LCC HQ1752 (ebook) |
DDC 305.409598—dc23
LC record available at https://lccn.loc.gov/2021012166
LC ebook record available at https://lccn.loc.gov/2021012167

Cover art: Safina (Kirana Larasati) in a faceoff with schoolboy
bullies, in a still by Dianti Andajani, from the omnibus film
Perempuan Punya Cerita (*Chants of Lotus*, 2007), produced by
Nia Dinata. Cinematography by Teoh Gay Hian.

To Saenah

Contents

Acknowledgments

So many people have helped me in myriad ways. I offer thanks to my parents, who gave me the keys to the world of reading and research. I am grateful to them for their sacrifice and support. I offer appreciation to all my teachers for their generosity and guidance. I offer heartfelt gratitude to all of my family in Indonesia and all over the world. *Terima kasih atas dukungan dan bantuan keluarga.* Any mistakes and omissions in this book are entirely my own.

I am indebted to my editor, Ken Wissoker, at Duke University Press, who believed in this project long before it was even written, and to Camera Obscura series editor Patricia White for her acumen and kind exigence. To those who tirelessly read early drafts, I thank you, especially Anitra Grisales and Timothy Hoekstra, who edited several versions, as well as Kellie Jones, Kristen Hatch, Susan Maldovan, and Bliss Cua Lim. Credit goes as well as to editors Joshua Gutterman Tranen, Elizabeth Ault, and Annie Lubinsky of Duke University Press, and to Diana L. Witt for indexing.

Acknowledgments go to the libraries and archives, and the scholars, curators, librarians, and archivists who gave so much of their time to me, including the late Mary Wolfskill of the Library of Congress; Gregory Jecman and Ginger Crockett Hammer of the National Gallery of Art; Jodi Hauptman and Starr Figura of the Museum of Modern Art; Wolfgang Apelt and Julia Besten of the Archive and Museum Foundation of the United Evangelical Mission in Wuppertal, Germany; Tomoko Sato, Marcus Mucha, and Sarah Mucha of the Mucha Foundation; the Bibliothèque nationale de France and the Bibliothèque historique de la ville de Paris in France; Emilee Mathews and Jenna Dufour of the Langson Library at the University of California, Irvine; and Laurie Sears of the University of Washington, Seattle.

Much appreciation goes to two production houses for their generosity and for providing me with a community of filmmakers. The first one is Kalyana Shira Films: thank you Nia Dinata, Constantin Papadimitriou, and your entire team. The second one is Flashcuts: thank you Walt Louie, Eurie Chung, Emma Berliner, and Fred.

I would like to thank those who invited me to give talks that helped me think critically through ideas that became a part of this book, including Gregg Mitman, Kelly Wilder, Sara Stukenbrock and the Max Planck Institute; Ariel Rogers of Northwestern University; Deborah Dorotinsky and David Wood of Universidad Nacional Autonóma de México; Renee Hoogland of Wayne State University; Kathleen McHugh of the University of California, Los Angeles; Lisa Cartwright of the University of California, San Diego; Sophia Wagner Serrano, Lorien Hunter, Anikó Imre, Akira Mizuta Lippit, and Nitin Govil at the University of Southern California; and Armando Garcia and Gonzalo Lamana of the University of Pittsburgh. I also thank Pooja Rangan, Rachmi Diyah Larasati, Lan Duong, and Viola Lasmana for collaborating with me on conference panels and for an open exchange of ideas. Thank you Raquel Loran Hill and Alice Pawley for always keeping me accountable!

I am grateful to all my former students, including Shelleen Greene and Mariana Botey, and especially to Corella DiFede, who opened my eyes to theories of biopolitics. Research for this book was made possible by grants from the School of Humanities at the University of California, Irvine. Deep appreciation goes to Julia Lupton, Judy Wu, Amanda Swain, Douglas Haynes, Tyrus Miller, and Andrzej Warminski for their support. Thank you to Film and Media Studies, Visual Studies, and the School of Humanities at the University of California, Irvine for all the assistance and encouragement, especially Desha Dauchan, Aglaya Glebova, Lucas Hilderbrand, Victoria Johnson, Trevor Jue, Heather Layton, Adrienne Lipscomb, Sylvia Meza-Tallada, Nikki Normandia, Elizabeth Pace, Allison Perlman, Clara Quijano, Stan Woo-Sam, and Eva Yonas. For kinship, sustenance, and faith:

Cesar José Alvarez and Steven Wicht; Kellie Jones and Guthrie Ramsay; Jodi Hauptman and Greg Clarick; Chantal Riss and Rachid Bachi; Carol Ockman and Margaret Waller; Angela Dalle Vacche; Susan Lee; Miya Elise Desjardins; Eileen Cabiling; Carol Young and Peter Kim; Helen Yoon; Jane Oak and Harry Yoon; Helen Haeyoung Lee and Todd Jones; Cindy Lin; Dot and Lloyd Hoekstra; Gene and Carolyn LeMaire; Misha Hoekstra; Kinch and Heather Hoekstra; Katie and Tom King; Ursula Angell; Tony and Amy Boch; Azusa Oda, Akira Boch, and Kiyona Boch; and Marie-Josée Cantin-Johnson and Kirk Johnson.

Finally, my greatest debt is to the family that lived with me through the writing of the book. I thank Tim for his never-ending respect for the project and for wryly comprehending that, as André Breton once put it, *"la littérature est un des plus tristes chemins qui mènent à tout."* I thank Saenah for bringing me joy, creativity, and inspiration, and for always asking me the question writers never want to hear: "Is your book done yet?"

Saenah, it's done.

TONGUE

I hear her voice first, my mother whispering to me to wake up. It is still dark, not yet dawn. She is holding a kerosene lamp, and there is a big black shadow of a man at the door. "Daughter, you must get dressed." "Hurry," the man waiting at the door says. "The boat is leaving soon." My mother takes out her comb and, bending down, parts my hair in the middle and briskly braids it. She wipes my face with a cloth, and then lifts my chin and looks me in the eyes: "Listen to the man. May God bless you." I look up at her, questioning, but I don't speak. She says, "We will be together again soon," but she looks away when the man's coarse hand grabs mine and pulls me away. I can't believe that my feet are moving, but there I am, walking out the door, past my father, who does not get up from his mat, out of the only house I have ever known, past the shadows of my sleeping brothers and sisters. Only much later—as I had all the time in the world to think about it, after countless nights of crying and shivering from the bitter cold as I lay in the black hold of the very large ship that took me away from my small little world to Paris,

France—only much, much later did I realize that my mother had sold me off to pay for my father's gambling debts.

I don't blame her. I was the oldest and I was a girl.

When I arrive in France, I see snow for the first time. I look up at the falling snowflakes as the large man in charge puts a handwritten sign around my neck, and then pushes me out to walk onto the pier. I wait an eternity. Nobody comes to meet me. I return to find the large man, but the ship has left, and I am all alone, until a policeman picks me up and takes me to the station. Later, the servant of Madame comes to collect me.

"What's her name?" he asks the policeman.

"Hell if I know. Call her whatever you want. You can call her Broom for all I care."

The servant looks at me and says, "The mistress has been wanting a *négresse* from the islands. We'll call you Annah. Annah la Javanaise."

And straightaway I lost my name and my mother tongue. I never hear my language again, except in the few instances when I dream that I am back home and free.

How Do We Look?

All your buried corpses are beginning to speak.
—JAMES BALDWIN, *I Am Not Your Negro*

The loss of stories sharpens the hunger for them. So it is tempting
to fill in the gaps and to provide closure where there is none. To
create a space for mourning where it is prohibited. To fabricate a
witness to a death not much noticed.
—SAIDIYA HARTMAN, "Venus in Two Acts"

ANNAH AND JUMILAH

Our story is inspired by a brown-skinned girl, age thirteen, who is called
Annah, *une négresse,* or a black girl. The year is 1893; the place is Paris, France.
The girl is found wandering the streets with a handwritten sign around her
neck stating that she is a package for a certain opera singer, Madame Nina
Pack, who had requested "une négresse" from the East Indies to be a maid.
Unhappy with Annah's housework, Pack fires her. Annah is sent to the studio of postimpressionist painter Paul Gauguin, known for his predilection
for black and brown girls. There she is forced to service him sexually and to
provide labor as a domestic servant, until she runs away in 1894. In a painting of 1893, *Aita tamari vahine Judith te parari,* Paul Gauguin painted Annah's
nude portrait over the nude portrait of another thirteen-year-old girl, this

one white, Judith Molard, whose mother forbade her from continuing to model for Gauguin (Figure 1.1).

To understand the story that enmeshed the girl who was called Annah, one has to go back to 1889, to four young Javanese girls dancing, at the Javanese Pavilion of the Exposition Universelle, in the shadow of the Eiffel Tower. When the bejeweled Wakiem, Seriem, Taminah, and Soekia danced, French observers mythologized the girls as harem dancers and nubile courtesans from the Solo (Surakarta) court.[1] These girls became so famous that it started a French vogue for "la Java"—*faire la java* still means to have a party, to get wicked—and it is that myth or story that was imposed on the thirteen-year-old girl Annah in 1893. To call Annah "la Javanaise" was to call her "the wicked girl." By metonymy, she was hung with the name, like the title of a circus performer. Except there are two things to point out: Annah was probably not Javanese, and indeed, Annah was most likely not her given name. A visual myth held her in place that justified her exploitation and likely early death, a concept that I call *visual biopolitics*.

Now fast forward to 1965, Indonesia, and the beginning of the autocratic reign of military general Suharto. There is a dancer from Java. Her name is Jumilah, but like Annah, another name is forced upon her. Jumilah is snatched up and tortured at a time when women dancers seen as allied with Gerakan Wanita Indonesia, the Indonesian Women's Movement, and thus unruly feminists, began to be scapegoated as the scourge of a righteous nation. This formative representation, seen in the newspaper media, radio reports, monuments, history books, and later Indonesian cinema, depicts the dancer as a monstrous, sexual communist female. In I. G. P. Wiranegara's documentary film of 2006, *Menyemai Terang Dalam Kelam*, Jumilah testifies how she was seized and forced to confess to crimes that she did not commit (Figure 2.9). The soldiers beat her to force her to confess that she was the supposedly wanton and wanted person named Atikah Jamilah, when her name was actually Jumilah. They forced her to declare that she had castrated and sadistically tortured government military officers and had a sexual orgy with their murdered bodies, when she had done no such thing.

This story, fabricated by the future regime and visualized in film, national monuments, history books, and government speeches, justified the creation of the Indonesian republic under the dictatorship of President Suharto, who used it to legitimize his seizure of power and the subsequent torture, rape, and genocide of up to a million people labeled members of the Partai Komunis Indonesia (PKI, the Communist Party of Indonesia), and the subsequent aftermath for children of political prisoners who are cast out from society and denied civil rights. But along with committing these heinous acts against humanity, the Suharto regime erased the freedom to question state power. Remaking history and visually archiving life in this way annihilates political imagination and puts fear or apathy in its place.

Since 1965, this image has been constructed and circulated over and over again; even to the present day, it is difficult to erase the taint of communism and its association with a dancing wanton woman from Indonesian minds. Virulently anticommunist and thus firmly in the US camp that supported and abetted the coup, President Suharto exploited the thousands of islands rich in vast resources of oil, tin, coffee, cotton, rubber, tea, timber, and labor. The nation's postcolonial economy embraced a vast expansion of capitalism and inaugurated the reign of homo economicus, the masculinist advocate of free-market capitalism and hyperconsumerism, which was used to justify the military dictatorship, shored up by the story of the PKI dancer as killer woman.[2] The United States has a culture that is violent to the lives of people of color due to the legacy of black chattel slavery, colonization of Indian lands, and American ignorance of history; Indonesia, even under Reformasi (the post-Suharto Reformation), has not adequately confronted its own killings from 1965 onward, and thus the trope of the dancing, murderous, sexual woman is used again and again and became imprinted in the nation's deep unconscious. To see the creation of the Republic of Indonesia is to see the battle against the unruly female dancer by the righteous Suharto-led army, much like the good-versus-evil Balinese dance of the good dragon Barong pitted against the monstrous witch Rangda. Such negative images become, then, what James Baldwin describes as "the fixed star" by which we learn to navigate our worlds.[3]

I begin this book by introducing two mythoi of two girls from two different centuries, both false. The tapestry of images (in painting, photography, historical monuments, film) of how Indonesian women are represented is transnational and globalized. The stories that are told through the network of what I call visual biopolitics, which makes certain populations more vulnerable to child rape, violence, or early death, have only become more entrenched, despite the rise of independence movements and the end of the Cold War. Visual biopolitics is the system, shored up by iconographies of justification found in photography, cinema, television, national monuments, and the internet, that underscores preexisting structural race and gender representations in language, politics, and the unconscious. It is an indictment by sight, to paraphrase filmmaker Ava DuVernay.[4] It is the concatenation and web of imaging networks that systematize who is allowed to live and who is allowed to die and, by extension, who is allowed to be raped and who is not.

In *The Third Eye: Race, Cinema, and Ethnographic Spectacle*, I wrote about how colonialism created a divide between the Historical and the Ethnographic, the Civilized and the Savage, and how these divides were inscribed in film, photography, and other visual technologies. These categories served biopolitics by producing a logic whereby the life of one group was nourished at the expense of another. Much to my dismay, more than twenty years on, I find that this divide is just as persistent and pernicious in our era of neoliberalism and globalization. In this book I trace the legacy of one particular aspect of visual biopolitics—the representation of the Indonesian woman—into the twenty-first century of globalization. I chose this particular representation because of my own investment as a filmmaker looking for representations of myself, which I could never find growing up in the United States. To my surprise, this figure is contested, highly vilified, and politicized, and has served the visual biopolitics of the colonial period from nationalism, to postcolonialism, to the present-day era of neoliberalism. I show why these images have such a strong valence and how they still persist.

Building on *The Third Eye*, this book ties critical race theory to a legacy in visual anthropology whose vast and varied archive I identify and interpret. The genealogy of this representation is based in historical and anthropological discourses of primitivism/savagery/colonialism/exoticism/genocide. The specificity of the figure of the Indonesian woman and the reality of Indonesian women artists, including myself, is inextricably tied to the genealogy of colonial/ethnographic discourse, which is why I pay particular attention to ethnographic film pioneer Margaret Mead, whose filming and editing of dancing Indonesian women reveals a particular network of looking that traces its foundations in colonialism, tourism, exoticism, and primitivism. Joshua Oppenheimer, the director of *The Act of Killing* (2012), is the documentary heir to this legacy, and this explains the acts of resistance of the dancing Indonesian woman that I will show in my discussion of Rachmi Diyah Larasati's book *The Dance That Makes You Vanish*. The Indonesian woman (the model, the dancer, the object of display) is not just an example of visual biopolitics: it is a palimpsest like no other, through which the centrality of the visuality of display, painting, photography, and film to biopolitics is established.[5] My goal is to show how discourses of resistance in acts of female creativity and embodiment can undermine and potentially topple such genealogies.

This book, then, is also about acts of resistance to visual biopolitics, specifically but not exclusively using examples from film. While I historicize and theorize the contexts and mechanisms of visual biopolitics and the archiving of the Indonesian woman and the divides and subjectivities it has perpetuated, I also show how those same tools can be and are being used to challenge power. Our work is to examine the representations so that we can visualize ourselves, in terms of both theory and practice.

In a 2009 interview, Jill Lepore declared that her task as a historian is to understand the vocabulary of justification: "I'm interested in our capacity to justify acts of tremendous, unspeakable cruelty. It's not obvious, at least not to me. And the way I have always tried to puzzle it out is by thinking mainly about language. What, literally, is the vocabulary of justification?"[6] Instead of language and the early eighteenth-century histories of North America that Lepore was describing, this book examines visual representations of and by Indonesian women within the histories of colonialism, postcolonialism, and biopolitics. Instead of words, I trace images across media as diverse as painting, photography, and film to understand visual and textual vocabularies of justification.

Media from Indonesia, the fourth most populous country in the world, and the most populous Muslim country in the world, are largely ignored in the field of film and media studies, and yet studying Indonesian media provides an interesting test case for how visual biopolitics can be dismantled. During the period of relative freedom after 1998, when the country suffered an economic crisis that led to the withdrawal of Suharto from the presidency, the figure of the Indonesian woman became the subject of much innovation in filmmaking, production, distribution, and exhibition, a subject that I explore later in this book. Finally, as a filmmaker who has worked with an Indonesian production house involved in this movement, I also provide a practical perspective on a topic and a field that I know experientially. The broader application of the theory of visual biopolitics is developed through the specific case of the Indonesian woman.

Visual biopolitics does not just produce empty signifiers: these visual myths contain the resemblances of the historical real. Visual biopolitics collapses the effects of the present, past, and future, and it is therein that an artist, a filmmaker, a writer can wield and take back her power. Thus, what shook me about the gorgeous painting *Aita tamari vahine Judith te parari* by Gauguin of Annah la Javanaise, recontextualized more than 125 years later, is the dead girl at the center of the painting, whose real name and origin we do not know, but who called out to me nevertheless.

Do not leave me in the archive.

The genesis of theories of biopolitics lay in an overlooked section of Michel Foucault's *The History of Sexuality*, vol. 1, that began to be read closely in the 1990s. The chapter, "Right of Death and Power over Life," described biopolitics as a new form of modern state power. If the sovereign could command deaths with "off with his head" impunity, power under the modern state was more secretive, purporting to foster life but also disallowing it to the point of death. Power was woven into the fabric of the commonplace, inhering in two ways, as disciplinary power over the body as machine (the prison, the police, the military, schools, hospitals, the factory, the plantation) and as regulatory power over the body as species (the medical, scientific, and sociological institutions that regularize population control, mortality, effects of environment, biological disabilities, etc.).[7]

Central to biopolitics is the production of a norm. In a lecture in the book *Society Must Be Defended*, Foucault writes, "The norm is something that can be applied to both a body one wishes to discipline and a population one wishes to regularize."[8] But this presents a conundrum: how does the democracy make in/visible who will be allowed to live and who will be allowed to die? What I call the archiving of life is synonymous with this construction of the norm, seen in the ethnographic film *Trance and Dance in Bali*, directed by anthropologists Margaret Mead and Gregory Bateson (discussed in chapter 2), and the innumerable reels of colonial footage archiving the movements of "primitive" peoples, or colonial films, like those assemblaged together in Vincent Monnikendam's found-footage feature film *Mother Dao* (discussed in chapter 3). This archive reinforces, reassures, and creates an ever-fixed mark of who is allied with life and who is allied with death. And this polarity between the Savage and the Civilized continues even in acclaimed new films, like Joshua Oppenheimer's performative documentary *The Act of Killing* (discussed in chapter 2). Foucault states that it is racism that provides the norm or "the indispensable precondition that allows someone to be killed," a killing that can simply be "the fact of exposing someone to death, increasing the risk of death for some people, or, quite simply, political death, expulsion, rejection, and so on."[9] Biopolitics means not just the politics of whether one lives or dies, but the terms upon which one is allowed to live.

Foucault's description of the norm that allows one to be killed is relevant for any person of color growing up in the United States, as well as for the Indonesian New Order regime's systematic use of violent torture, rape, imprisonment, and death against anyone labeled leftist; it also describes women's sexuality in Indonesia and how the state and the local religious culture make one vulnerable to premature death. The sovereign right to kill still inheres in modern state power through what Giorgio Agamben calls states of exception, in which the law protecting citizens is suspended in declared states of emergency and war.[10] Ironically, although biopolitics' purported goal is sustaining life through regulation, at the crux of biopolitics is this aporia: certain populations are allowed to die at the expense of other populations.

To make that palatable, visual biopolitics interpellates citizens, so that we perceive these norms as a natural, God-given right. Here I find a great source in the critical race theory of thinkers like Sylvia Wynter. Drawing upon Frantz Fanon and neuroscience, Wynter explains that we humans use stories as a way of inventing ourselves as a biological species, with story lines like Darwinian evolution, Malthusian overpopulation, consumerism, and ghetto communities posited as common sense.[11] We are social beings that narrate. Life as seen through biology is undergirded by story. To Wynter, I add that we sew the bios into the mythos, in the visual image web that makes up visual biopolitics. The particular narration that we have chosen, one that undergirds modernity and the secular liberal subject that she refers to as homo economicus, is monohumanism, a Darwinian Malthusian one that narrates the world into symbolic life and symbolic death, or what I have described in my own work as those who are seen as historifiable, belonging to history, and those who are seen as ethnographiable, or belonging to ethnography. Or, plainly stated, the Civilized versus the Savage.[12] The archiving of life in biopolitics informs the way we see and interpret ourselves: it undergirds the story and it makes the story seem like common sense.

Theory itself has its biopolitics: Alexander Weheliye lambasts how critical theory has ignored the work of black feminist theorists Sylvia Wynter and Hortense Spillers, who delineate how the Human is, in fact, the norm: the white male allied with life. The discourse of race functions by determining who is to be conceived of as Human, Subhuman, or Nonhuman, Visible and In/visible.[13] Race is crucial to the subjectivity of what "human" means: Agamben's "bare life," or life reduced to biology and deprived of rights, and Foucault on "biopolitics," naturalize race and overlook what Weheliye terms "the racializing assemblages" that affect difference, creating Man (capital M) or the human as the universalizing Self. The rational individual Subject, in other words, is still aligned with white male subjectivity. To race, I would also add gender and sexuality, extending who is allowed to live and who is let die to who is allowed to be raped and who is not—rape and death often being perpetrated together.

The stories that we tell about ourselves can be classified as genres, and like genres are possibly capable of being transformed. Wynter argues, "We need to speak instead of our *genres of being human*. Once you redefine being human in hybrid *mythoi* and *bios* terms, and therefore in terms that draw attention to the relativity and original multiplicity of our *genres* of being human, all of a sudden what you begin to recognize is the central role that our discursive *formations*, aesthetic fields, and systems of knowledge must play in the performative enactment of all such genres of being hybridly human."[14] This textualization, a kind of weaving or storytelling of life, is part of what I call visual biopolitics. Categories and ideologies work to designate populations that are allowed to die or even encouraged to die. The visual underscores these markers of difference by telling us what to see.

Wynter illuminates that homo economicus is a global phenomenon among middle classes all around the world who have embraced this model from the West in a neocolonial process of interpellation: "The West *reincorporate[s]* us neocolonially, and thereby mimetically, by telling us that the problem with us *wasn't* that we'd been *imperially* subordinated, *wasn't* that we'd been both socioculturally dominated and economically exploited, but that we were *underdeveloped*. The West said: 'Oh, well, no longer be a *native* but come and be Man like us! Become *homo economicus!*'"[15] The Civilized versus the Savage has thus become the enlightened versus the undeveloped (or what Wynter calls the selected versus the "dysselected"). Life became the object of vigilance by the state in modern society, bolstered by visual discourse that renders certain populations more likely to encounter early death and sexual violence.

And now, in the context of neoliberalism and globalization, the colonies are no longer distant but situated within the metropolises. Death-worlds, to paraphrase Achille Mbembe, are contained under and near the overpasses on which those who have, those who matter, drive every day.[16] This is one major way visual biopolitics has changed under globalization: the ghetto of the casbah is no longer walled off from the European quarter, thus making vocabularies of visualization even more important for the state to control and restrain. While the actual walls keeping one group in or out may have crumbled, other structures of power have taken their place. We can understand the persistence of the subjective gaze and the disciplining of the bodies of populations through analyzing visual biopolitics, the visual and aural constructions that govern life and death, the body, subjectivity, and relations of periphery and center. In a sense, the visual—whether it is painting, photography, or film—mythologizes the work of biopolitics. Moreover, biopower operates through ways of seeing, valorizations of the visual, and hegemonic representational practices.

Ruth Wilson Gilmore's definition of racism expresses the function of racialized biopolitics: "Racism, specifically, is the state-sanctioned or extralegal production and exploitation of group-differentiated vulnerability to premature death."[17] Visual biopolitics is what shores up this racism so that it appears to be and becomes dominant power's common sense, instinct, and science. In particular, it defines the moment before the trigger is pulled; the moment when a female dancer is grabbed off the street to be tortured and scapegoated; the moment when a child worker is labeled Javanese and thus rape-able. What vocabularies or stories of justification occur in that moment when a person decides that he needs to kill another? Visual biopolitics helps to create the categories of people whose lives and histories should be valued and those whose should not—of whose lives matter.

How do we look? My understanding of visual biopolitics is inspired by two practices of thinking. The first body of theory is by those who engage in what I have called the third eye, akin to Du Bois's double consciousness, or Fanon's third space, emerging from postcolonial theory and black studies, and expanded upon by James Baldwin, Sylvia Wynter, Saidiya Hartman, and Alexander Weheliye, which develop biopolitics into the realms of visual culture and gender and race. In describing paradigms of looking, I turn to critical race theory, a theory derived from the experiential, and thus a living, breathing theory, where the past is always prologue, to paraphrase the title of the book by Sohail Daulatzai.[18] This is the heart of my writing: when denied humanity and thus symbolic life—by language, by culture, by history, by common sense—how does one regain subjectivity or agency? How does that change? So although my topic is ostensibly the figure of the Indonesian woman, what I am describing can be used to interrogate other systems of visualizing power to create other acts of resistance.

Following that purpose, how can one resist visual biopolitics? In particular, I look at the practice of reading in the archive of art history, with the example of Annah la Javanaise; in the missionary archive, with the example of the photograph of Raja Pontas; through dance, in films as seemingly disparate as the ethnographic film of Margaret Mead and the contemporary art documentary of Joshua Oppenheimer; in the found-footage film in *Mother Dao* by Vincent Monnikendam, and in examples from contemporary Indonesian cinema made in the Reformasi (Reformation) period following Suharto's downfall in 1998, which use collective practice to transform the very notion of ideal viewer or auteur filmmaker. Critical to this theory of resistance is one of the most profound works resisting visual biopolitics that I have ever encountered, the dancer and choreographer Rachmi Diyah Larasati's book, *The Dance That Makes You Vanish: Cultural Reconstruction in Post-genocide Indonesia.*

The "you" in the title refers to both Larasati, a government dancer who was sent around the world to perform Javanese dance during the Suharto regime, and the "you" of her aunts, mother, and "sister" female dancers who went missing in the wake of the killings in Indonesia of 1965. Larasati has herself become, as she poignantly explains, a replica, the whole dancer who replaces those who were disappeared. As Larasati explains, unlike Baudrillard's simulacra of hyperreality, which are empty signifiers, the replicas of the bodies of dancers contain a trace of the dead: "The overlaid 'hyperreality,' despite its purported leveling and destruction of that which came before, is nonetheless inextricably tied to the historical 'real,' which remains embedded as collective unconscious, even as it is wiped from public discourse. Replica bodies, then, while defining the audience's perception of reality, necessarily take on uncanny resemblances to their forebears, creating flashes of vivid connection in which the unseen disappeared becomes visible, even if not always consciously readable as such."[19] I stress that visual biopolitics does not just produce empty signifiers: these visual myths contain the resemblances of the historical real.

My task in this book is to gently unravel the skein of visual vocabularies in media that reinforce biopolitics. My concern is in how visual materials across genre and time reinforce habitual ways of seeing and not seeing, but can also be used as resistance. In particular, I look at what happens when we are put in a place of impossible subjectivity. How can that become a space of empowerment? As I argue in *The Third Eye*, inspired by Frantz Fanon and W. E. B. Du Bois, there is a moment in the person of color's consciousness when we find ourselves sitting in an impossible space, what anthropologist Stefania Pandolfo has described as the Cut, or the thin line of modernity.[20] To constantly have to prove our humanity (to be at once patient and doctor) is exhausting and demoralizing, and yet because of that impossible space of subjectivity, we are able to critique and unsettle the matrix of biopolitics.

FABULATING

The archiving of life is a biopolitical endeavor: from anthropological archives like those of Margaret Mead and Gregory Bateson to cross-study so-called primitive tribes, to medical and colonial archives, to the genetic data popularized today for general consumerism and consumption, biopolitics showcases the archive as an absolute empirical apparatus. As a historian of media, I have always been aware of the fascinating cannibalism of the media consumer who is entertained by the retelling of the story of savagery[21] At the heart of one's endeavor lies the history of the image of the dead black girl's face, which is also the image of one's own face. At the center of "Venus in Two Acts," Saidiya Hartman's revelatory essay on the failure of the archive, is a cruelly murdered African girl on a slave ship. She is referred to in the archive and thus the history book as "Venus." As women of color reading the archive, we are also doubly injured: we cannot reach Venus, just as we cannot reach Annah, and so they die another death, one of silence. The tragedy that led to the abuse, exploitation, and sexual violence they experienced is still part of our culture today.

The archive of history is particularly cruel to black girls. As Hartman explains about US historical evidence, female slaves are often called Venus, and the archive has only this distorted trace of their subjectivities, and so the historian is in a dilemma: to write about Venus may be to keep perpetuating the silencing of her story. The Annahs and the Venuses are still present in the fact that thirteen-year-old black girls continue to be exploited and brutalized. They are trafficked for sexual exploitation, with Italy being the primary entry point for a prostitution trade that encompasses all the major cities of Europe. As Father Enzo Volpe, a priest who runs a center for migrant children in Palermo, Italy, states, "There's an extraordinary level of implicit racism here, and it's evident in the fact that there are no underage Italian girls working the streets. . . . Society dictates that it's bad to sleep with a girl of thirteen or fourteen years. But if she's African? . . . They don't think of her as a person."[22] This is the story of Annah and her great-great-granddaughters. This story, of the sale and trafficking of the black girl, has enormous political and economic relevance today.

How do we create subjectivity when it has been erased? Hartman presents a new possibility when the reader searches for stories of Venus in the archive:

The intention here isn't anything as miraculous as recovering the lives of the enslaved or redeeming the dead, but rather laboring to paint as full a picture of the lives of the captives as possible. This double gesture can be described as straining against the limits of the archive to write a cultural history of the captive, and, at the same time, enacting the impossibility of representing the lives of the captives precisely through the process of narration.

The method guiding this writing practice is best described as critical fabulation.[23]

Therefore, to dissect, analyze, and understand the images of people of color that have left them more vulnerable to premature death or sexual violence is to understand not only how we are mirrored in our societies, but also how to participate and take part in the making of art that will upset, challenge, and in Hartman's words, critically fabulate.[24]

Scholars and filmmakers have focused on many aspects of black representation. The scholarship around representations of black men has shown how D. W. Griffith's cinematic image of Gus, in what is considered the first great Hollywood feature film, *The Birth of a Nation* (1915), as a raping black monster, a bogeyman who lusts after innocent white virgins, continued in later images, such as the 1988 anti-Dukakis political ad that featured Willie Horton as another black monster. These, as scholar Michelle Alexander and filmmaker Ava DuVernay show, have affected the lives of black men and boys, such as seventeen-year-old Trayvon Martin, shot by George Zimmerman in 2012 on the pretext of self-defense, or George Floyd, who perished under the knee of Derek Chauvin, a Minneapolis police officer, in 2020.[25] I believe that we can begin a discourse around the study of visual biopolitics in critical race studies, and my project to look at what the representation of Indonesian women does and has done sheds light on visual biopolitics as a whole.

Indonesian film is a relatively understudied field, and yet I find many exciting films from Indonesia that also critically fabulate: diverse forms such as montage video found on YouTube that I compare to the found-footage feature by documentarian Vincent Monnikendam (discussed in chapter 3); or the multistory narrative and omnibus films produced by contemporary Indonesian filmmaker Nia Dinata (discussed in chapter 4), combined with new forms of distribution and exhibition.

I am passionate about examining how media is used to transform our minds and our world, both so that we can understand visual culture and history and so that we can make media that will transform visual culture. I have written this book from the point of view of someone who does film, in every sense of the word, as a film historian and as a filmmaker. Film is a perfect medium for critical fabulation because of its special relationship with time, reality, and realism. Born of the trace of what is recorded by the camera, the shutter opens, and what is fixed on the emulsification of the film is what passed or stood in front of the camera shutter, a ghostly trace. These imprints, these recordings, these traces, are then compiled, stitched, sutured together by an editor, to create an apparently organic beast that is actually inherently full of gaps and holes. "Persistence of vision" is how film theorists have explained how the viewer does not see the black spaces between the twenty-four frames per second. We put the images together and see the reality of the recording; but in truth, they are compiled by montage. Finally, the film that gets seen is not the one that the filmmaker makes, but the one that catalyzes and provokes the memory-scape of images, experiences, and sounds that make up the viewers' unconscious. Filmmakers can excite that combination and transform it, not merely by changing subject matter and narratives, but by triggering different temporal and spatial limits of the mind, by configuring new subjectivities.

Like Hartman, my goal is to show the limits of the archive: the limits of language that called her Annah, made her Javanese, and still calls her a mistress; the limits of ethnographic film that always already visualizes; the limit of the contemporary documentary film that still produces a subjectivity by and for homo economicus. My work here: to raid the archiving of life to write about critical fabulations, to show how we can make film as a form of critical fabulation.

DAE'ANNA'S EYES

St. Anthony, Minnesota, July 6, 2016. Her name is Lavish, given name Diamond Reynolds. She stares into the camera, her cell phone livestreaming onto her Facebook page: in the backseat behind her is her boyfriend, Philando Castile, dying, his white T-shirt soaked bright red with his blood. Through a window we see the shaking gun held by a police officer. Lavish is talking to him in a calm manner in an effort to de-escalate the policeman's panic. Underlying her attempt to pacify him, however, is another effort: to report to us, the viewer, what has just happened.

Please, officer, don't tell me that you just did that to him. You shot four bullets into him, sir. He was just getting his license and registration, sir.

Lavish calls the man waving a gun at her "sir." She volleys "sir" five times. The horror of this scene is that she cannot allow herself to react normally to the gunning down of her beloved: to scream, to cry, to grieve, to panic, to become angry.

How do we look? We must always be seeing with a third eye, the eye that rises out of one's mind and watches the scene, detached: I am watching myself trying to calm a cop; I am speaking in a clear, calm cadence; I am observing how to protect my four-year-old daughter, Dae'anna, in the backseat from seeing even more violence than Philando's possible death, that of my own death or hers. That is how the third eye works: it involves an interaction with the observer and another, and it is the watching of that interaction, the awareness of one's responses, that defines a third-eye experience. What happens in that moment when the police officer looks at an African American man and sees and decides that he must be annihilated? Even before the traffic stop, a story has already been impressed upon Philando Castile, to justify his murder, and the vocabulary of the story is the basis of and feeds into visual biopolitics.

There are three temporal zones here: the past, which taught Lavish that to be African American meant to always be faced with the possibility of a violent, dangerous reaction from police officers and other whites (James Baldwin once said to an uncomprehending Margaret Mead that he was born on a slave boat[26]); the present, in which the police officer is shouting and waving his gun at her; and the future, the growing up too fast of the little four-year-old Dae'anna with the impossibly big eyes.

At the end of the video, the police have forced Lavish to leave the car; they have handcuffed her, and she prays out loud for her boyfriend to be spared, not to die. Her calm is fraying: she panics because she cannot see her daughter. The police finally put mother and daughter in the police car.

Dae'anna tells her, "It's okay, Mommy."

"I can't believe they did this," exclaims Lavish.

Calmly her daughter says, "It's okay, I'm right here with you."

Dae'anna is the fourth eye.

Examples of split subjectivities are rife in theories about race, and are important to my discussion of how to resist visual biopolitics. Fanon talks about learning he is black from being pointed at by a little white girl: "Look, a Negro." Du Bois calls it double consciousness. A four-year-old African American girl is forced to grow up and learn about race and biopolitics under the muzzle of a police officer's gun. Unlike Du Bois's and Fanon's world, the twenty-first century has yet more eyes in the form of social media and surveillance. Lavish's video reveals the true consequences of the third eye, the split, cracked identity, but she uses the camera as a record and as a testimony of that experience: it is an example par excellence of resisting visual biopolitics. The fourth eye is the witness, the eye that sees the violence of visual biopolitics, and how one's self is constituted by it. It can be the eye of the child that watches her mother trying to contain the violence of visual biopolitics, but it can also be the artist who refuses that straitjacketing and silencing death, or the historian or scholar. The fourth eye sees the triangulation of the loved one being constituted as Other and thus annihilated, and then this fourth eye, which may retreat and wait for a more opportune time, is able to resist, attack, and refuse the subjectivity granted to the third eye. The fourth eye comforts, the fourth eye confounds, and the fourth eye survives.

What makes it seem reasonable for police officers in the United States to shoot unarmed black men? Or for Los Angeles County hospital doctors to automatically sterilize Latina women after they are done giving birth, as seen in Renee Tajima-Peña's film *No Más Bebés*?[27] Or for the murders of indigenous women in North America not even to be investigated?[28] How has this cultural logic been produced and reproduced through images? There is actually no justification for using a young girl called Annah la Javanaise as a maid and sexual servant. In the cultural logic of nineteenth-century France, however, this unjustifiable treatment of a child labeled "une négresse" or "la Javanaise" seemed reasonable and natural, so much so that it needed no justification, and continues to inform, given the ways that she is currently regarded in twenty-first-century art history.

In point of fact, justification, which suggests an argument, vindication, plea, apology, excuse, or alibi, suggests a moment of doubt in which an actor (a police officer, a doctor) provides the reason for committing a certain act. This justification does not necessarily occur on a wholly conscious level in the moment when these offenses are committed. Visual biopolitics makes this justification unnecessary or post facto, the articulation of the reason for an act; but the act, once committed, still may require explicit justification. Biopolitics generally, and visual biopolitics in particular, is the predicate; it is what sanctioned the categories of those who matter and those who don't. And if a life does not matter, then one need not have to justify taking it. In a sense, then, visual biopolitics substitutes for justification.[29]

What do I mean by visibility and the visual? First, the visual encompasses categories of seeing around race, gender, class, and sexuality that are signaled by constructed definitions of appearances, such as skin color. Philando Castile is shot because he is seen as a black man. Annah la Javanaise is exploited because she seen as black, "une négresse." Jumilah's difference cannot be racialized. Jumilah is tortured because she is seen as expendable: a poor woman, she could embody the evil feminist leftist dancer necessary for Indonesian historiography. Her difference is made visible by media representations of the venal communist woman. Biopolitics is a visualizing technology, and it must continuously operate and reassure us that, yes, race is empirical, and, yes, the communist is pathological, and, yes, the girl is Javanese. Second, the visual includes those who are not seen. Mechanisms (reglementary, cultural, political) determine who is not seen, as an individual or a community, whose story is not told, whose individuality is not recognized. One can be marked as black or Mexican or Javanese, and not be seen as an individual. Third, visual biopolitics also determines who engenders an indifferent gaze, those seen as landscape. Visual biopolitics determines who can be visualized and who can't, and how they are visualized; who has subjectivity and what kind (and thus what can happen to them), and for what purposes.

I posit that film and digital media provide critical forums for engaging with the image to rewrite history, to foreground that which was forced to be in the margins or eradicated by discourse. Filmmaking has the potential to undo or resist that, using some of the same tools, techniques, or functions. It is with film that one can reframe both our nonbeing and overpresence. But we cannot write or make film, or create art or music, if we do not begin to understand the visual and textual vocabulary of justification that continues to allow women of color to reside in what are essentially phantom realms of nonrecognition. Visual biopolitics needs to be theorized so we can understand how filmmaking can be used to undo it, so that certain subjectivities can be visualized finally, or anew.

My concept of visual biopolitics differs from the theory that Laura Mulvey set out in her 1976 polemic "Visual Pleasure and Narrative," which posited the male gaze in cinema as sadistic and fetishistic.[30] Mulvey's theory is still the dominant framework through which film studies has understood images of women. Mulvey argued that Hollywood cinema encourages spectators to identify with a male gaze, that Hollywood associates subjectivity with masculinity and relegates women to the position of object (which echoes Foucault's idea of the light that constitutes the viewer's gaze).[31] Visual biopolitics builds on this but goes beyond it, linking this subject/object, viewer/image dichotomy with matters of life and death. Examining how visual biopolitics works matters, because it is intersectional, recognizing that Indonesian women, for example, are framed through the lenses of gender, race, class, sexuality, caste, and disability, and that this produces different effects from those that Mulvey describes. Also, while Mulvey's was a call to action for (white) feminist filmmakers to resist "visual pleasure," I document a very different type of resistant filmmaking, one that is focused not on destroying visual pleasure but on producing a collective subjectivity that works to undo some of visual biopolitics' damaging effects. The power networks of biopolitics work invisibly. But homo economicus must conceive and visualize an enemy, the corrupt, evil monster who must be rooted out. Here is where visual biopolitics comes in. This is part of the weft of society, woven by media, narrative, and politics to become the reality of a culture.

The Annahs, the Jumilahs, the Lavishes, the Dae'annas of the world are both seen and unseen at the same time. They are phantoms relegated to the shadows, the worlds of hidden labor, poverty, the death-worlds that Mbembe talks about, and, on the other hand, they are everywhere, banalized, the dancing native girl, the Budweiser calendar girl, the bare-breasted woman toiling and carrying children on her back in ethnographic film. This improbably impossible oscillation (described in film theory as "I know very well, but just the same") is at the heart of my project, which is to consider the variations, to use Michele Wallace's term, in the visual representation of women of color—in this case, the figure of the Indonesian woman—that can be seen across media and that defy the discursive straitjacket of the ethnographic.[32]

LOOKING BACK

Salty sweat pours into her mouth as Nur raises the rock above her head and smashes it down to break stones, her legs splayed in front of her. Middle-aged and East Javanese, Nur's black hair is cut short in a no-nonsense style, and she wears a blazing red T-shirt, the same color as the blood that wells up on her finger after a stone cuts her. Huge heaps of large stones loom behind her. The sun is unrelenting. Behind her, her young daughter who toddles in a red dress is also playing with the stones. After the work is done, Nur gathers the child up in one hand, a bucket in another, so that she can go home and get ready for her night's work as a prostitute in a Chinese cemetery.

In this scene from *Ragat'e Anak*, the last segment from the Indonesian omnibus film *Pertaruhan* (At Stake, 2008), directed by Ucu Agustin and produced by Nia Dinata, we see Nur as a hardworking middle-aged woman who is simply trying to feed and educate her children, belying the myth of the sexually wanton prostitute. Just as the idealized Annah looked at the viewer from Gauguin's canvas in his 1892 painting *Aita tamari vahine Judith te parari*, director Ucu Agustin presents us with a realist portrait of Nur looking calmly at the camera as she explains what she does for a living in order to feed and educate her children. Instead of being a metonym for an entire, timeless, ahistoric Ethnographic, Nur is firmly rooted in the Historical, her life determined by the transnational labor forces that compelled many wives in East Java to leave Indonesia and work abroad, of which the illegal prostitution in which Nur takes part is a direct result.

The visual is much more difficult to pin down than a text is, since it always requires textual explanation, an act or form of translation or ventriloquism.

As any film historian knows, it is an impossible task to truly or even adequately describe a film in words, like trying to capture an uncontainable beast of moving image, sound, dialogue, music, narrative, and mise-en-scène colliding with the viewer's memory and subconscious, and whose very essence cannot be contained by words. Our memory coils around the body of the film and swallows it whole. And yet we keep on trying to figure film out, seeking to explain it, contain it; and the more films we see, the more we carry within ourselves, like a battered old suitcase of images and sounds and fragments. We speak of the whole film as a unitary thing, but what do we remember? A phrase here, an image there, sometimes a feeling like a punch in the stomach—was that love or a punishment? The effort of describing a film is like that of describing love—impossible, ineffable, and infuriating—but like love, it's urgent.

Lavish Reynolds explained, in an interview conducted following the recording of the death of Philando Castile, that she wanted her story told, and she knew that without her filming it, it would not be told. The camera becomes another eye in the situation, along with her eyes and those of her daughter, Dae'anna. How it is interpreted will be up to the persons who view it; experiences and words cannot be fully contained by film and media, and each of us sees the film with the baggage that we carry in our unconscious.

Long ago, James Baldwin wrote a letter to his nephew in which he advised him that integration is not the issue. He wrote that it is not difficult to be accepted into the society of the white man. What is difficult is for us to accept and love and forgive the white man, for he is not aware of the mask that he wears, while we are always aware of our mask, our third eye. "Try to imagine how you would feel if you woke up one morning to find the sun shivering and all the stars aflame. You would be frightened because it is out of the order of nature. Any upheaval in the universe is terrifying because it so profoundly attacks one's sense of one's own reality. Well, the black man has functioned in the white man's world as a fixed star, as an immovable pillar, and as he moves out of his place, heaven and earth are shaken to their foundations."[33]

How the norm functions as a fixed star is brilliantly stated here. The star can no longer be fixed, and the foundations must be shaken. Visual biopolitics determines subjectivity and reinforces visual vocabularies; it determines the technology of the self, how we learn subjectivity that is individual and ego-based versus collective and community-based, and it shapes how that subjectivity is produced in media, whether it be film, painting, photography, or television, maintaining categories of identity. This book is about visual biopolitics, why certain populations are allowed to live and others are allowed to die, and how that is accomplished with technologies that provide a visual vocabulary of justification. It is a subject important enough for us to consider across race and gender and sexuality, wherever and whenever people are engaged in a life-or-death battle over how we look.

ANNAH AND HER DAUGHTERS

We begin with the story of Annah la Javanaise, the thirteen-year-old girl found wandering the streets of Paris in 1893 with a sign around her neck. Chapter 1 thus evokes the haunting of gendered visual biopolitics. The title in Tahitian of her portrait *Aita tamari vahine Judith te parari* refers to the name of the original model, the white girl who was Gauguin's neighbor, Judith, the one whose image is painted over with Annah's. In chapter 1, I push the divide between those who are left alone (in this case Judith) and those who are allowed to be raped (Annah) by looking at the relationships between sexuality, visuality, race, and primitivism. Visibility is one of the enabling conditions of the extended, racialized, and gendered concept of visual biopolitics. By scrutinizing archival photographs, texts, and the Gauguin painting itself, I explore the discursive complexity of what it means to be framed, and how Annah is framed through visual biopolitics. In discussing how she poses and performs, I analyze how a subject can exert some agency or resistance against how she is framed. Brown girls that worked for Gauguin were part of an archaic structure: they were there to cook for him and be used sexually by him for a short time, after which he replaced them with new girls. I consider the construction and legacy of the figure of the black maid and la Javanaise as a form of serial equalization of women, as Bliss Cua Lim has explained, which we will see later in other figures of Indonesian women, both colonial and postcolonial.[34]

Dancer, choreographer, and historian Rachmi Diyah Larasati brilliantly goes further with the idea of serial equalization by charging that these replicas of Indonesian women contain a remnant of the murdered one within them. In her masterful book, *The Dance That Makes You Vanish*, Larasati writes a counternarrative that reveals what is at stake with the exoticization of trance, dance, and the Indonesian woman. The second chapter explains the importance of the ethnographic and colonial representation of the dancer as exotic primitive from Margaret Mead's ethnographic film *Trance and Dance in Bali* (1955) and from her heir Joshua Oppenheimer's award-winning documentary portrait of Sumatran gangsters, *The Act of Killing* (2012), to show how visual biopolitics is carefully constructed using nonsynchronous representations of the Savage and the Pathological; this erases the historical and political presence of the ethnographic and/or documentary filmmaker, even when the filmmaker purports to collaborate with the subjects in the film. Using the focus of the dancer, I show how two seemingly disparate films and genres actually share similar characteristics as examples of visual biopolitics: eliding the implications of colonialism, in the case of *Trance and Dance in Bali*, and US support of the coup in Indonesia in 1965 and the New Order government of Suharto that ruled with a bloody fist for thirty-two years, in *The Act of Killing*. Although Oppenheimer's film criticizes the visual biopolitics of the Suharto regime and subsequent Indonesian governments, it has been highly successful in feeding into the West's own appetite for the entertainment of fascinating cannibalism. Finally, I look at other media made by Indonesians, before and after Oppenheimer, that rewrite the history of the killings of those associated with communism.

Continuing to examine acts of resistance to visual biopolitics such as Larasati's, chapter 3 looks at how one can interrogate the nature of photography and film through unsettling and raiding the archive. In the first example, a YouTube montage of historic photographs of the period after 1965 reveals how official history can be disrupted by video editing and found footage. In the second example, a missionary photograph that also happens to be my great-great-grandfather looks at the shimmering of first contact, an event of missionary photography in 1853, and how that image became codified as a norm that also was used as a form of familial and ancestral history. Vincent Monnikendam's devastating found-footage film *Mother Dao, the Turtlelike* (1995) is the third example. This film, which raided the Dutch colonial archive for images of Indonesia, disregards the authority of the auteur that we saw in chapter 2 with Mead and Oppenheimer, and through recontextualization, editing, and sound juxtapositions, *Mother Dao* draws from the archive and transforms what is previously seen as the pathological. Bringing the past of the colonial archive into the present becomes a form of resistance.

With an emphasis on communing, chapter 4 sets the stage for demonstrating how Indonesian women make film and engender new forms of filmmaking, thus unraveling the fabric of the normalized image of the native woman and sexuality. My particular focus is on the feature films of Nia Dinata. Very little has been written on this innovative filmmaker, whose diverse genres and styles of directing, as well as collaborations with other directors, break new ground in the directing of feature films. Her collaborative practice includes exhibition, in the ways that the films get screened on road shows to nonprofit organizations, local communities, and universities. Although this may appear to be a forward leap, it is with this goal to seek out how one figures oneself as part of a community that the title of this book is *How Do We Look?* Visual biopolitics determines who has individual subjectivity versus who must always think as a collective subjectivity; and film, in the ways it expresses subjectivity in its subject matter and elicits it in its reception, is part of that storytelling process.

Spanning various eras—colonialism, nationalism, postcolonialism, and neoliberal globalization—I illustrate how history bears the traces of the past in the present and carries them into the future.[35] If I come back to the Indonesian women, who are there to be painted, to be pried open, or to be covered, it is to ask another set of questions than those generally posed in art history, namely, how do we look to you, the viewer? This is the first and most traditional line of inquiry, that of representation, that of framing. How do we (the objects posited in the representation) look to you, the consumers of representation? I add three other lines of inquiry. The first has to do with performance and posing: How do we compose ourselves for your view? Performance and posing are not just a form of subjectivity; they are also a making and a playing of subjectivity. The second has to do with recomposing: How do we take the media offered of ourselves and recombine them, recompose them, reedit them, review them to offer another set of views? And the third line of inquiry has to do with how we—as writers, filmmakers, and producers of art and media—look. There is more than one way to answer the question of how we look in and how we look at photographs, films, painting, media. As Sylvia Wynter writes, "Humanness is no longer a noun. Being human is a praxis."[36]

THE PEONIES

"Wait here for Madame."

I was left alone in the foyer.

There on a lace doily, on a round table, sat a vase. It was beautiful, a pure ivory-colored china with a design painted in blue, of peonies and a pair of lovers caressing each other by a pavilion. I stood next to it and stared. It looked cool and inviting.

I heard Madame before I saw her, practicing her scales, as well as singing. A man would interrupt and talk to her, and a piano was playing. The sound of her voice was like an alarming wind before a storm. Woo-woo-woo-woo-woo-woo-woo.

I looked around for the presence of children. But the apartment was dark and formal, and the chairs looked uninviting, as if nobody ever sat in them.

Finally in swept Madame. Her eyes narrowed when she caught sight of me, with the gaze of someone shopping at the market, making quick calculations about how much to bargain. She had glittering blue eyes, and with the tight carapace of her deep red velvet fitted dress, she reminded me of an iridescent beetle. Where I lived, only very old people had blue eyes, after going blind, but here, it was not odd to see someone with eyes that color.

"Tiny huh."

She looked into my eyes as if to appraise their quality, then opened my hands, and looked at my palms. She made me turn around.

"Well, I suppose it means that I won't have to feed you very much."

She kept her word. I was not fed much. I was not paid either. And I never saw any children. Instead, I woke before everyone and went to bed after everyone, and did all the cleaning, laundering, and cooking. I made many mistakes because there was no one to teach me the correct way to do things. Because of this, Madame liked to hit me, and with her sharp tongue, accused me of terrible things. I was lazy. I was clumsy. I was stupid. From her I learned the vocabulary of very bad words to say in French. She would come home with a headache—things hadn't turned out right—and then she would see me and start yelling. She would hit me. On the legs. On the arms. Sometimes on the face.

One morning, I was in the foyer, dusting her table, which held the beautiful vase with the two lovers among the peonies, and I don't know what happened. Maybe I was not concentrating, maybe I was too sleepy, maybe my hands were too sweaty, but the vase all of a sudden tipped, in suspended time, and then crashed to the floor.

I knelt down and looked at the shards that lay on the ground. Irreparable. My heart sank.

Looking up, I listened for the inevitable reaction. And then I realized something. As luck would have it, I was alone in the house. Madame was rehearsing at the theater and the other servant was out.

I heard the horses of the carriages outside. The people walking on the street. The klaxon of a carriage. A hawker selling vegetables from a cart.

I didn't wait for the screaming aria that would, I knew, greet me later, just as surely as the sun would set and the sun would rise.

Somehow, I had the temerity, or the stupidity, to take off my apron, straighten my skirt, exit the foyer, and open the front door. I looked up and the sky was blue. I took it as a good sign and stepped out into the street.

ANNAH LA JAVANAISE

A man needs a maid.

—NEIL YOUNG

She sits naked on a blue armchair against a pink wall, her bare brown feet propped on a plush green footstool jutting into the viewer's space in the bottom foreground of an interior vibrating with other colors—the purples on the left of the floor, the yellow of the lower right corner encroaching upon the orange monkey seated at the foot of the chair. The unfamiliar energy of the colors blurs the borders between the representational and the symbolic. This is Paul Gauguin's painting *Aita tamari vahine Judith te parari* (The child-woman Judith is not yet breached, 1893–94; figure 1.1), of the thirteen-year-old girl known as Annah la Javanaise, who calmly gazes at the viewer. It is a conflation of both the white prostitute and the black maid in Édouard Manet's *Olympia* (1863), the painting that Western art historians mark as the beginning of modernity. It is not the type of canonical Gauguin painting we are familiar with, of mythical brown girls in their *pareos* near the beach or on a terrace fanning themselves. This may in part be due to the fact that the painting is not well known, having disappeared during his lifetime and only resurfacing in the 1920s.[1] But it can also be attributed to the striking, perhaps disturbing,

FIGURE 1.1 Paul Gauguin, *Aita tamari vahine Judith te parari* (The child-woman Judith is not yet breached, 1893–94), private collection.

modernity of the image: seated in an elaborately carved wooden armchair, the girl, like Olympia, looks frankly and steadily at the viewer. Unlike Olympia, however, her skin is dark. This is the shock of the new, the loss of certainty that Charles Baudelaire characterized as the new relationship of the painter to modern life: "By modernity I mean the transitory, the fugitive, the contingent which make up one half of art, the other being the eternal and the immutable."[2]

Paul Gauguin, the painter of this image of Annah la Javanaise, was born in France in 1848 and, as a child, lived briefly with his mother and sister in Lima, Peru—his grandfather was Peruvian. He then grew up in France and served for two years as a colonial naval officer; married a Danish woman, Mette, with whom he had five children; and worked as a trader at the Bourse in Paris. He abandoned his responsibilities as a family man when he set his mind upon the idea of becoming a great painter and traveled to Tahiti in 1891. He died in 1903, on the island of Hiva Oa in the Marquesas, riddled with syphilis. The fame that he sought came only after his death.

After his first trip to Tahiti from 1891 to 1893, in which he made some of his most famous paintings—including *Ia orana Maria* (Hail Mary, 1891–92), *Fatata te miti* (Near the sea, 1892), and *Manao Tupapau* (The specter watches over her, 1892)—Paul Gauguin returned to Paris in August 1893 to establish his reputation as an avant-garde painter. He only stayed until June 1895. One of his literary friends, Charles Morice, said this about Gauguin and the first exhibition of his Tahitian paintings, the Durand-Ruel exhibition of November 10–25, 1893: "In Tahiti, the painter had 'rediscovered the land of his dreams. . . . He became a savage, was naturalized a Maori—without ever ceasing to be himself, to be an artist.'"[3]

Here is the myth of Gauguin writ large: he is the Savage artist, a white man who has rejected modern life to embrace a purer, more authentic existence. Receiving an unexpected inheritance from his Uncle Isidore (Zizi), Gauguin established a studio, what he called a "living museum," at 6, rue Vercingétorix in the Montparnasse section of Paris. Built from the repurposed pavilions of the 1889 World's Fair, which Gauguin had frequented, the studio housed his Uncle Zizi's ethnographic collection of carvings, Gauguin's own paintings, reproductions of Japanese prints, other artists' paintings, photographs, flea market finds, a piano, and a camera.[4] The camera is important, as I will explain later, since habitués of the "museum" helped stage "selfies" of a sort, portraying the lifestyle of Gauguin and the artists, musicians, composers, and writers in attendance—including Swedish playwright August Strindberg, English composer Frederick Delius, and Czech art nouveau painter Alphonse Mucha—who met there every Thursday to drink, party, and make music in this "studio of the South Seas." Inscribed on one of the windows were the words *Ici faruru* (Here we make love).[5] Amid these white male members of European high culture one face stands out: Annah.

In 1893, a very small, chocolate-colored girl, age thirteen, with long black hair and fiery, darting eyes, was found by a policeman wandering the streets of Paris with a sign around her neck that read "Madame Nina Pack, rue de la Rochefoucauld. Paris. Consignment from Java."[6] Apparently Pack had, months earlier, mentioned to a business acquaintance who had dealings in Southeast Asia that she was looking for "une petite négresse," "négresse" being the term for any girl or woman with brown skin, including those from the Dutch East Indies, now known as Indonesia. But "négresse" also meant "female slave," so she was also asking, implicitly, for "a little slave girl."[7] Annah was often referred to as "une négresse" or sometimes *une mulâtresse*. Here is art dealer Ambroise Vollard's account of what happened to the girl, whom he described as a young mulatta, half Indian, half Malaysian:

> She was given the name Anna. Some time later, in consequence of a little domestic drama in which Anna was implicated, she was dismissed. She came to me, as I had known her at her employer's house, to ask me to find her a good situation. I judged her qualifications as a housemaid to be very middling, and thought she stood more chance of succeeding as a model. I told Gauguin about her.
> "Send her to me. I'll try her," he said.
> Anna pleased him, and he kept her.[8]

There: "I'll try her." "Anna pleased him, and he kept her." Annah la Javanaise, as she came to be known, has been reduced to a snigger in an eccentric anecdote, a picturesque detail. Visitors to Gauguin's salon described her by her function in the household: one who "keeps house" and "serves drinks," "wife," "attendant," "mistress," "model." She lived with and worked for him during the brief period between December 1893 and August or September 1894.

That Annah, a thirteen-year-old alone in Paris with no parents or relatives to protect her, of mysterious origins, was sent to the house of a forty-five-year-old man known for his sexual predilection for very young nonwhite girls raised no alarm, and that this was considered an apt situation for a fired maid, reveals the different mores around children and sexuality, and, as we shall see, native girls in particular. The age of consent in France at the time was thirteen. It was not raised to the age of fifteen until 1945. A little "négresse." One of whom we would know nothing if not for a painting of her.[9] But Annah's tale is not unique in the Gauguin canon of muses: there are innumerable tales of other girls and women, caught up in an apparatus of framing, posing, painting, seeing, and being. What is celebrated about Gauguin's art is the story of the civilized man's return to Savage life. But this story of modernity is haunted by the story of the life of the girl, and if we elect to excavate it, how the story of her was made, with paintings, photographs, and text, so that she is everywhere present and nowhere to be found. What if we chose to see the revenant of the girl left behind?

The history of art is generally introduced as a chronology of names, a history of "begats," as author Rebecca Solnit puts it:

> Art history in particular is often cast as an almost biblical lineage, a long line of begats in which painters descend purely from painters. Just as the purely patrilineal Old Testament genealogies leave out the mothers and even the fathers of the mothers, so these tidy stories leave out all the sources and inspirations that come from other media and other encounters, from poems, dreams, politics, doubts, a childhood experience, a sense of place, leave out the fact that history is made more of crossroads, branchings, and tangles than straight lines. These other sources I called the grandmothers.[10]

In scholarship we concern ourselves with the painters, the bards, the authors, not the mothers or the grandmothers. In this chapter, though, I will excavate the discourses around Annah la Javanaise. I can state from the start that finding the truth about Annah is a nearly impossible task, for the girl left no textual or visual evidence. It is a flawed archive. Or should I say, it is an archive that works—it maintains the subjectivity of the homo economicus—in its creation of the norm.

Although we have no evidence of anything Annah wrote or made, exhuming her traces in the archive reveals a haunting. As I explained in the introduction, inspired by Rachmi Diyah Larasati's conception of the replica that contains revenants of the dead, the girl who is now long dead haunts the signifiers that we have left of her. Not to recognize her ghostly traces is to be complicit in the serial equalization of exotic women in the historiography of Gauguin studies, and which I question.[11] In general, the historiography and criticism of the work of Gauguin has been either (1) to praise him as a great modernist painter who defied bourgeois mores to paint a truer vision of the world; or (2) to denounce him as a colonial expatriate pederast who exploited native women; or (3) as a postmodern ironic genius whose work revealed the slippages and instability of colonialism and heterosexuality. My intervention will be different, because my claim is that Annah la Javanaise is a portrait of two girls, Annah who is black, and Judith (the original model for the painting) who is white, and the histories of the two girls allow us to parse the relationships of sexuality, race, and primitivism that are latent in the painting. Visual biopolitics determines who is visible and who remains invisible, who can and cannot be raped, who is protected and who is not.

Who gets framed and how? A frame determines a space, and a frame determines a narrative. In the 1970s, film theorists posited how narrative cinema is historically determined by a genealogy that conceives of seeing as knowing, from a godlike monocular vantage point, beginning with Italian Renaissance perspective. As Stephen Heath famously wrote, "Frame space . . . is constructed as narrative space."[12] The frame is the structuring device of the painting, and later it will become the "material unit of film."[13] I contend that the framing of Annah la Javanaise is an example of gendered visual biopolitics.

This chapter takes up the visual framing of subjectivity in words, painting, and photography, and how we can disrupt it by looking closely at the subject who is posing and performing. Described as Gauguin's mistress or maid, Annah's assigned image came from French cultural definitions of la Javanaise and the nude in painting, but the textual and photographic evidence reveals an identity at odds with this, which leads to larger questions: What is a mistress? And if she was not a mistress, then what is sexual coercion? What is rape? And what do we do with great art that reveals a whole imaging mechanism of visual biopolitics for how women of color exist for service and sex?

A TALE OF JAVA

She was always referred to as Annah the Javanese, already racialized as a metonym for an entire culture and people. This identity was ascribed to her, as if she were a walking live figure model, a performer from the Javanese village of the World's Fair exposition. But was Annah even Javanese? There are so many conflicting reports about her origins. The terms "Indian" and "Malaysian" are also thrown around, with no evidence for these claims. She is first conjured as Javanese by the imperious opera singer Nina Pack, who wanted a "négresse" from the East Indies. Historians Billy Kluver and Julie Martin characterize Annah as Malaysian.[14] Art historian Jehanne Teilhet-Fisk refers to her as "an exotic mistress of Indian and Malaysian descent."[15] Paul Gauguin's son, Pola Gauguin, explains, "And for attendant and mistress, a handsome Javanese named Annah, a well-known model from the studios of Montparnasse."[16] Hungarian painter József Rippl-Rónai erroneously referred to Annah as Gauguin's wife, Noa Noa, also the title of his beautifully illustrated book seen by most scholars as a fictionalized, romanticized version of Gauguin's time in Tahiti.[17]

Here is how Jiří Mucha, the son of Gauguin's former roommate, the artist Alphonse Mucha, described Annah:

At the time of Gauguin's exhibition at Durand-Ruel's, a small and rather ugly half-caste girl of about fourteen called Anna la Javannaise [sic] appeared at my father's studio. Officially she was Gauguin's model. He dressed her in fancy oriental clothes, made her serve drinks at the rue Vercingétorix, and once even painted her. . . .

Gauguin, who claimed to be descended from the Incas, had a weakness for dark-coloured women. Although Anna was not pretty, she was at least very young, and brought back to Gauguin some of the atmosphere of the South Seas. She kept house for him at the studio with its chrome yellow walls, Tahitian pictures and weird exotic objects.[18]

She keeps house for him, and she is his weakness. Gauguin's own power over her is disguised as a "weakness." In labor terms, she is his maid and sex worker. While we do not know Annah's true name or ethnicity, what is certain is that her life was shaped by a tale of four other very young, brown-skinned girls who were Javanese, and who lived in the shadow of the Eiffel Tower four years earlier, in 1889 (figure 1.2).

Their names are mellifluous: Wakiem. Seriem. Taminah. Soekia.

These four girls, ranging in age from thirteen to seventeen, were royal dancers from the court of Surakarta, Java, then part of the East Indies, a colony of the Netherlands. From April to November 1889, they became the object of fascination for thousands of visitors to the 1889 World's Fair in Paris. This is the genesis of the French myth of la java: mystical, precious, refined, beautiful, exotic, sensual. Java was above all la Javanaise, but la java was also French.

In the shadow of the Eiffel Tower, then the tallest building in the world, which was built for the World's Fair to celebrate the technological might and power of France, Wakiem, Seriem, Taminah, and Soekia lived with sixty-one other Javanese men, women, and children in the Javanese village or kampong javanais (figure 1.3). The European power to colonize was displayed in the "native villages" that were arrayed around the grounds, many from French colonies. The fair was itself a form of time travel. Julien Tiersot wrote at the time: "Rome is no longer in Rome; Cairo no longer in Egypt and Java no longer in the East Indies. All of that has come to the Champ de Mars, on the Esplanade des Invalides, and to the Trocadéro. Thus, without leaving Paris, we have the leisure to study for the next six months, at least in their exterior manifestations, the practices and customs of the most distant peoples."[19] Annegret Fauser has written an illuminating book on the soundscape of the 1889

FIGURE 1.2 The four Javanese dancers (Wakiem, Seriem, Taminah, and Soekia). City of Paris Historical Library (Bibliothèque Historique de la Ville de Paris), Dossier photographique Divers XXI, 364.

World's Fair, noting that in places such as the Javanese village, sometimes "the performances could also transgress the limitations of their institutional framing."[20] In a café that could seat as many as 100–150 people, visitors could, while indulging in Dutch beer, Lucas Bola spirits, and Van Houten hot chocolate, watch daily dance performances accompanied by a gamelan orchestra.[21]

The image of Java was sexualized. When the bejeweled Wakiem, Seriem, Taminah, and Soekia danced, observers mythologized the girls as harem dancers and nubile courtesans from the Solo (Surakarta) court.[22] Artists and musicians of different camps were inspired, including impressionists, symbolists, and Académie artists: "Every day, one can see dessinateurs and watercolorists that use [the dancers] as models during the performance. As for the musicians, they are struck by the unfamiliar rhythms and bizarre sonorities of the two orchestras, which play in the background and at one side of the stage."[23] Gauguin, who loved to frequent the fair, described them as "a troupe of temple dancers, little girls aged from twelve to sixteen, dressed in exquisitely bejeweled costumes, performing temple dances whose movements

FIGURE 1.3 Photograph of the Javanese village, Kampong Javanais, 1889 Exposition Universelle, Paris, France.

mirror the Khmer figures on the temple next door," the temple being a replica of Angkor Wat in Cambodia, a French colony.[24]

Suggesting harem dancers, concubines, and Khmer figures, the girls halted time. One contemporary observer, Judith Gautier, wrote that viewers were so spellbound that "the foam of the beer withered and the sorbet melted under distracted spoons."[25] Their performance was slow, exquisite, refined. The gamelan music with its haunting pentatonic scale was unlike any visitors had ever heard before: it seems to have put them in an ecstatic trance.

This new discourse on Java will have larger ramifications, even for a little girl who comes to Paris. As I have argued in *The Third Eye*, the World's Fair, with its fenced-off display of native villages, was a form of disciplining the body but also a means of setting apart what was the Savage and what was the Civilized, making confinement, apartheid, and race appear natural. These others living behind the fence are conjured up to perform and pose for you while you sip or slurp on delicacies of the colonies, a means of explaining empire and the naturalness of colonial domination.

Wakiem, Seriem, Taminah, and Soekia became stars of the exposition: 876,000 visitors came to see them, and writers and photographers followed their every move.[26] Here is how Fauser explains the Parisian passion for la Javanaise as the Parisian's antidote to modern life: "The fact that the four dancers came from the princely court of Surakarta only added to the fantasy of catching a glimpse of a hidden world of mysterious exotic beauty, even if, as the symbolist writer Joris-Karl Huysmans observed in truly Parisian fashion, these goddesses had dirty feet."[27]

Like the prostitute Olympia with her dirty heels, the "dirty feet" of Wakiem, Seriem, Taminah, and Soekia connoted the other side of the myth: sexuality. Gauguin visited the Javanese village several times in 1889, and in a letter to his friend, the painter Émile Bernard, we see how it became associated in his mind with art and sex.[28] "You missed something in not coming the other day. In the Java village there are Hindoo dances. All the art of India can be seen there, and it is exactly like the photos I have. I go there again on Thursday as I have an appointment with a mulatto girl [*une mulâtresse*]. Come on Thursday, but I don't want to be too late."[29] Long before his first trip to Tahiti, Gauguin was making appointments with women of color. Indonesian or Javanese women were described as "négresse" and/or "mulâtresse," so it is possible that the woman he was meeting was Javanese.[30]

Another telling part of Gauguin's description is how he sees the girls and the village through the lens of photography: "it is exactly like the photos that I have." Elizabeth Childs has written extensively on Gauguin's use of ethnographic and colonial photography (some of naked women) as legitimization for his aesthetic choices, as communication to other artists, and as decoration for his studio's ethnographic museum decor, his "*musée imaginaire.*"[31] Photography frames and shores up what one sees, a form of "seeing anthropology."[32]

From that moment on, la java became a part of the French cultural imagination. Even today the colloquial, if slightly outdated, phrase "faire la java" means "to live it up," "to party," "to have a wild time." La Java, a fast waltz, was born in the early part of the twentieth century at the *bal-musettes*, dance cafés that first became popular in the 1880s. La Java took on the tone of the sexual and the forbidden. Many French popular songs feature the figure of la java, including Georgette Plana's "La Java Bleu" of 1938 and Edith Piaf's "L'Accordéoniste" of 1942; another famous version was pop singer Serge Gainsbourg's "La Javanaise" of 1962 (figure 1.4).

The dance of the four Javanese girls was not in itself sexual, but was interpreted as such. Put another way, French society's focus on sex is perfectly compatible with, and even the corollary of, a simultaneous focus on chastity. They are the flip sides of an obsession with the sexual dimension, and we will see this structure again with Gauguin's *Aita tamari vahine Judith te parari*. Sexuality is the rubric under which biopolitics plays out: "Sex was a means of access both to the life of the body and the life of the species."[33] French society, as Michel Foucault explained, was obsessed with sex: "the mechanisms of

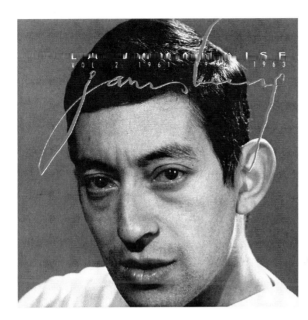

FIGURE 1.4 Album cover for Serge Gainsbourg compilation CD, *La Javanaise, vol. 2, 1961–1963* (song "La Javanaise" originally released on 45 rpm record in March 1963; CD in 2006).

power are addressed to the body, to life, to what causes it to proliferate, to what reinforces the species, its stamina, its ability to dominate, or its capacity for being used."[34] Sexuality is intertwined with race at the World's Fair: the visitors look at those enclosed behind the fence and may have dalliances with "négresses," but it is the libertine who has agency to choose a sexual partner who is not white. In a sense, this village built in the shadow of the Eiffel Tower prepares for the twentieth- and twenty-first-century industry of sex tourism.

The image of Java that the French had in mind when Annah walked onto the Paris scene in 1893 was the perfumed dream of an unfolding dance to gamelan music by tiny Javanese girls in batik splendor. It is about desire, and the association is with the otherworldly, the sensual, and the small brown girl. As Boris Vian sang in his song of 1957, "La Java Javanaise":

> All roads
> Lead to Rome
> Even if it is Rome that one has left
> But the javas
> Even the Javanese [girls]
> All of them will take you back to Paris.[35]

This is the story then: Annah la Javanaise. Annah the Wicked Girl.

As Foucault writes, sex was everywhere, to be feared and causing excitement: "Power delineated it, aroused it, and employed it as the proliferating meaning that had always to be taken control of again lest it escape; it was an effect with a meaning-value."[36] Yet, as Ann Stoler has pointed out in *Race and the Education of Desire*, race and the colonial body are elided in Foucault's work on the history of sexuality. Stoler writes, "In locating the power of the discourse of sexuality in the affirmation of the bourgeois self, Foucault short-circuited the discursive and practical field of empire in which Western notions of self and other were worked out for centuries and continue to be drawn."[37] Pertinent to our analysis of the discourse that constrained the girl who was called Annah la Javanaise is Stoler's thesis concerning the Dutch colonial context for a pornographic racial taxonomy that Dr. C. H. Stratz wrote and produced in 1895, after Annah's period working for Gauguin. This taxonomy, titled *Women in Java*, reveals another European discourse on the sexual Javanese female. Inasmuch as Annah's life was shaped by the discourse of la java in France and in the Netherlands, the representational apparatus of sex and sexuality in nineteenth-century French painting also determined it.

If you were a time traveler and encountered nineteenth-century French culture for the first time, and in particular the culture of painters, both Salon and avant-garde, one thing that you would find striking about this culture is its obsession with naked (mostly white) women. If you knew nothing about the people, you might assume from the paintings that this was indeed the mode of dress for these women, that they shaved their pubic hair, that their bodies were as polished as precious marble, for the idealized nude was a goddess of love. There are scores of Salon paintings that present writhing Venuses like so many luminescent pieces of flesh. And then there are the paintings by artists that scorned the Salon, and their images are of women inviting you to look at them, to have sex with them, whether sitting on a lawn naked with two men in black suits, or in a boudoir inviting you into their chamber with a black maid holding a bouquet you brought, or stretching backstage before dancing *en pointe* for you. For the avant-garde, the shock of the new is borne on the bodies that are often those of working girls and women. The audience that receives these outrageous spectacles is not the girls or women depicted, but the men who desire them.

The gaze that ushered in French modernity and spat in the face of all that pearly Salon flesh was Édouard Manet's *Olympia* of 1863 (figure 1.5). Unlike the idealized nudes of Titian and Ingres, Olympia, with the black ribbon around her neck and the dirty soles of her feet, is a prostitute who looks back at the viewer. Her startling modernity is in her frank gaze, but if we unpack the history behind this painting, we can see that the model for Olympia was Victorine Meurent, who later went on to be a painter who showed her works in the Salon, although she died in obscurity and poverty. Meurent's own vision of the world—her paintings—did not get archived, nor did her paintings become a part of the art historical archive. Next to Olympia is a black maid, modeled by another woman, Laure, who holds the bouquet that the client has brought and stands at the side.[38]

Foucault explains that the scandal of the painting is the light that strikes Olympia, a light that he characterizes as violent. That light, he proffers, is the spectator, who stands in the place of the light source, so that our gaze appears to illuminate Olympia:

> It is we who render it visible; our gaze upon the Olympia is a lantern, it is that which carries the light; we are responsible for the visibility and for the nudity of Olympia. She is nude only for us since it is we who render her nude and we do so because, in looking at her, we illuminate her. . . . We are—every viewer finds this—necessarily implicated in this nudity and we are to a certain extent responsible. You see how an aesthetic transformation can, in a case such as this, provoke a moral scandal.[39]

But even as the light emanates from us, the viewer, Olympia also creates us, the viewer, and that is its scandal. It is a painting that reflects upon our agency. But what about those of us who notice and identify with the black maid?

Performance artist Lorraine O'Grady in her brilliant reproof "Olympia's Maid" asks the question: What happened to that black maid when she was brought here? She reminds us that the black maid buffered the representation of the white woman as ideal beauty, and that is why her presence is such a contrast.[40] Darcy Grigsby has also written a detailed article about how Laure worked for Manet as a model. Although her representation in Olympia is associated with that of a black slave, Grigsby argues that she is a working-class woman just as Victorine Meurent is.[41] Laure's blackness, given France's derision of black women, made her invisible to art historians, explains Grigsby.

Olympia contains the two poles of visualizing modernity—sexuality and race—as does Gauguin's Aita tamari vahine Judith te parari, the portrait of Annah/Judith. What is both explicit and implicit about this presentation of Olympia is how it depends upon the spoils of colonialism, for without the wealth that colonialist expansion brought, the flâneur would not have

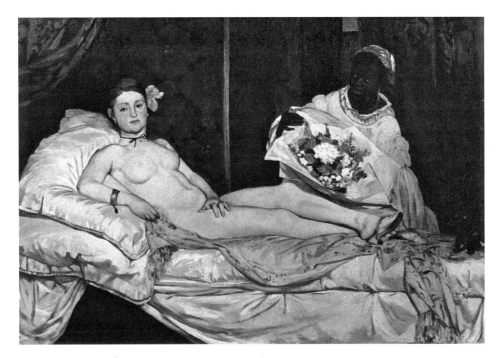

FIGURE 1.5 Édouard Manet, *Olympia* (1863), Musée d'Orsay, Paris, France.

had the leisure or means to frequent the boudoir of a beribboned prostitute. Both Olympia and the maid are the alternating signs of this privilege, the light versus the dark: in the modern city of Paris the shock of the new is in the conflation of visuality and sex and commerce. In other words, here I am tracing a function of visual biopolitics and how it developed.[42]

Without colonialism, the trope of savagery could not adorn the prostitute. Later on, the tropes of savagery and race begin to signify the prostitute. In Picasso's painting of 1907, *Les demoiselles d'Avignon*, perhaps the primitivist modernist painting par excellence, a curtain is pulled back at left to reveal prostitutes in a brothel who are in a room, some of their faces wearing or becoming African masks. Modern art emerges through the encounter with non-Western art, in the possibility of emphasizing the materiality of the brush stroke rather than the yoke of figure representation. Ironically, what is antimodern (the Savage) makes the work modern. This is a standard argument of the self being defined as existing because of the other. The framing of lightness versus darkness and the narrative that is conveyed are bound to a power relation that implicitly sanctions who can be raped and who cannot.

The history of *Aita tamari vahine Judith te parari* (The child-woman Judith is not yet breached), the title of which is inscribed at the painting's upper right, is one of mystery, according to art historian Richard Brettell.[43] Unsigned and undated, the painting was unknown during Gauguin's lifetime and not mentioned until twenty years after his death.

In the actual portrait itself, Annah is, as I have said, already a shocking conflation, an Olympia who is also the black maid, naked, with a monkey at her feet. In 1893–94 it would have violated so many genres: here is a Primitive sitting in an armchair transgressing the dichotomy between the Primitive and the Civilized, which, according to the doctor Félix Regnault—credited as the first ethnographic filmmaker—is those who squat versus those who sit.[44] There is a frankness but also a menhir-like quality to this image, a result of her majestic stylized head, modeled after the fourth-century Javanese Buddhas of the temple of Borobudur, photos of which Gauguin liked to copy (figure 1.6).[45] Her head is idealized, noble, and beholden: like Wakiem, Seriem, Taminah, and Soekia, she is represented as timeless. The detailed pubic hair, which Gauguin used for all his Tahitian nudes and which would not have been seen in a Salon painting of a nude white woman, makes explicit, though, that she is no prepubescent girl, but a sexual woman. But it also shares provenance from the ubiquitous colonial and ethnographic postcards of naked native women of the same period, which he used as sources for his paintings.[46]

And this is how primitivism works, as a kind of modernist antimodernism: there's both a nostalgia for the past—the Primitive—and an exaltation of colonial privilege in the form of the gaze. Elizabeth Childs details Gauguin's use of photography as a control over time, a control over "collapse in the wake of Western imperialism."[47] She suggests he preferred photography to the real:

> The implications and convenience of the temporal dualism of photography for an artist are obvious: why should Gauguin, on a self-declared mission to recover primitive authenticity, deal with the messy contingencies of live models and the disappointing hybrid of colonialism when such an appealing simulacrum of the exotic was available to him in the imagery of colonial photography? Granted, neither he nor any other primitivist resorted exclusively to the authority of photographic renderings of the visible Polynesian world. But that Gauguin returned to this mediating

FIGURE 1.6 Stupa of Buddha, Borobudur Temple, 775–835 CE, Indonesia. Photographed by Fatimah Tobing Rony, 2007.

image-world repeatedly throughout his Polynesian career suggests that in the realm of the photographer, he had found some satisfying comfort and reaffirmation of his vision of Tahiti as it should have been.[48]

Photographs, she notes, like Cézanne's apples, do not talk back to you.[49] Savage life must be kept separate from civilized life or a hybrid colonial life. And the rich complexity of what it means to be a native woman during colonialism or in Paris is rejected for a less complicated exoticism and primitivism.

Like the black cat in *Olympia*, Gauguin's painting also has a domesticated animal at the subject's feet. The monkey—Annah was said to have a pet monkey, Taoa—sits in profile, with long fingers, not dissimilar to Annah's, a reminder of the evolutionary ladder that was seen as beginning with the Savage who, in turn, was represented as not so far off from a monkey. We can see the implied linking of the Savage to the monkey in other representations of colonial others, and it is also there as a reminder of what was perceived as the closeness of the colonized to the animal.[50]

Unlike the space of Gauguin's studio, which Brettell writes was yellow and olive and full of paintings, the space in *Aita tamari vahine Judith te parari* is empty and stylized: the walls are pink with a kind of tile pattern at the bottom. The interior is not the only thing empty and stylized here. Modeled after a Borobudur Buddha, part of a long line of female nudes, a conflation of the prostitute Olympia and the maid Laure, the tale of Annah would seem to be of a woman, full figured, with breasts and pubic hair, gloriously naked, who must be venerated. She stares brazenly back at the viewer. This is how she is framed. Was Annah anything like this portrait? The evidence, both textual and visual, reveals a different sort of Annah, and this is what I want to sift and analyze.

She was, we can definitively say, very alone, very small, and very young. Drawings of Annah by Gauguin bring into relief all of these facts, not visible in the painting. In *Reclining Nude* (1894 or 1895), the recto side is an image of Annah sleeping (figure 1.7).[51] In addition, there are two counterproofs from a design in pastel, *Reclining Nude* (1895), which is dedicated and signed with the inscription, "à Amedée Schuffenecker/Paul Gauguin-1895,"[52] and a watercolor monotype titled *Reclining Tahitian* (1894), which I believe is misnamed and is actually *Annah la Javanaise*.[53] In both works, the model is sleeping on her stomach, and is rather thin and boyish in figure, with an earring in one ear.

What is startling about *Reclining Nude* (recto), *Reclining Nude*, and *Reclining Tahitian* is that here Annah is sexless, sleeping, rather lithe, almost like a

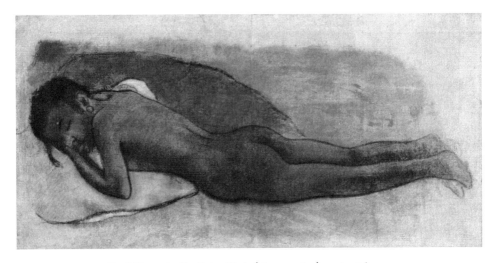

FIGURE 1.7 Paul Gauguin, *Reclining Nude* (1894 or 1895), recto side, National Gallery of Art, Washington, DC.

boy, and vulnerable. Several art historians and critics have examined what is seen as Gauguin's sexual desires and fascination with boyish girls, and also note his fascination with a young male woodcutter in his memoir *Noa Noa*.[54] Before this, Annah mirrors the figure of his own favorite child, Aline, who was four when she was also painted recumbent in *The Little Dreamer* of 1881 (figure 1.8). Aline sleeps with her back to the viewer, in the opposite direction of Tehura in Gauguin's famous painting *Manao Tupapau* (The specter watches over her; figure 1.9).[55] My interest here is not to provide evidence of Gauguin's known fetishism, but to show a view of Annah that contradicts the image of the bold sexual woman of *Aita tamari vahine Judith te parari*. If Brettell is indeed correct about the dating of this drawing, then Annah truly is a mere child.

It is also an image of a sleeping girl very different from Tehura of *Manao Tupapau* (figure 1.9).[56] In *Manao Tupapau* of 1892, a painting that Alfred Jarry dubbed "the brown Olympia," this same recumbent position, albeit in a mirrored direction, was assumed by a thirteen-year-old girl named Tehura (sometimes referred to as Teha'amana), who lived with Gauguin during his first stay in Tahiti and serviced his sexual and domestic needs.[57] *Olympia* was a painting that had a strong influence on Gauguin: he made studies of it, and a reproduction was often hanging wherever he lived. Gauguin wrote of the thirteen-year-old Tehura, "[She] told me that this Olympia was very lovely; I smiled at her remark, and was much moved. She had a sense of what was beautiful (the École des Beaux-Arts thinks the picture's horrible). Then she suddenly spoke again, breaking the silence brought on by these thoughts. 'Is she your wife?' she asked. 'Yes,' I lied. Me! the lover of Olympia!"[58] Instead, Gauguin created his own brown Olympia, with Tehura as the model. In his largely fictional memoir, *Noa Noa*, Gauguin borrows the essential structure of Pierre Loti's *The Marriage of Loti*, in which an English officer falls in love with and then abandons a fourteen-year-old Tahitian girl named Rarahu. (He and Loti had sailed in the same colonial boat when Gauguin was in the navy.) Gauguin describes coming home to find Tehura in a kind of trance:

> Tehura lay motionless, naked, belly down on the bed: she stared up at me, her eyes wide with fear; and she seemed not to know who I was. For a moment I too felt a strange uncertainty. Tehura's dread was contagious: it seemed to me that a phosphorescent light poured from her staring eyes. I had never seen her so lovely; above all, I had never seen her beauty so moving. And in the half-shadow, which no doubt settled with dangerous apparitions and ambiguous shapes, I feared to make the slightest movement, in case the child should be terrified out of her mind. Did I know what she thought I was in that instant? Perhaps she took me, with my anguished face, for one of those legendary demons or specters, the *Tupapaus* that filled the sleepless nights of her people.[59]

The painting *Manao Tupapau*, although ostensibly about a Tahitian girl fearing a spirit or tupapau, also presents Tehura for the viewer's pleasure. Patty O'Brien explains that the shocking element of the painting to conservatives and libertines would be the idea that she, like Olympia, is sexually experienced. The body turned over increases her vulnerability, and the exposure of her buttocks signifies her primitiveness, explains O'Brien, although Gauguin later disguised this meaning by explaining that her posture was born out of fear.[60] To his wife, Mette, Gauguin wrote that her position was "indecent." "Yet, I wanted her that way. . . . One of our own young women would be startled if I surprised her in such a posture. Not so a woman here."[61] This is the defining myth for Gauguin: he is a white native, cognizant of Tahitian myths and religions, and the girls, although only thirteen, desire to be taken. This framing myth is used again in *Aita tamari vahine Judith te parari*.

Besides *Eve Exotique*, a nude portrait of his mother with detailed pubic hair (figure 1.10), another nude he made before he left for his first trip to Tahiti was a symbolist portrait of the seamstress Juliette Huet, lying in a Breton landscape, when she was two months pregnant by Gauguin and posed for him for *The Loss of Virginity* (1891; figure 1.11). Like *The Little Dreamer* with

FIGURE 1.8 Paul Gauguin, *The Little Dreamer* (1881), oil on canvas, Ordrupgaard Collection, Copenhagen.

its strange doll at the right, or the black tupapau or spirit in *Manao Tupa-pau*, and later the orange monkey in *Aita tamari vahine Judith te parari*, this painting, *The Loss of Virginity*, reveals a supine nude flanked by a small un-canny figure—here, an orange fox. This painting was made in the same year that Gauguin copied Manet's *Olympia*, and Brettell asserts that he reprised *Olympia* as a challenge. The black cat in *Olympia* is here an orange fox who has a paw on Juliette's breast and looks right out at the viewer, a symbol not just of lust but also of the artist himself, letting us in on the secret (her loss of virginity symbolized by the red-tipped flower in her right hand).[62] We can see that the images of naked girls in a color-saturated landscape, many of whom are sexual-ized, were often of women with whom he was intimate: Aline, his mother, as a girl; Aline, his daughter; Judith, the neighbor's daughter; Juliette, his girlfriend; and Annah.[63] The title of the painting of Juliette presages that of *Aita tamari vahine Judith te parari* in its theme of the breaching of virginity. It appears that not just brown girls but white working-class girls were there to be violated. (Later, when Gauguin returned to Paris in 1893 and their daughter Germaine

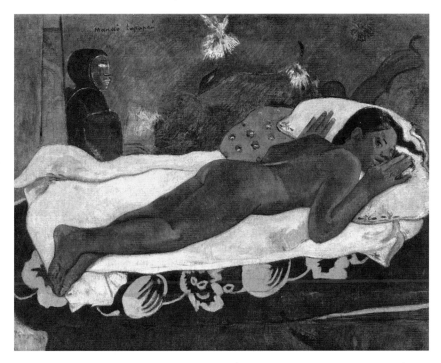

FIGURE 1.9 Paul Gauguin, *Manao Tupapao* (The specter watches over her, 1892), oil on canvas, Albright-Knox Art Gallery, Buffalo, New York.

was age two, he resumed relations with Huet).[64] In the much later painting of 1902, *Contes barbares*, the orange uncanny figure is made explicit: it is a white male devil with red hair, like the painter himself.[65] Annah's body was just one among many bodies of girls and women Gauguin painted throughout his career. Like the violent light that constitutes the viewer's gaze upon Olympia, as delineated by Foucault, these paintings are in essence portraits of Gauguin, a kind of collection or what Bliss Cua Lim would call a serial equalization of the women and girls of his life, a Bluebeard's closet.[66] These works reveal Gauguin's subjectivity, and the bright light of the viewer is his own.

The first wave of art historians who established Gauguin as a modernist hero reveled in his sexuality, seen as integral to rejecting the stale conservative values of fin-de-siècle France and part of his persona as a great radical painter. Later on, art historians such as Abigail Solomon-Godeau lambasted Gauguin as a colonialist living out his fantasies through his representations of Tahitian and Marquesan girls.[67] As if seeking to pacify both sides, recent art historians seek to claim him as a postmodernist hero who reveals the

FIGURE 1.10 Paul
Gauguin, *Eve Exotique*
(1890), gouache, private
collection, Paris.

ambivalence of the colonialist position. Art historians Stephen Eisenman and
Nancy Mowll Mathews, among others, have posited that Gauguin actually subverted sexual binaries. Many critics, including Chris Bongie and Rod Edmond,
claim that he is an ironic fetishist involved in a process of affirmative deconstruction.[68] Regardless, Gauguin remains a great maker of myth, as the block-
buster exhibit of 2010 at the National Gallery in Washington, DC, and the Tate
Modern in London, and the 2014 show at the Museum of Modern Art attest.

In general, art historians have glossed over the divide between those who
see (who are the light, who illuminate, as Foucault put it) and those who are
seen (Olympia, Tehura, Annah, Juliette, Aline); but what is interesting about

FIGURE 1.11 Paul Gauguin, *The Loss of Virginity* (1891), oil on canvas, Chrysler Museum of Art, Norfolk, Virginia.

Aita tamari vahine Judith te parari is that the brown girl Annah and the white girl Judith are conflated in a willful misnaming and doubling. Visual biopolitics works through this complexity: the real rape of the brown girl is obfuscated by the naming of the white girl who is not raped.

Even in studies of how colonized or enslaved people are represented, there is often a normalizing of the critic's own biases. Perhaps the most cited essay on reading the performance of subjugated peoples in photography is Alan Trachtenberg's from 1990, in which he reads the photographs of African American slaves from South Carolina commissioned by anthropologist Louis Agassiz in 1850. J. T. Zealy photographed the subjects naked, or partially naked. Trachtenberg admits to being aroused, what he calls "imaginative liberation," which is the white male viewer's liberation from American ideologies of class and race. "We know how to view conventional portraits—but to gaze upon naked bodies, male and female, of persons dispossessed of themselves, is another matter. The effect even now can be confusing, erotic response mingling with moral disgust and outrage."[69] If one looks at the subjects in the photographs as one's grandfather or grandmother, that kind of liberation that he describes is not primary. Instead these photographs mirror one's own image in the skein of visual biopolitics, whose legacy is still felt today in what film theory would call identification, the investment of the viewer in the emotional energy of the main characters on the screen.[70]

Besides the study of Annah lying down, there are several striking photographs that include her. These photographs appear to be nineteenth-century "selfies," self-portraits of fabulous, spectacularly posed selves, which celebrate the libertine, the louche, and the artist who spits in the face of conservative society. Before Gauguin moved to rue Vercingétorix after inheriting his Uncle Isidore's money, he had rented a small studio at 8, rue de la Grande Chaumiere, which he shared with painter Alphonse Mucha.[71] The photographs that include Annah were probably taken in the Grande Chaumiere studio before Mucha's move in 1896 to Val-du-Grâce.[72]

In one photo, Gauguin plays the harmonium wearing a jacket without pants, perched on a stool atop a shaggy rug at Mucha's studio: "his white feet extending from a pair of hairy legs and resting elegantly on the pedals" (figure 1.12).[73] Another photograph by Mucha shows an unidentified man (whom son Jiří Mucha identifies as Gauguin, the same man in figure 1.12), Alphonse Mucha in an embroidered shirt, the Czech artist Luděk Marold, and Annah dressed for costume tableau, standing in front of a mirror (figure 1.13).[74]

In fact, there are at least three photographs of Mucha's studio that include a very young and a very small Annah. Unsmiling, alarmed, suspicious, her fiery eyes say something to us across the centuries: I am here. What the photographs give is evidence that Annah existed in the same moment as Gauguin and the others, and she cannot be reduced to some idealized image. She is coeval with them, not a Savage, simply by being caught in the same frame, at the same moment that the camera shutter opened to capture the group's likeness on film. The photo asserts her existence in a way that the painting does not, and this is because she can represent herself through her facial expression and her look, and the way that she poses (instead of being posed). They also reveal Annah's difference, but not just in her gender, her clothes, or her dress—after all, Gauguin is without pants, and another man is in a dress;

FIGURE 1.12 Gauguin at a harmonium, probably taken in the Grande Chaumiere studio of Alphonse Mucha before 1896. Photograph: Mucha Trust/Bridgeman Images.

FIGURE 1.13 Gauguin, Alphonse Mucha, Marold, and Annah la Javanaise. Photograph: Mucha Trust/Bridgeman Images.

what signals it is the agony in her eyes. They are alarmed, furtive, guarded. This is her look. And this is how she represents herself. Unlike the men in their bohemian costume dress, Annah's hands are crossed in front of her chest, a bizarre gesture, like an unsmiling corpse. The men's dissoluteness and ease—oh, what fun to be a bohemian man, to be a libertine—contrast with her stiffness and startled expression. She is not in on the joke; she is the joke. And this is what, drawing from Larasati's description of the replica of the Indonesian female dancer who stands in for the other murdered girl, constitutes the haunting.

This is how Mucha's son, Jiří, described the photograph:

> My father's friendship with Gauguin actually started before his [Gauguin's] first trip to Tahiti and lasted until his final departure in 1895. A photograph of the two of them taken by my father (who operated the camera by pulling a string) in his studio shows Gauguin wearing a Moravian peasant's hat, his mistress, Annah la Javannaise [sic], in a white headdress, and Marold, a Czech painter, who until his premature death was father's closest associate, wearing a Renaissance jacket. . . . What they were all dressed up for is anybody's guess—a fancy dress ball perhaps, or to pose for one of my father's historical illustrations.[75]

The men look at the camera in a very direct and casual manner. Annah's manner is intense and agitated. The casualness with which she is identified as Gauguin's mistress is belied by the intensity of her gaze. She is thirteen and looks caught in a game that she does not want to play.

In another photograph, probably taken at the same time, we again see Annah, in the same dress, same studio, this time with a dog and with Alphonse Mucha wearing the same embroidered shirt (figure 1.14).[76] Here we see her long hair flowing past her shoulders. In the photograph it is hard to tell her age; it is possible that she is a teenager, but possible as well that she is older. She appears awkward and upset; she has the look of someone who does not want to be photographed. Her gaze is averted, in contrast to Mucha's happy-go-lucky gaze. He appears casual and relaxed; he looks at the camera, but his gaze is not fixed. She is resisting, and her pose is one of resistance.

And in another photograph, this time taken by Gauguin in his studio at 6, rue Vercingétorix, Annah's extremely tiny, thin hands contrast sharply to her disembodied presence in a flowing, dark dress (figure 1.15). In this photograph, whose subjects are identified by Richard Brettell, she is flanked by the postimpressionist painter and sculptor Paul Sérusier (one of Les Nabis) and the postimpressionist painter Georges Lacombe (also part of the Les Nabis group) in the back row, with the Swedish cellist Fritz Schneklud (center) and

FIGURE 1.14 Alphonse Mucha and Annah la Javanaise. Photograph: Mucha Trust/Bridgeman Images.

the musician Larrivel (right) in the front row.[77] She sits with her hands on her knees, again revealing her tiny stature. In all the photographs she is wearing a very loose gown, as if to hide the fact that she is a mere child. She is still gazing guardedly, while the musicians appear relaxed, hamming it up.

"How do we look?" the celebrated male artists and musicians seem to ask, crowing as the sexually liberated avant-garde. But it is the look of the child—anxious, guarded—that disturbs the spectacle of entertainment. How do we look at such a photograph? In contrast to the direct Olympia-like gaze in the painting *Aita tamari vahine Judith te parari*, that of the sexually experienced prostitute looking fixedly at the viewer, the male client, Annah's look in the photographs reveals . . . a child. Left behind in the archive.

What we have then is the inverse of Gauguin's paintings of Tahitian women. In this photograph the white men are the main subjects, and Annah becomes the uncanny side figure, the spirit that disturbs. She stands out. She looks uncomfortable, even upset, never relaxed, but she is also engaged in the

FIGURE 1.15 Photograph by Gauguin, at the studio of 6, rue Vercingétorix. Front row, Swedish cellist Fritz Schneklud (center) and the musician Larrivel (right), with postimpressionist painter and sculptor Paul Sérusier, Annah la Javanaise, and the postimpressionist painter Georges Lacomb in the back row. Photograph: ©Museé du Pont Aven, Pont Aven, France.

dress-up; she becomes the fox, or orange monkey, or tupapau who watches over the scene of these men involved in their own self-portraiture. She is the ghost, the phantom that sits watchfully, on her guard, among the men who are proud to show off their spectacular Western subjectivity. This is the image that could never be painted within one frame. This is Annah's resistant eye, her look back and her challenge.

A TALE OF JUDITH

What do you call a thirteen-year-old girl who works for you and has sex with you and whom you paint? Can we call her a mistress if she is that young and poor and without protection of a mother or a community to shield her from harm? For isn't a mistress in this situation one who is allowed to be raped? With Annah la Javanaise, what we have is a figure who contravenes the ethnographic template of those who squat and those who sit. In the modern world of subjectivity, the rational I, the Civilized is constituted through making an other the Noncivilized, the non-I. Annah is constrained by the disciplinary apparatus of what it means to be a Parisian; she can be the dancing girl in the Javanese village or she can be the black maid, but she can never be the modern Parisienne. Her subjectivity is thus circumscribed. *Aita tamari vahine Judith te parari*, then, is a visual rape, the actual rape of a girl (the trace of her relations with Gauguin, which involved habitual and normalized rape), and an image that shows the girl inviting rape. It is about who may be raped, and how the one who is raped is framed.

Like Annah and Gauguin's daughter, Aline (whom he adored, but who lived far away with her mother in Copenhagen), Judith was thirteen years old; biographer David Sweetman writes that this is "the mythical age which seems to have represented for [Gauguin] the hallowed point when a girl became a woman, rather than any very precise chronological moment."[78] The tale of Annah cannot be told without that of the blonde-haired Judith, the illegitimate daughter of Swedish sculptor Ida Molard and Swedish opera singer Fritz Arlberg.[79] Judith also lived at 6, rue Vercingétorix. Judith hated her stepfather, William Molard, an unsuccessful composer who loved to drink with Gauguin, but she adored and desired Gauguin.

A photograph of Judith taken around 1896 is indeed not dissimilar to the painting of "Judith," *Aita tamari vahine Judith te parari*.[80] Sweetman suggests that the painter was trying to work some likeness of Judith into the painting, and that is why the Annah of the painting does not resemble the Annah of the photographs:

> It is also true that Annah is not quite Annah—she does not quite resemble her photographs and there is good cause to believe that Gauguin slightly modified her appearance so as to work in some resemblance to his original model Judith. This notion is reinforced by the title he eventually gave the painting: *Aita tamari vahine Judith te parari*, this time using the Tahitian to deliberately ensure that no one, especially the Molards, would understand the meaning, which can be translated as "the child-woman Judith is not yet breached." If nothing else, this confirms Judith's assertion that he did no more than kiss and fondle her.[81]

At the far right of the painting one can see the title and the vestiges of her original portrait, according to Thomas Millroth.[82] Judith is like the spirit or tupapau in the background of *Manao Tupapau*—the spirit that watches over, the specter of sexuality, the one who is untouched—but she is also the real subject of the painting. Much later in her life, Judith wrote a memoir, never published, which she titled *The Young Girl and the Tupapau*. Gauguin was the specter that watched over her. Judith seems to have wanted to be desired by Gauguin in the same way he desired Tehura or Annah, in a triangular formation of looks.

Here is how Judith describes Gauguin's attentions. Ida Molard had ordered Judith to get her stepfather, William, from Gauguin's studio, due to Molard's fear that "he would be unfaithful to her in his thoughts, as he talked to Gauguin about Negresses":

> I went quietly up to Gauguin. He slipped his arms round my waist, and laying his hand like a shell round my budding breast repeated in his gruff voice, which was barely audible:
> "This is mine, all this."
> Everything was his, indeed: my affection, my as yet unaroused sensuousness, my whole soul. I stood up on tiptoe and raised my lips towards his cheek, but met his lips. I offered him my whole soul, as I offered him my lips, and all he had to do was take it.[83]

But Gauguin does not "take" Judith, in large part, because she is under Ida's watch. Judith is replaced in the painting with the figure of Annah. Like *javanais*, the French secret language that hid the meaning of words by adding -av infixed inside a word after every consonant that is followed by a vowel, the title is pseudo-Tahitian, and hidden code for "the child-woman Judith is not yet breached." The white girl Judith's virginity is left intact and replaced by that of a brown girl, who in her frank gaze, naked body sitting upon an armchair in a living room, an exotic monkey at her feet, is iconographically decidedly not a virgin. Judith is not breached because Annah is breached: therein lies the irony of the painting. Like Olympia, Annah invites the breach; she is the "child-woman who desires to be breached." The language is one of sexualized assault. The verb "breach" is, literally, to break through, as through a wall.[84]

In an earlier version of *Noa Noa*, Gauguin wrote that the young native women of Mataiea "look at you with such . . . utterly fearless dignity, that I was really intimidated."[85] Literary scholar Rod Edmond explains that Gauguin wrote that he wanted these "calm-eyed young women to be willing to be taken without a word: taken brutally. In a way, a longing to rape. The old men said to me, speaking of one of them: '*Maü téra* [take that one].' I was timid and dared not resign myself to the effort."[86] An inversion is going on here where Gauguin's timidity is overwhelmed by the native elders' authority to "take that one."[87]

Edmond also explains that in a later *Noa Noa* manuscript (now at the Louvre) Gauguin's desire to rape has been sublimated into the more predictable sentiment that the women wish to be raped. Here is how Gauguin describes the girls as desiring to be raped:

> Indeed, I saw in the district young women and young girls, tranquil of eye, pure Tahitians, some of whom would perhaps gladly have shared my life.—However, I did not dare approach them. They actually made me timid with their sure look, their dignity of bearing, and their pride of gait.
>
> All, indeed, wish to be "taken," literally, brutally taken (*Maü*, to seize), without a single word. All have the secret desire for violence, because this act of authority on the part of the male leaves to the woman-will its full share of irresponsibility. For in this way she has not given her consent for the beginning of a permanent love. It is possible that there is a deeper meaning in this violence that at first sight seems so revolting. It is possible also that it has a savage sort of charm. I pondered the matter, indeed, but I did not dare.
>
> Then, too, some were said to be ill, ill with that malady which Europeans confer upon savages, doubtless as the first degree of their initiation into civilized life. . . .
>
> And when the older among them said to me, pointing to one of them, "*Maü téra* (take that one)," I had neither the necessary audacity nor the confidence.[88]

What is fascinating about Gauguin's alteration in the text is that it is their calm look back that intimidates the painter, and that in taking them, in raping them, he is doing them the favor (of not having to commit to a relationship). A few years later, in 1897, Gauguin was more blunt about his relations with young native girls. In a letter of January 15, 1897, to painter Armand Séguin, Gauguin wrote,

> Just to sit here at the open door, smoking a cigarette and drinking a glass of absinth, is an unmixed pleasure which I have every day. And then I have a fifteen-year-old wife who cooks my simple everyday fare and gets down on her back for me whenever I want, all for the modest reward of a frock, worth ten francs, a month. . . . You have no idea how far 125 francs will go here. I can ride or drive round in a trap as often as I feel like it. The horse and trap are my own, like the house and all the rest.[89]

The breach, the rape, the rift, the violation . . . Abigail Solomon-Godeau implicates the layout of the World's Fair with rape, and writes, "The importance of this lexicon of exoticism for Gauguin should not be—but usually is—underestimated."[90] The rape is there, even when the discourse constructs the woman's willingness. Solomon-Godeau continues,

> Thus, the experience of the primitive "framed" within the Pavilion of the colonies or the History of Human Habitation is analogous to the primitivist discourse "framed" by the imperialism that is its condition of existence and the content of its articulation.
>
> To acknowledge this framing is but a first step in demythifying what it meant for Gauguin to "go native." There is, in short, a darker side to primitivist desire, one implicated in fantasies of imaginary knowledge, power and rape, and these fantasies, moreover, are sometimes underpinned by real power, by real rape.[91]

I go further than Solomon-Godeau and state that the biopolitics of who may live and who may let die can be extended to the power relation of who may be left alone (Judith) and who may be raped (Annah). There are two kinds of thirteen-year-olds, and one of them is there to be breached, which is the fate of Annah la Javanaise, without a mother or a father or friends to protect her, in Gauguin's "living museum" studio in 1893. Rape, and its presentation as normal, is an example of the effects of the visual aspect of biopolitics, and this painting valorizes it.

What are the enabling conditions of this biopolitics? One is visibility. Apparatuses such as the native village set up a way of looking that allows for the way that Annah is not ever really seen; she is always already a Javanese girl, which is how Gauguin will see any of the black girls, be they from Tahiti, the Marquesas, Java, or Paris—girls to party with, or girls to rape. These apparatuses are a form of visual biopolitics. Annah is a metonym for a wider culture; she is Annah the Javanese girl, la Javanaise. The second is primitivism and exoticism, which is seen by the discourse that constructs her as desiring to be raped, which obfuscates the other girl's, Judith's, actual desire for Gauguin. However, the obverse could be true under primitivism and exoticism, that she is incapable of being raped. She has no subjectivity; therefore the rules of consent or lack of consent don't apply. Also, at that time, rape was a crime against the father or husband who had an interest in the daughter or wife's virginity/monogamy for the purposes of primogeniture (which is why the law did not recognize marital rape). In a sense, Annah could not be raped because there was no father or husband whose property rights would be threatened if she bore an illegitimate child.[92] And finally, the discourse must be one sided: the only text from this history is that of Gauguin, other European visitors to his salon, and Judith's memoir. Annah has left no text behind, which is the final enabling condition: that she is not allowed, must not be allowed, to speak—and also must not be allowed to look; for as we saw in the *Noa Noa* memoir, it is the calm look back on the part of the native girls that intimidates Gauguin and leads him to change the narrative from his desire to rape to their desire to be raped. Not looking is also part of the looking connection. For the thirteen-year-old black girl found wandering the streets of Paris, who may or may not have been Javanese, it was this discourse of Java and Tahiti that constrained her as much as her dire straits.

Achille Mbembe renames Foucault's concept of the "power and the capacity to dictate who may live and who must die" *necropolitics*, which has incurred the genocide of indigenous people, chattel slavery, and colonialism, a regulation of life over death. There are two aspects that I want to point out in terms of necropolitics. The first is that the newfound freedom of the artist is at the expense of the safety, security, and health of the colonized girl or woman, like Annah. The light that Foucault talks about that reveals the position of the viewer, in relation to the spectator of *Olympia*, is a violent light, the light of the colonizer. Freedom requires violence, and not just that of war, but violence against the subjects who are not seen as agentive, Western liberal rational subjects. The agency to act as a rational liberal subject, in a sense the freedom of the liberal subject—that is Man, or homo economicus—ironically requires slavery, apartheid, and violence. Talal Asad, citing Max Weber, explains that freedom and democracy in Europe were engendered by "the forcible expansion of the West over many centuries into the non-European world—and in spite of the simultaneous growth of a standardizing capitalism," and ironically, it is that drive for freedom that may be what compromises freedom and democracy.[93]

But to continue the historiography of Gauguin, to render all the women in his life—wives, daughters, daughters of friends, girlfriends—as without will, there to be taken, is to continue to deny them agency. While I do not want to ventriloquize Annah's voice in any sense, she is in many ways a perfect example of how the subaltern woman cannot speak.[94] Yet Annah did look at the camera, and in her pose she communicates something that does not mesh neatly with the narrative of la Javanaise.

Let me turn now to the construction of subjectivity through visual biopolitics, and in particular to the idea of the mistress. The narrative of the framed image encodes a society's system of repression, and thus this narrative literally permits violence against those denied the right to their own words, their own language. Like the fence that delineates the colonial village at the World's Fair from the Parisian visitor, the historiography of Gauguin calls Annah, like the others—Juliette, Tehura (Teha'amana), Pau'ura a Tai, and Marie-Rose Vaeoho—a mistress.[95]

The question of authenticity comes to the fore, not just a physical fence to delimit the Savage from the Civilized, but also a discursive one. Gauguin is not a real savage, lamented a critic after Gauguin's return to Paris. What the critic really yearned for was "the arrival in Paris of a real Tahitian painter, who, while his works are at Durand-Ruel or somewhere else, will camp out in the Paris Zoo—a real Maori, in other words."[96] The apartheid of the native artist is apparent, behind bars. Consequently, Annah could not be a real Parisienne. At this point in time, Savages in Paris were seen as inhabitants of zoos or a World's Fair. The same mentality that yearned to see a "real Maori" could not fathom Annah as a real Parisienne. Nobody, except perhaps Annah herself, really saw Annah as a modern Parisienne.

Gauguin and his cohorts are proud to be flouting modernity, their subjectivity, with the narrative of who is posing for whom. Neither the photos of themselves cavorting and hamming it up in Mucha's studio nor the paintings of the brown girls are intended for the girls and women themselves, but, rather, for each other. These artists see themselves as the Western secular subject, without realizing that they do not exist, they cannot constitute themselves, without the nonsubject, the non-I, who, to paraphrase James Baldwin, constitutes their fixed star. Homo economicus exists because of his freedom to take. If there is fear in Annah's eyes, then it is probably of rape or sexual coercion, or at least sexual harassment; not just by Gauguin, but by his buddies, like Judith's stepfather, William, whom Gauguin regales with tales of "négresses."

I would like to expand upon Ruth Wilson Gilmore's definition of racism, elaborated in the introduction, to include the state-sanctioned or extralegal production and exploitation of group-differentiated vulnerability to rape.[97] In this case the colonial man or the sex tourist is the sovereign: he has the right to force someone to have sex or to be let alone. When Vollard sends Annah to Gauguin, he sends her to be raped. Judith, who was totally infatuated with Gauguin, desired Gauguin, offering herself to him when he kissed her and groped her breasts, was thwarted in her desire. Instead Annah's desire is created as a fascinating visual subterfuge. A culture long used to valorizing genius cannot see that she was a young girl involved in an abusive relationship with a famous artist, as writer Joyce Maynard has expounded.[98]

I have detailed the discourses around the nude in Gauguin's oeuvre, in part to show that to Annah, whose real name we do not even know, was ascribed an image that was already formed before she even appeared on the threshold of Gauguin's studio at rue Vercingétorix. And while I can tell you is how she is framed, I cannot say how she perceived herself. Nevertheless, there are definitely points of resistance in Annah's actions and the story told about her that reveal that her own spirit was, to use Barthes's words, light, divided, and dispersed.[99] It is an identity that haunts the myth of modernity and Gauguin.

If in the painting Annah appears as a brown Olympia, and if in the drawings she appears to be an androgynous young child, in Judith's memoir Annah is revealed to be insolent and proud. This is apparent even in her provenance: Nina Pack had hoped to have a little black girl to clean her house: she was to fire Annah for a domestic incident. She begins in this tale as a failed maid, or as a girl who refused to clean house.

What did Judith make of Annah? They appear to have gotten along well, but Judith describes Annah as an exotic, picturesque animal or alien. In her memoir, Judith recounts coming into Gauguin's salon one day and finding Annah in his bed. She accepted Gauguin's explanation that Annah was sick.[100] The point that Judith in her memoir was making is that she, as a thirteen-year-old girl, did not realize Annah and the forty-five-year-old Gauguin might be having intercourse.[101] It becomes an anecdote about Judith's naïveté, but in looking back it could very well be that Annah was lying in bed not because she was lazy or promiscuous. She may indeed have been sick or injured, in every sense of the word, from being forced to have sex with a man who would nine years later die of advanced syphilis. We can only speculate but cannot be sure, since there are no recorded traces of Annah's agency or wishes, and questions of consent and compliance in rape are complicated. Moreover, a kind of sexual triad that we see in slave societies, like that of the colonial South, is formed here, where a white girl (like Judith) can grow up with a black girl (like Annah), and be close in age, like sisters, but the master will have sex with the black girl, who may be his own daughter (like Aline). Thus, the cult of white femininity is upheld.

Judith's remembrances of Annah also reveal a girl who resists the shadow-figure role into which she had been cast. Again, we are reading traces here; just as there are traces of Judith in Annah's portrait, there are traces of Annah in Judith's memoir, just like the overlaying of the two girls in the painting. In the painting and in the memoir, they are conjoined, Judith and Annah, two types of girls, one let alone, one who is violated, who become merged in one figure.

Judith's memoir describe a girl whose French was good enough to take to task jealous ex-girlfriends. Juliette Huet, the mother of Gauguin's two-year-old daughter, Germaine, attempted to reestablish a relationship with Gauguin by coming to the studio one day. To her dismay, she found Annah there. Huet was furious and spent some time cursing Annah, with the assumption that she could not understand French. Judith relates that after Huet's tirade was over, Annah finally replied, "Has Madame finished?" This made Huet even more furious and, according to Judith's memoir, she stormed out and never came back again. What is so strange about this anecdote is that one assumes that Annah, if she had indeed just appeared from Java, could not speak French that well, but her French was good enough for her to have the last word with an enraged French mother trying to get her man back and, presumably, child support for her toddler daughter. Annah at least knew enough French to render Huet speechless.

Judith also relates that Annah, like any self-respecting modern Parisienne of the time, loved to stroll, to look at and to be seen. She was, in other words, a *flâneuse*. Gauguin presented both Annah and Judith with rolls of plaited leaf so that they could get hats made. Here is what Judith wrote about the two of them visiting two rival spring art salons at the Champs de Mars in 1894:

> At the opening of the spring show we were dressed differently; for though Annah, like me, was only thirteen, she had rigged herself in grand style, while I wore a short dress. We had arranged to meet outside the entrance to the Palais des Beaux-Arts, as we were two to a ticket. The odd crowd, which gathered around Gauguin, consisted of a "bodyguard" of thin men— Morice, Leclercq, Ranson, Roinard, and Monfreid—and a troupe of little people—my mother, myself, the Maufras, Paco, and Anna [sic]. We cannot have averaged more than five feet in height.
>
> Once through the turnstiles, each followed his own glittering lodestar; some beginning to look round for useful acquaintances, others trying mainly to attract attention, the rest bent on discovering the latest master-piece by Rodin, Besnard, or Gauguin. Anna [sic] looked as if she meant to lay the world at her feet, walking determinedly erect with her head in the air and thrusting out her little pointed chin over her stiff, embroidered collar. Her straw hat rested at the back of her head on a great knot of blue-

black hair and so inclined at an angle of forty-five degrees in the direction of her nose, which was as flat as that of a baby chimpanzee. She was wearing a tight-fitting blouse of checked silk with puff sleeves and ample decorative folds and a long gown with a train, which she held at waist height in her silk-gloved hand.[102]

Judith denigrates Annah's style: she makes fun of her for looking like a monkey in a woman's clothes. She is anything but a "chimpanzee," although Judith chooses to describe her in that way. Her description reminds us of the kitschy American oil paintings by Donald Roller Wilson of chimpanzees in old-fashioned girls' dresses. Here again, Annah is the joke. But regardless, it is clear that Annah is set on presenting herself in her own way: "Anna looked as if she meant to lay the world at her feet." Here, she is posing and performing, not being posed.

Two things seem to belie the story of Annah as a girl who was just dropped onto the streets of Paris: her command of French (to the chagrin of Juliette Huet) and her incredible style as a flâneuse who loved walking around imperiously in the latest fashions. It was probably that fierceness that led to the incident that would allow Annah to leave Gauguin forever.

In the provinces and outside of Paris, her appearance, a brown girl in Parisian finery, walking with a white forty-five-year-old French man and a monkey, would have been seen as unacceptable and intolerable. On May 25, 1894, Gauguin, Annah, and monkey Taoa, accompanied by Roderick O'Conor and Armand Séguin and their girlfriends, went for a walk in the small Breton fishing village of Concarneau. It seems that the sight of them provoked a fight, and in particular the sight of Annah and her monkey with Gauguin. Pretty soon children were taunting them. Here is Bengt Danielsson's account: "The youngsters soon grew bolder and more aggressive. Anna may have upset them more than was necessary by sticking out her tongue at them or thumbing her nose, the way she used to do when annoyed, for suddenly they began to throw stones."[103] One of the men of the party, Séguin, pinched a boy's ear, and his father came out to defend him. A fight ensued. Other men came out from taverns to assist. Danielsson writes, "These new assailants also went for the screaming Annah, though the other women nobly did their best to shield her."[104]

According to another account, it all came to a head in Brittany when the local residents attempted to stone Annah as a witch: "She was the cause of Gauguin's memorable battle with the Breton peasants, who threw stones at the little Javanese girl, accusing her of being a witch. In the course of the fray the painter had his foot broken. He never got over this accident."[105] The wicked girl, the Javanese girl, who walks on the same plane with the white French man, must be expelled. Writing to William Molard, Gauguin also seems to imply that it was the sight of Annah that caused the conflagration:

> I feel too seedy to write much. My leg is broken close to the ankle. They started throwing stones at Concarneau, when I was walking with Annah. I knocked down with two punches a pilot who attacked me. He then rallied the crew of his boat and fifteen men fell on me. I took them all on, and kept the upper hand, until my foot caught in a hole and in falling I broke my leg. Whilst on the ground I was kicked mercilessly but at last I was extricated. I had to be carried to Pont-Aven, and am nursing my wounds. Cannot more—.[106]

Gauguin had to stay behind in Brittany because his leg had been broken, but Annah insisted on returning to Paris, so he paid her fare. And that was the last time he saw her. Upon returning to his studio in November, Gauguin found that "Anna had been there already and made off with all his valuables—everything, that is, except his pictures."[107] Again, Annah has the last word. Her decision not to steal his paintings is the ultimate snub: she did not deem Gauguin's work valuable enough to sell. The next year Gauguin left for Tahiti, never to return to Paris.

Brettell speculates that perhaps Annah did take one painting, *Aita tamari vahine Judith te parari*:

> We know that Annah returned to Paris from Pont-Aven in the late summer of 1894 and that she looted Gauguin's studio of everything but his paintings. Is it possible that she took just one, this portrait of her? If so, we have only the negative evidence that no one seems to have mentioned it within the artist's lifetime. In 1922, the painting was purchased by the great Swiss collector Émile Hahnloser of Bern, where it was undoubtedly admired by Félix Vallotton, whose own nude or seminude figures owe a profound debt to this painting by Gauguin.[108]

From Annah's point of view, it might not have been looting. From her point of view, it might have been her due wages. Or as an escape from Gauguin, possibly it attests to her strength of character, and her assertion of sovereignty after only a few months in Paris.

Finally, one last photo remains of Annah, taken by Mucha (figure 1.16). She is much changed. Now working as a model for Alphonse Mucha, it is striking to see how much Annah poses similarly to the figure in *Aita tamari vahine Judith te parari.* Her chair even appears to be perched on the same shag rug we saw in Gauguin's half-naked portrait at the harmonium taken several years earlier. Her dress is European, long, velvet; she appears to have her hair up, with a flower by her right ear, and her hands are still extremely thin and small. Behind her are the attributes of a studio parlor: a stone bust, a lamp, a vase of flowers, and a few canvases. She is still unsmiling, but here she looks right at the camera, and there is a resignation about her. Her eyes are no longer ablaze. It is perhaps the alcohol that has changed her; according to Judith, she had taken up drink. After Gauguin left Paris for Tahiti, never to return, Judith went on to marry Edouard Gérard, who became governor of Algeria, and thus she lived as a colonialist in Algeria for two years. On their return to France, the Gérards decided to live apart, and Judith went on to become a painter.[109] Her memoir was titled *The Young Girl and the Tupapau,* but the young girl who desired Gauguin would grow up instead to be like Gauguin, an artist.

After Gauguin's departure for Tahiti, Judith was devastated, and in 1905, ten years after Gauguin had left Paris, Judith decided to see her old friend Annah, according to David Sweetman:

> Annah the Javanese . . . was still modeling—an ideal occupation, as she put it, as it meant she had to do nothing but lie around. Fascinated to see her again, after all that time, Judith hired Annah to pose for her, intrigued to listen to the incessant chatter about their mutual past. Annah revealed how Gauguin had given her one of his portraits of her but that she had been angry when they parted and had poked out the eyes and then burned it. Now she was truly furious because she had been told it was worth a lot of money. There is a curious twist to this story for the nude portrait of her that Gauguin had made disappeared from the public view for many years until it turned up with Vollard, so it may be that it was the one picture which Annah took when she looted his studio, a fact that she was now trying to hide by claiming it had been destroyed when she was in fact planning to sell it to the dealer.
>
> As her new portrait took shape, Annah chatted on and on until Judith told her servant to let the poor thing sit in the kitchen and drink herself to sleep so that there could be some peace at last.[110]

Thus, Vollard, who had pimped Annah to Gauguin in the first place, profited in the end with the painting of Annah, whose myth he helped create. Nobody listens to Annah, least of all her childhood friend Judith. She chatters away into the night, and there is the irony of this story: she speaks but

FIGURE 1.16
Alphonse Mucha,
photograph of
Annah la Javanaise
(1898). Photo-
graph: Mucha
Trust/Bridgeman
Images.

nobody listens, or cares to hear. Judith writes, and paints, and Annah speaks
but does not write. We only know of her from others, their photographs and
their memoirs. Because she is seen as a "négresse," like her sisters in Tahiti
who also became sex partners of Gauguin, most Gauguin commentary tends
to naturalize, normalize, or rationalize her story.

   After years of being silent over her sexual and physical abuse by directors
(Quentin Tarantino) and producers (Harvey Weinstein), actor Uma Thurman said this when she finally recognized what had been done to her, and
declared it to be wrong: "I am one of the reasons that a young girl would
walk into his room alone, the way I did. . . . And all these lambs walked into
slaughter because they were convinced nobody rises to such a position who
would do something illegal to you, but they do. . . . I stand as both a person

who was subjected to it and a person who was then also part of the cloud cover, so that's a super weird split to have."[111]

That a proclaimed "goddess" like Uma Thurman could be the subject of such abuse is already shocking, but what is interesting is also her ability to see that by keeping silent about the abuse, she may have been complicit in the abuse of other girls. By talking about Annah la Javanaise, I am invoking not just that girl but all the Annahs, her granddaughters and great-great-granddaughters, whose lives are made vulnerable to early death or sexual trauma. The tale of Annah can be seen in stories of the other maids, like Nafissatou Diallo, the Senegalese hotel maid who in 2011 charged that International Monetary Fund director Dominique Strauss-Kahn had raped her while she was working. The other maids, the other mistresses, still reflect Annah.

You may say that the parallel is too far-fetched: it is not rigorous or scholarly to jump from 1893 to 2011. But I would like to end with another tale.

BARBARIC TALES: EPILOGUE

When I was growing up, above my small trundle bed, affixed to the wall, was a framed Gauguin poster, in which two brown-skinned, sloe-eyed women sit stolidly majestic (figure 1.17). The two women are very young (one is perhaps even a boy, not yet adolescent) and the other has long, wavy, curly russet-colored hair. I was fascinated by them: they were beautiful, and the colors of purple and orange and green of the landscape were so vibrant, so succulent, that they made me long for other things.

That they are bare-breasted and that that might be seen as sexually provocative did not really occur to me, because my house was full of such images from Indonesia or, to be more specific, from Bali. On a side table in the living room sat a *suar* wood torso of a woman, wearing only a rice farmer's hat. Another painting on the living room wall depicted a group of Balinese villagers resting on the side of the road, including women who were similarly wearing only a sarong, and no *kebaya* (fitted blouse). When I was twelve, I first learned that these images were odd for a Maryland subdivision, when a neighbor girl named Kitty came over to visit: she stared and then giggled at the sculpture and painting, shocked by the show of breasts. I was confused. No one before that in my parents' circle of Indonesians and Malaysians had ever had such a strong reaction to the objects in my parents' living room. I remember thinking, "But my Auntie Martina breast-feeds her babies in front of me, so why are they a problem?" Suddenly, I saw the Balinese art in my parents' home with different eyes.

FIGURE 1.17 Paul Gauguin, *Contes barbares* (Barbaric fairy tales, 1902). Museum Folkwang, Essen, Germany.

The fact that in my bedroom poster of the painting by Gauguin, titled *Contes barbares*, there was a small red-headed white man, crouched in the corner, like a little malevolent fox, did not really disturb my little arcadia (figure 1.17). A scholar could call the man an intruder into this paradise, the figure of colonialism, of patriarchy, of patrilineal authorship. But it wasn't Gauguin that I loved—it was the girls he painted. Later when I studied art history in college, I fell under the spell of the history of painting: in the blackness of the darkened room, one could be transported through the projection of slides accompanied by the disembodied voice of my erudite professor with her lilting Ukrainian accent, light shining through the celluloid frames, to other times, other worlds. I fell in love with art history. One could become expert in identifying and placing the history of paintings. One could hide in the darkness.

I tell this tale about a bedroom poster because I think it is significant that I identified with the women who posed. Certainly one could make the criticism that a university professor living in Los Angeles has nothing in common with a thirteen-year-old girl who came to Paris more than a hundred years ago. But let me wrap this tale up with another tale.

It's about my first day at Yale.

It was a beautiful, sunny September day. I was excited to be embarking upon my studies of art history in the PhD program. I dressed appropriately: dark skirt and a blouse, with sensible shoes, the kind of bookish stockinged look that my art history professors wore when I was an undergraduate. Arriving at the imposing gate of the Hall of Graduate Studies, an ivy-covered Gothic stone building, I rang the bell. I heard footsteps hurrying behind the shut entrance. Suddenly the door swung open. A tall man looked at me impatiently.

"Where have you been?" he bellowed.

I looked at him. Quizzically.

"We've been waiting for you!"

"Excuse me?" I asked.

He looked at me again and then cocked his head.

He thought I was the new maid.

UNDER THE TREE

I was hiding under the Tree on the day the Girl came over and found me in bed. I could not walk because the Man had hurt me so bad. I was still bleeding from it.

In my head I would go back to my village. I would leave the yellow and olive-painted studio, packed full of odd wood sculptures, paintings, photographs, and engravings, and I would travel back home, where I would be watching over my younger brothers and sisters. I would sit under a huge tree whose roots spread so far and wide. I could hear the sound of the children playing, yelling, laughing. I would look up at the sky and marvel at the branches of the Tree crisscrossing over me, protecting me. A tree is so strong. You make houses from trees. You make furniture from trees. There I could sigh and feel the warm sun mingled with the sea breeze. It felt so good.

Suddenly I was torn from my reverie. It was the Girl.

"Why is Annah still in bed?"

I heard his voice, murmuring while he painted. "She's sick. Lazy girl."

I pretended to sleep but even with my eyes closed I could feel the Girl's eyes gazing at me. She knelt down to caress my forehead. She would not ignore me.

"Poor Annah. Are you sick?"

Her eyes were large and brown. She reminded me of my youngest sister, the baby. Something in the way she tilted her head and considered me gravely made me decide right then and there that I would protect her. She would find out soon enough what men do, and how they hurt you. But let her still remain a child even if it was only for a little while longer.

"Bring me the cards," I told her.

I sat up. And so we played cards in bed while he painted.

I was good at cards.

THE STILL DANCER

What does endangered life do for documentary?
—POOJA RANGAN, *Immediations*

She is a dark flame. Tiny, immaculate, compact, her face powdered, hair raked into a chignon, very still, she flicks her hands, waist, legs, feet, and her large, bright eyes with extremely slow, precise, impossible, yet elegant movements. The dancer from what will be called Indonesia is sent in the 1880s all over the world to represent the colonies; in the late twentieth and twenty-first centuries, she is sent to represent the nation, dancing a repertoire of courtly dances known for their moments of great stillness and refined movement from Bali and Java, but rarely including dances from the outer islands, and rarer still the folk dances, feared to be somehow communist, that were banned after the rise of the Suharto regime in 1965. She is the girl you watch at the World's Fair in 1889 under the recently built Eiffel Tower, while slurping on half-melted sorbet and drinking beer, and whose image was forced upon a trafficked girl who was called Annah la Javanaise. She is that girl in the ethnographic film, a plumeria flower tucked behind her ear, bare-breasted with unfurled hair, stabbing herself with the jagged sword, in trance, for God's sake, in Margaret Mead and Gregory Bateson's *Trance and Dance in Bali* (filmed in 1936–39, edited in 1950). She is the castrating sexual predator of the good generals, a member of the Indonesian Women's Movement or Gerwani (Gerakan Wanita Indonesia), wielding a slashing razor in her scarlet red *kebaya*, or fitted blouse, in Arifin C. Noer's birth-of-the-Indonesian-nation film *Pengkhianatan G30S/PKI* of 1982, a film that was mandatory viewing for students and seen by anyone watching television every September 30 in Indonesia in the 1980s and 1990s (figure 2.1).[1] She is the young woman in the strapless gold lamé dress shimmying to an internal, silent score at the edge of Lake Toba by the ruined wreck of a large signpost shaped like a fish, in US filmmaker Joshua Oppenheimer's stunningly visceral and lauded art film, *The Act of Killing* of 2012 (figure 2.2).

Visual biopolitics is underscored by the figure of the Indonesian dancing girl across media and political regimes and historical periods, a figure who must be ordered, repressed, controlled, limited, and, in some cases, violated or made to disappear. The first thing that must be said about the still dancer as a figure of visual biopolitics is that she must not speak. She is there to entertain, to be looked at, to act as your muse, the launching pad for your imagination, your painting, your music, your film, to be used as a national figure of excoriation, but not, it appears, to speak.

How does visual biopolitics shape the image of the Indonesian female dancer and what are the consequences of that image, those stories that are told about her? But most importantly, as this book interrogates, how does one challenge the biopolitical tendency in visual culture and politics? How does one resist visual biopolitics?

The theorist who can best answer that question is not a master painter from France, or a world-renowned anthropologist, or a MacArthur Fellow genius (yet).

She is a dancer herself.

The daughter of a dancer who vanished after 1965 during the years of the killings of any Indonesian accused of being communist or leftist, Rachmi Diyah Larasati was spared because her aunt had married a military man, and thus she was protected by this uncle, who adopted her.[2] He would also suffer the consequences of loving a woman tainted by a family of dancers who were purported communists, as we learn in the opening of Larasati's riveting scholarly masterpiece, *The Dance That Makes You Vanish*, perhaps the finest writing ever on the history of visual biopolitics and how to muster the will to resist it (figure 2.3). That this book, written by an Indonesian woman, in the field of dance studies, remains largely obscure is another form of biopolitics: there are those who are read and those whose writings are ignored.

FIGURE 2.1 Poster for *Penghianatan G30S/PKI* (Arifin C. Noer, 1984).

FIGURE 2.2 Poster for *The Act of Killing* (Joshua Oppenheimer, 2012).

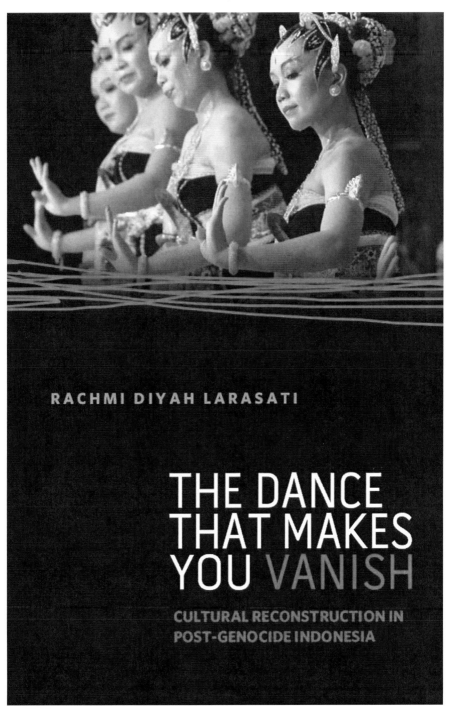

FIGURE 2.3 Cover of Rachmi Diyah Larasati, *The Dance That Makes You Vanish* (University of Minnesota Press, 2012).

The influence of Margaret Mead in offering the "truth" to the West, with anthropological discourse overdetermining the contemporary image of Indonesia updating earlier colonial images, also informed and was informed by the iconography of tourism. Visual biopolitics has a particular relationship with the Real. It plays with genres of realism that purport to reveal the Truth, so that when you see these images of the dancer, whether in the late nineteenth- and early twentieth-century World's Fair exhibits, or in the present day as carved friezes in historical monuments, or in films, news reports, historic film, and government-sponsored performances, you "know" what you are being told is true. It is the very "endangered-ness" of subjects of documentary, as film theorist Pooja Rangan points out, that provides the frisson of the Real upon which so much documentary depends. That is why ethnographic film did not begin with an anthropologist going out into the field but instead traces its roots to Félix-Louis Regnault's protocinema of West Africans performing movements such as walking and jumping, staged under the shadow of the Eiffel Tower.[3] The World's Fair satisfies the public's desire to see the Other in the flesh, and cinema is a much less labor-intensive and expensive way to circulate native bodies for the public's entertainment. Actual bodies are known to resist, to talk back, to leave, and to die (of diseases against which many native populations had no immunities, as in the example of Minik Wallace, the Inuit boy whose family was displayed at the American Museum of Natural History).[4]

The mode that envisions the West as the historifiable and the Rest as ethnographiable, to use Claude Lévi-Strauss's distinction, is still ingrained, and made even stronger by technologies like film that align the ethnographic Other or Savage with the Primitive, the Endangered, and the Authentic, which means that the Other is always already known.[5] In this chapter I examine varied discourses around the dancer, the small native girl that one finds in the World's Fair, to show how visual biopolitics is entrenched in seemingly objective media like ethnographic (Margaret Mead and Gregory Bateson's *Trance and Dance in Bali*) and documentary (Joshua Oppenheimer's *The Act of Killing*) film, as well as the national historical film (*Pengkhinatan G30S/PKI*). In conclusion, I carefully examine *The Dance That Makes You Vanish* and explain why this overlooked book that situates dancing as a political tool profoundly resists the visual biopolitics that would control the writer/dancer. It is a book that speaks truth to power.

Margaret Mead and Gregory Bateson's *Trance and Dance in Bali* is a classic ethnographic film that was viewed by multiple generations of Indonesian-ists and anthropologists.[6] It has thus had a profound influence on the visual biopolitics that ultimately endangered (and endangers) the dancer as female artist. This twenty-two-minute, black-and-white, 16 mm film shows one day's classical temple dance and trance in Pagutan (Dutch spelling Pagoetan), Bali (although it was shot over several periods between 1936 and 1939). Narrated by Mead in a dry, cool voice-over, it has a gamelan music track recorded by Colin McPhee.[7]

Aesthetically, what is most impressive about the film are the sections in which the dancers stab themselves in slow motion, all filmed by anthropolo-gist Jane Belo. Its ultimate structure is an encounter between the empirical (the scientific tool of film) and the supernatural (the Balinese in trance gyrating and stabbing themselves without drawing blood) along with what the West would see as sexual (young, half-naked women dancing). Although presented in the guise of education, it is pure entertainment, an example of fascinating canni-balism.[8] Bateson, who had hoped to use the film to create a cross-cultural ar-chive of movement, wanted nothing to do with Mead's edited version of 1951 (the footage he shot was intended for archival study), which was screened in schools, churches, natural history museums, and anthropology and South-east Asian studies classes.[9] As I explain in *The Third Eye*, Mead's philosophy of ethnographic film was that it was an inscription of the body and of real-ity: "[Mead] believed that long takes and an immobile camera could study nonverbal behavior objectively. . . . Mead thought that film could provide an important record of the ways of life of vanishing races; she also endorsed the idea that by collecting and examining an enormous amount of film ma-terial, the anthropologist could make anthropology a science."[10] Yet how she recorded the Balinese dancers in her film, the historical context of their being colonized people performing for European and North American tour-ists, how she contextualized them in voice-over, and the venues in which she chose to show the film were used to exoticize Bali and were all intrinsically part of larger discourses around colonialism and exoticism (figure 2.4).

Educational ethnographic film did not rely on marketing but on out-side funding, and Mead's film was funded by the Committee for Research in Dementia Praecox (now known as schizophrenia). *Trance and Dance in Bali* laid significant groundwork for the visual biopolitics of the cinematic

FIGURE 2.4 Margaret Mead and Gregory Bateson filming, Pagoetan, Bali, Indonesia, 1936–39.

and scientific visualization of Bali as a sexual pathologized Other.[11] Thus the film's anthropological twist is its linkage of the Balinese dancer not only with *goona goona* ("black magic," the Hollywood film industry trade papers' term for native bare breasts) but also with what the anthropologists saw as pathology (schizophrenia) and the fraudulent supernatural (trance). As in other films about the Ethnographic Other, such as Jean Rouch's film *Les Maîtres Fous* (1955) of Hauka men in Accra going into trance and mimicking their colonial masters, or Maya Deren's film *Divine Horsemen: The Living Gods of Haiti* (shot 1947–54 and edited in 1985) of vodun trance in Haiti, trance presents a vision of the opposite of modernity, in which native people inhabit the supernatural world and the present simultaneously. This use of film to record and rout out what is true about trance is something that we will see as well in Oppenheimer's *The Act of Killing*, which contains scenes where Indonesian actors fall into trance during reenactments of mass murder.

Trance and Dance in Bali is not a film about the impoverished and malnourished villagers of Bayung Gede (Dutch spelling: Bajoeng Gede), the site of Mead and Bateson's primary research in the 1930s for their book *Balinese Character*, but instead about a commissioned theater group from the south of Bali who danced for tourists. Like the commercial colonial visual biopolitics of the World's Fair, the female dancer in *Trance and Dance in Bali* is contextualized in a story of exoticism and sexuality. The Balinese are represented as creatures of an erotic, exotic past, seen at a geographical and temporal distance. The dances in the film were normally performed at night by older men, but Mead and Bateson made the directorial choice to film them performed in the day (so they could film) and by teenage girls and young women, as well as young men, who had never performed them before. This casting of young men and women, according to Belo, was an "unprecedented variation."[12] Mead later explained that the trance they filmed was changed by filming in daylight and by casting young, beautiful women so that they could record "how women who had never before been in trance flawlessly replicated the customary behavior they had watched all their lives."[13] Despite Mead's rationalizing, the voice-over in the film makes no such disclaimer. By displaying long-haired teenage girls in tight sarongs gyrating in trance, Mead was tapping into the nineteenth-century visualization of the exotic Indonesian dancer, à la Annah la Javanaise (figure 2.5).

In chapter 1, I explored how exoticism and sexuality yoked to Dutch colonial propaganda and commercialism made up the structural framework against which the story of the four young court dancers from Surakarta, Java, was told: Seriem, Taminah, Wakiem, and Soekia became the rage of Paris in 1889, performing every day to visitors who drank Dutch hot chocolate or Dutch beer. The official intention of the Javanese village, like all the other exhibited villages at the Exposition Universelle—Dahomey, Tonkin, and so on—was to display the might of the French to bring back and display the world to the Parisian public.

Exporting people for exhibition was difficult and expensive, thus film was and is a cheaper way of bringing the colonized Other to the West, but, traversing in the other direction, Americans and Europeans were traveling to Bali as tourists. Bali in the mid-1930s, according to Tessel Pollmann, was already seen as a fashionable tropical paradise, attracting thirty thousand tourists a year, often enticed by its reputation as a sexual paradise of nude girls and charming boys.[14] As Mr. Wijaksuma, a fighter during the Indonesian Revolution, explained many years later, "For us Bali is the place where everything is holy—we pray to the gods, as well as to the plants, the animals, the flowers. That's our religion. But for them [Western tourists and expatriates] Bali is a paradise because they have a beautiful house, many servants, beautiful gamelan, a lot of food. And they have the girls with the bare breasts."[15] The bare breasts of the young female dancers provided sexual titillation and were used in early cinema as a marketing tool to Western audiences, the goona goona.[16]

Following a trend that Paul Gauguin had already made romantic in his search for a modern paradise, tourists and expatriates stayed (and continue to stay) for years in Bali, establishing a kind of tropical café society that

FIGURE 2.5 Still from
*Trance and Dance in
Bali* (Margaret Mead
and Gregory Bateson,
1954; shot 1936–39).

burgeoned into the largest industry in Bali today.[17] Dutch art collectors Walter Spies and Beryl de Zoete, the self-educated anthropologist Jane Belo and her husband, musicologist Colin McPhee, the Mexican illustrator Miguel Covarrubias, and the filmmaker André Roosevelt all lived a comfortable life in the Bali of the 1930s. This is what Ibu Gedong Bagus Oka ironically describes as "Baliitis," the blindness and thus collusion of visual biopolitics (including the anthropologist and the expatriate artistic community) to colonial oppression:

> Margaret Mead, Gregory Bateson, Walter Spies, Katharine Mershon, Jane Belo, Colin McPhee, they all didn't come to Bali to render us a service. They came only in their own interest, and that means they never integrated, never participated in our society. We as young girls imitated them: oooh, Bali is so beautiful, Bali is such a paradise. We said that they had an illness: the Bali-it-is. Look they paid their interpreters and guides and informants, so these people confirmed everything their employers said. All these Europeans were frustrated Westerners who wanted to believe Bali was a paradise. It was their flight from the West, which gave them this so-called insight.[18]

Ironically, Balinese observers ascribed pathology (Baliitis) to the white outsiders/tourists/anthropologists, who in turn saw the dancers as the pathological.

The science that the film represents blurs history. The elegant violence of the self-stabbing dancing girl obfuscates the several historic *puputan* that occurred earlier in Bali, when entire courts refused to surrender to the Dutch colonizers and were gunned down dressed in their ritual finest. Furthermore,

Mead who offers film as the empirical recorder of reality, helped solidify the narrative of the pathological sexual exotic female dancer, by speaking of the dancers in the ethnographic present (the third person, present tense, as if the actions filmed were not recorded in the past). Mead does not entertain the possibility that the Balinese men and women in the film are indeed inhabited by spirits or gods. In other words, trance is anthropologized away, to use Dipesh Chakrabarty's term, "that is, converted into somebody's belief or made into an object of anthropological analysis."[19]

In the cultural relativism of the Boasian school of anthropology, of which Mead was a student, the study of other cultures was often justified as a way to correct what was decadent about the Western body (hence Mead's earlier hypothesis that Samoan society was more sexually free in order to argue for the need for less sexual repressiveness in American society).[20] The normalization that biopolitics requires is upheld through the visualization of difference, of race, and that is what Bateson and Mead's obsessive photographic and cinematic archive of the Balinese provided.[21] What could be learned from a culture identified as schizoid could be applied, so Mead's logic went, to an American society that was fearful of this disease.[22]

The idea that one can truly understand a people through the copious use of recording—textual, photographic, and filmic—is connected to the primacy of science. Mead described her interest in creating a kind of archive of cross-referencing, with "notes made against time":

> Gradually we developed a style of recording in which I kept track of the main events while Gregory took both moving pictures and stills—we had no means of recording sound and had to rely on musical recordings made by others—and our youthful Balinese secretary Made Kaler kept a record in Balinese, which provided us with vocabulary and a cross-check on my observations. We soon realized that notes made against time provided the only means by which the work of three people could be fitted together and which would enable us, later, to match the photographic records of a scene with the notes. For special events, such as trance, we used stopwatches.[23]

This use of the stopwatch is a fascinating example of how American social rationality and efficiency could be yoked to the idea of trance. Time was also collected here, rigorously archived and noted. Thus, for Mead and Bateson, the truth about the Balinese could be graphed, firmly placed on x-y-z-axes so that even years later, knowledge could be apprehended. The key axes were time and space: if time and space were rationalized, even people in trance could be catalogued, classified, and archived. The hubris was that if it is recorded, then it is forever captured for the use of scholars in a cross-cultural visual archive. This archive requires the technology of storage, with its filing and classification systems, which means that it is rarely seen, access is controlled, and its meanings are predetermined and enforced. Those who shoot are those who archive. Those who are shot are archivable, there to be delimited, discussed. The colonial archive, a subject that I take up again in chapter 3, legitimizes colonial power—"the natives are too ignorant to archive"—and rationalizes the annihilation of culture and peoples—"the natives may vanish, but they live forever: in the archive."

PATHOLOGY OR PERFORMANCE? THE LOOK OF THE REAL

Is it possible to think of the idea of schizophrenia, or the inability to distinguish reality from fantasy, as a projection of the anthropologists' inability to be in the present? The schizoid is seen as being of fantasy, while the modern is seen as the real. Why were the signs of colonialism and expatriate culture that had a significant impact on the trance ritual so assiduously erased from the book and the film? What *Trance and Dance in Bali* presents to us is the limits of historiography and cinematic practice, a test of the real. Why were these anthropologists creating this fantasy?

In contrast to Mead and Bateson, Jane Belo did note the intrusive presence of tourism. The Pagoetan troupe was so well loved by tourists that they sometimes performed three or more trance dances in a single week.[24] Edited out of Mead and Bateson's film are the other Western tourists, as well as the two filmmakers (Bateson and Belo), and the note takers (Mead, I Made Kaler, and Katherine Mershon). Belo, who later made films with Zora Neale Hurston about African American churchgoers who went into trance, and who herself later suffered from schizophrenia, explains that the kris dance involving the dragon Barong and the witch Rangda was highly successful, often with twenty tourists in the audience. It was advantageous to record the Pagoetan troupe precisely because they were always performing for tourists, "so that we as observers were not forced to wait until a calendrical event came round to see the subjects once more in action."[25] At the end of the performance as the trancers gyrated (*ngoerek*), the tourists who at first believed it was a hoax "came away breathless and startled, convinced that something extraordinary and unexplainable had taken place before their eyes. In not a few cases, the observers remarked the peculiar sexual undertone of the trance behavior, to them suggestive of sexual activity without being in any obvious or surface way connected with a sexual idea or purpose."[26]

The problem, wrote Belo, and as Mead herself noted, was that the Balinese were, in real life, genuinely good actors: "In Bali, not only would the entranced behave as if he were acting, but the actor would behave almost as if he were in trance."[27] Belo asks if the section where the men appear unconscious but are wildly self-stabbing is "but one more stylized figure of the dance, and in its way, a group fake, a simulation of trance in which the entire number takes part?"[28] In underlining this anxiety about the real and the false, Belo uses an example of a boy in the middle of trance who looks up into the camera during another film, made by Plessen. Looking into the camera was a sign of consciousness and hence of performed trance.[29]

The performers themselves despised those who were not really performing in trance. In particular, there was one villager, Rawa, who loved to shake hands and toady up to the white anthropologists and tourists, and who was notorious for sleeping with married women. In one described performance, he stabbed himself, producing blood. The other performers denounced him as not really being in trance, complaining that he was "unclean" for being promiscuous. Belo describes how, during the filming of *Trance and Dance in Bali*, Rawa was brutally attacked by two other male performers. In addition, Belo comments that the older dancer, Ni Ngales, was not conscious of the violent assault on Rawa, which occurred during her coming-out period, and so was not "performing" trance: "I also came up to her at this very time and took a close-up of her with a cine camera, at three feet. The film shows the man supporting her turning his head in surprise, his attention attracted by the sound of the camera's mechanism. But on Ni Ngales's face is no sign of response."[30] What is so telling is this desire to dichotomize the fake and the real; they cannot exist together.

The rule of ethnographic film is not to include the look. Indeed, the look back at the camera proves inauthenticity. When the Balinese in trance look at the camera, it cannot be read as an altered, passive state. The look back makes the Balinese active and asserts their subjectivity. And yet the ways that Dutch colonialism, tourism, and anthropology changed the trance performances were not seen as problematic to this criterion of authenticity.

There are many levels of conversion going on in the film *Trance and Dance in Bali*. Anthropologists are converting the Balinese into schizophrenics, and the bodies of those in trance are being converted into film so that the ethnographic filmmaker can distinguish the real from the fake. The scientific apparatus of the camera, the secretary, and the anthropologist translate what is also a spiritual experience and edit it later into the racialized, sexualized spectacle that is commonly known as a classic ethnographic film, a form of visual biopolitics.

Visual biopolitics must interrogate and penetrate the mystery of the Savage: Is it human? Is it a monster? Is it a show? Is it real? So much of the discourse around the Savage is tied up with whether the Savage is authentically savage, and this is true whether it is an early ethnographic film or a contemporary postmodern documentary film. Deities and spirits can refer not just to some Primitive past but also to one's life in the present, another notion these anthropologists do not entertain. One's religious background is adaptable, dynamic; one can go in and out of trance without being inauthentic. Anthropologist Stefania Pandolfo has theorized this split in subjectivity for the colonial subject forced to live in two worlds. In Morocco, a person suffering from mental illness might be seen as possessed by djinn (or demons) and therefore needing to be cured by a local healer, or they could be taken to a hospital and cured by a psychiatrist or psychoanalyst. Sometimes both practices could be used by the same person at once. Modernity, she argues, lies precisely in the form of unsettled speech: not the true speech that psychoanalysis seeks, or the speech that the djinn produces, but somewhere in between. She reflects on the possibility "of speaking, listening, and dwelling on the boundary of Moroccan modernity, that intermediate zone where the two stories of illness belong. That boundary of modernity sets as its limited aim to trace the implications of a specifically modernist Moroccan sense of temporality, the temporality of the 'cut' or the 'bridge,' related to the drawing of a line that separates and joins worlds experienced as at once contiguous and remote."[31] Pandolfo takes inspiration from Moroccan writer Driss Chraïbi's description in his novel *Le passé simple* (*The Simple Past*, 1954): "The Line— so thin, so impalpable, that it is unreal—is the classificatory boundary between East and West, black and white, tradition and modernity; the unreal limit that constitutes their reality, the limit that should not be crossed."[32]

It is with this goal to seek out how one figures oneself as part of a community that I ask, how do we look? Within the same body a colonization can occur, what Pandolfo refers to as the thin line of modernity, a willful destruction of boundaries between us and them; Pandolfo, Talal Asad, and Achille Mbembe theorize this in relation to the suicide bomber.[33] This is an even more complicated idea, but one I believe may constitute a different form of the body and subjectivity than what has been heretofore acknowledged by theorists of modernity. I would like to suggest that for those whom dominant society visualizes as subhuman or nonhuman, for formerly colonized and colonized selves, subjectivity lies in the Cut between what is seen as the rational and the supernatural. And this subjectivity is potentially liberating and radical. In other words, instead of hiding or denying the wounds, of having to speak through the voice and cultural structure of another—the language of the colonizer, the language of the regime—living in the Cut acknowledges the still-fresh wounds of the historical past and the present.

How can one track a Balinese woman's subjectivity across seemingly incompatible media, both visual and textual, as a rebellious speaking subject and pictured sexual object? To think of the Balinese women as understanding that they are performing exoticism or performing trance is anathema to visual biopolitics, which naturalizes the classification of subjugated populations. The functions of visual biopolitics dictate their subjectivity. Mead only remembers the women in the film as being young and beautiful, which is not quite true—several are older. Belo notes the names of the women and puts them in two categories: the old and the young. Of the older ones, Belo, and the film, focus on two: Mangkoe Tegeh, a priestess of the Tegeh temple, and Ni Ngales, who had the most extreme coming-out period, in which her spasms were accompanied with visual expressions "of painful ecstasy, very sexual." Belo continues to describe Ngales as the kind of trancer who performed at night:

Aged or unattractive women often went into an abandoned trance, surprising in its violence and in the completeness with which they gave themselves up to it. . . . These humble, mousy women, who did not sparkle as their sisters in youth or in bright raiment, became all at once aflame with desire and gave themselves up in forgetfulness to conduct which was the more exhibitionistic, because they were denied the minor, everyday exhibitionisms which are every women's need. This at least is the interpretation, which I, as a woman, put upon their behavior. It is significant that time after time, at temple festivals, when we had been watching the preliminary ritual for three or four hours, suddenly out of nowhere would appear the mousy women, hurling themselves into the center of things at the very height of the pitch of trance.[34]

These hurling, mousy women, some of whom were temple priestesses, were still sexualized: as failed sexual beings, overcompensating for their lack of masculine attention by extreme exhibitionism.

The ethnographic writing about the performances in *Trance and Dance in Bali* provides some point of contrast: the transcription of the conversation that the women dancers had before they went on to be filmed in trance did not serve the visual biopolitics of an ethnographic film. The women's subjectivity comes through in their discussions about performance and in acknowledging themselves as performers. Surprisingly, considering Mead's dry voice-over in the film, which turns the women trancers into grim self-stabbers, it is a dialogue full of coquettish talk and vanity.

The older woman priestess, Mangkoe Tegeh, for example, is interested only in how she looks and asks for powder to cover her dark skin.[35] The two young girls, Moenet and Soekoen, according to Belo, are concerned with what gestures they should use.[36] Soekoen is described as having "the reputation of a 'naughty' girl, and often varied the fixed pattern of her dance to approach and dance flirtatiously before the foreign guests—showing unheard of independence of a child dancer."[37] Both girls are aware of their sexuality and beauty, but it is Soekoen who at one point comments on their status as objects of anthropological recording. She teases Mead and Bateson's notebook-scribing secretary, I Made Kaler, who was sent to record their dialogue, by asking, "Are we all to be written down there?"[38]

The ethnographic film does not allow for the comments of a dancer like Soekoen. Seen as naughty by the anthropologists, the teenage Soekoen uses puns to comment on status, caste, and class in her word-play joke on the action of drinking arak (rice wine): "It makes my head swim to guzzle arak." She uses a very vulgar word for "guzzle." "This 'Sak Adé, she imbibes arak, I delicately partake of it."[39] A play on words here, as she uses first the vulgar word for how Desak Adé, who is of higher caste, drinks, and then, in fun, the word applied for the gods' refreshment for herself. Is Soekoen naughty, as Belo characterizes her? Or is she perceptively in the present, her comment subverting the anthropologist's endeavor to visualize her as the sexual Balinese dancing girl, unveiling the tenuousness of age, class, caste, and gender? She is a more complicated subject; in fact, she is an individual, something that the film and anthropology of that time cannot see.

Being turned into a "living museum," as Ida Bagus put it, was how the anthropologists visualized the Balinese by making them "photogenic."[40] This codifying of the photogenic, on the part of the colonizer (and then the Indonesian government), on the one hand, and the native, on the other hand, is certainly true of Balinization, a system of exoticization that works politically to erase signs of political and historical struggle, and a form of visual biopolitics that disciplines bodies.[41] Belo concludes, "On the whole it is clear that both the older women and the girls anticipated no very personal emotion to accompany their trance act; that whatever nervousness they felt was akin to stage fright and not the result of being keyed up to an intense emotional experience."[42] The girls and the women care more about how they look and will appear than how they will perform spiritually; they are aware of being photogenic. The documentarian cannot control all meanings. The tension here is between performing and directing; visual biopolitics divides the world into those who are real and those who perform. The real cannot be revealed as a construction; it can only be understood within the context of the archive, a subject on film brought back and edited and produced and shown not for the Balinese, but for the West. Is it trance? Is it performance? And can the supernatural coexist side by side with the real?

By considering the words of the women who were commissioned to dance before tourists and the scientists' cameras, we can move beyond always seeing them at a sharp distance of time, space, and status. In this way we can tentatively make a connection with Rawa the toady, Mangkoe Tegeh the priestess, Soekoen the flirt, and all the many others whose names we can find in Belo's accounts. We can attempt to remain in the Cut. These people's presence and their humanity trouble the archive. As Rebecca Schneider writes in "Performance Remains," "When we approach performance not as that which disappears (as the archive expects), but as both the act of remaining and a means of reappearance (though not a metaphysics of presence) we almost immediately are forced to admit that remains do not have to be isolated to the document, to the object, to bone versus flesh."[43] The women in the film convert themselves into spectacle, transform themselves for the gaze of an Other; they become their own translation. They take control over how they look to the viewer, and how they look by seeing.

NEW ORDER VISUAL BIOPOLITICS: THE VILIFICATION
OF GERWANI AND THE FEMALE DANCER

Fourteen years after *Trance and Dance in Bali* in 1965, local militias tortured, sexually mutilated, burned, slashed, and killed thousands of Balinese.[44] The image of Bali that Mead and Bateson's film had promulgated from the colonial Dutch legacy of the World's Fair and subsequent tourism served the New Order dictatorship well, and it helped cover up the massacre of 100,000 Balinese during 1965–66 so as to not scare off tourists. Balinese anthropologist Degung Santikarma lays the blame for this stereotype of Bali on both the Dutch colonial regime and Mead and Bateson.[45]

The New Order regime took up visual biopolitics; the exoticization of Bali (Balinization) lends itself well to this. Santikarma notes that after Independence, developers built hotels on land soaked with the blood of Balinese who had engaged in ritual suicide (puputan) against the Dutch. Violence, he explains, was also part of the image served up about Bali: stories about the evil of rajas, the burning of widows, the stabbing of knives into oneself during trance, as well as the magic of warring shamans, a violence that was acceptable as long as it was sterilized against the contamination of contemporary politics.[46] Violence can be part of the image of Bali, as long as it is temporalized as ritual and of an earlier Primitive era. This is a classical structure of visual biopolitics: the violence used against the endangered is represented as the endangered being the violent. There is thus a clear line between the colonial and anthropological gaze seeing the Balinese as photogenic and picturesque trancers going amok, and later, the government gaze seeing the Balinese as leftist terrorists the Indonesian state must kill and expel.[47] According to Leslie Dwyer and Degung Santikarma, during 1965 and after, "Most western news accounts of the time tended to strangely echo these claims by the state that the violence was a product of the frenzy, betraying their cultural propensity for falling into mass trance or running amok or simply demonstrating their Third World Savagery."[48] The killings of more than a million people that occurred during Major General Suharto and the Indonesian military's takeover of the Indonesian government, and the subsequent military dictatorship that assumed power and ruled for thirty-three years, became seen as either praiseworthy or something to be ignored, and thus Suharto was able to continue his repressive operations. Central to the mythology of the New Order was the female dancer.

She wore red, she was orgiastic, she was sexual, she was young, she castrated and devoured the penises of good generals. In bas relief on historical monuments, in newspapers, and in Arifin C. Noer's 1982 film, *Pengkhianatan G30S/PKI* (famously seared into the hippocampus of every Indonesian schoolchild who was forced to view it every September 30), the female dancer was set up as the epitome of sexual, pathological evil. According to film historian Katinka van Heeren, the Indonesian public saw *Pengkhianatan G30S/PKI* as a documentary film, even though it was a government-produced narrative film of historical fiction.[49] It was seen as real, which casts light on Western definitions of the documentary film, for arguably *Trance and Dance in Bali* and *The Act of Killing* are as culturally biased and myth making as Noer's film. The film is real, if it is said to be real, and watched so many times it becomes a memory of events past. In this film, Noer's last feature, the director brought to the screen the myth of the birth of the contemporary Indonesian state as a fight between the virtuous heroes of Suharto's party versus the evil, sexual communists. This film served as a mighty bulwark that shored up the origin myth of the state of Indonesia under Suharto: that on October 1, 1965, six generals and one lieutenant were kidnapped and brought to Lubang Buaya

(Crocodile Hole), where they were savagely tortured and murdered by the G30S Movement (the September 30th Movement). The inciting incident that the subsequent Indonesian government used—its birth of a nation, or grisly origin story of why Suharto legitimately came to power and created his military dictatorship—was that a group of lower-ranking officers with confirmed loyalty to President Sukarno attempted a military coup against CIA-backed generals. In the name of destroying what he labeled the evil PKI (Partai Komunis Indonesia, or Indonesian Communist Party), Suharto set about terrorizing citizens, Sukarno fell from power, and all leftist organizations and publications were destroyed. Propaganda was important to the campaign, but the regime's most important strategy, according to historian Geoffrey Robinson, "was a campaign of violence that entailed outright killing as well as mass detention, ill treatment, torture, and rape."[50] The military government was so virulently anticommunist—and thus US supported—that it murdered anyone associated with the left, and for decades this allowed the free flow of transnational capital and resources, such as Indonesian oil, gold, coffee, rice, tea, tin, cotton, and human labor that globalization required.

Pengkhianatan G30S/PKI is a well-crafted film of 271 minutes, following the lives of the army generals who were killed in the coup and establishing great sympathy for them and antipathy toward the communists (figure 2.1). The horrific excess and style of this film make it a cross between a horror film and Gillo Pontecorvo's 1966 film *The Battle of Algiers* (with its location shooting, use of suspenseful music along with elegiac classical score, and archival footage). The music of the gamelan that connotes the Savage in *Trance and Dance in Bali* plays during the torture scenes. A young woman wearing scarlet red brandishes a razor and slashes the face of a general, yelling, "Blood is red, General!" Other actions in *Pengkhianatan G30S/PKI* depict a PKI member grabbing a sickle and crying, "I am a sculptor. I will now sculpt your face General," and another PKI member exclaiming, "Enjoy the rust of this sickle" as she attacks the general's eye. As Annisa R. Beta, Inditian Latifa, and Nila Ayu Utami contend, viewers can only identify with the generals, who are shown to be upstanding family men defending their country.[51] It is impossible to identify with the PKI, who dance maniacally by candlelight to the popular song "Gendjer Gendjer," scored menacingly in a pentatonic minor scale. And thus the Suharto government created a pathological demon: communist women, often dancing, as evil, sexual murderers.

One of those Indonesian schoolchildren who was required to watch and write papers in class about *Pengkhianatan G30S/PKI* was Rachmi Diyah Larasati. She reveals:

The watching of the film, particularly its required viewing by schoolchildren, was embedded like a centerpiece in a specially tailored journey through national history lasting several days. On the mornings following the screening, the teachers . . . would review the details of the film, drawing parallels between its cinematic realism and the pages of our textbooks. From their precise, "empirical" lectures, we learned, again, exactly what we needed to remember about the rebirth of our proud nation, including the identities, roles, and qualities of all the major and minor characters, heroes, and villains.[52]

That includes the role of the women in the killings of the generals and the lieutenant at Lubang Buaya, which are graphically reenacted in the film.

REFLEXIVE DOCUMENTARY AND VISUAL BIOPOLITICS: TRANCE AND DANCE IN SUMATRA

Joshua Oppenheimer's *The Act of Killing* (2012) has been hailed as a new kind of documentary film: one that foregrounds the performance of its subjects in a film about performance through filmed reenactments of events around the mass killings. The crisis around the image ethics of documentary that media historians and critics have struggled with since the 1970s—that is, how to get around the lack of ethics in the differing power relations between those who can shoot and those who are shot—appears to be elided here. Not only did Oppenheimer make a film about his subjects, former murderers, making a film, but in the making of the film, the killers are forced to confront their own history of violence. The film has been lauded as revelatory, a clever and powerful new form of documentary, and a critical success that won an Oscar nomination. The Western audience no longer had to feel guilty about watching brown men behaving badly, since the brown men were consciously reenacting, for the viewer's gaze, their own retrospective look at their own brutality.

Set in the raucous city of Medan, Sumatra, *The Act of Killing* has a twist: the former gangsters Anwar Congo and Herman Koto are making a film about their past, inspired by the violent Hollywood films they used to watch as youngsters working the black market for movie tickets in Medan. It is a clever, brutal film that, before it can be decried as a construction, declares itself as a film all about construction. One of the truth claims of the film is that because these gangsters are just playing on desires acted out in Hollywood films, they are thus the products of the Hollywood nightmare thrown back in the face of the North American viewer (figure 2.6).

FIGURE 2.6 Anwar Congo and Herman Koto by Lake Toba, Sumatra, Indonesia. Still from *The Act of Killing* (Joshua Oppenheimer, 2012).

Given the very real status of *Pengkhianatan G30S/PKI* as the historical memory that replaces what actually happened in 1965—a national propaganda film that supersedes memory—it should come as no surprise that it is the film that former low-level gangster and aging murderer Anwar Congo is watching on television in *The Act of Killing*. This is then referenced but not explained when Congo's sidekick, gangster Herman Koto, cross-dresses as a scarlet-gowned character named Aminah who devours the human liver of a murdered body, played by Anwar Congo. Here, too, savagery is projected onto the Indonesian woman. As film scholar Intan Paramaditha has described, the Orde Baru or New Order world of Suharto from 1965 to 1998 was a hypermasculine world, and ironically *The Act of Killing* mimics its subject in that way. Women are sexualized: the term "Gerwani" (literally, a member of the Indonesian Women's Movement, Gerakan Wanita Indonesia) is in Oppenheimer's subtitles "Communist bitch," presumably a way to let non-Indonesian audiences understand the insult of Gerwani, yet without providing needed context.[53]

Instead of the sight of self-stabbing, bare-breasted, writhing trancers à la *Trance and Dance in Bali*, Oppenheimer's film puts its filmed subjects into trance by producing a reenactment of past violence from 1965 in order to lambaste the toxic and murderous machismo of the vigilantes. However, without explaining the Suharto regime's mythologizing of independent women artists and dancers as sexual predators, this postmodern documentary film engages in what I have called fascinating cannibalism. In the process of excoriating savagery, the film in fact reifies savagery—makes it titillating, replicating the visual strategies of who is human and who is nonhuman, or subhuman, through spectator identification with the male gaze.

As I theorized in my introduction, what visual biopolitics does, and does particularly well in the documentary format, is provide the visualization of how humanity is disciplined into full human, not-quite-human, or nonhuman beings. To add a corollary to Rangan's tenet that documentary feeds upon endangered humanity, there is a price that the Other must pay for documentary's focus on bodies disciplined as subhuman or nonhuman. That price is (1) the need to justify and prove one's own humanity as the subject of documentary, and (2) the interpellating of oneself as exotic, or pathological, or aberrant, the impossible position of the third eye.

In her book on visual biopolitics *In the Wake: On Blackness and Being*, Christina Sharpe resists and is aware of how the US history of slavery in the service of capitalism and its aftermath continues to affect black people's lives, leaving them vulnerable to death. Being in the wake conjures the space of the slave ship as well as those who mourn loved ones taken too soon due to systemic racism. The dysselected, to use Wynter's term, those who must prove their humanity in documentary, those who are endangered, in a state of precarity, are also in the hold of a history that does not let go. One example Sharpe gives is how black people are exhorted to become "Human" by the US media, even by President Obama in a speech she describes from 2013, ignoring the very infrastructural and historical position in which black people are allied with monstrosity, terrorism, and death: "The hold is what is taken as a given; it is the logic; it is the characterization of relation in that moment. Obama has succumbed to the logic of the hold. I am, we are, held and held. *Wake; in the line of recoil of (a gun).*"[54]

Similarly, documentary ignores the hold of what is taken as common sense, as our norm, as our Real, that the subjectivity of the rational individual subject (homo economicus) is aligned with the director/documentarian. This is tied directly to the West's very strong mythology of the documentary director, as Mead and Oppenheimer exemplified. For Mead, the documentary subjects are described, written about, and visualized as the pathological, and she uses film to rout out the real, those who are truly in trance versus the fakers. For Oppenheimer, the documentary subjects—the aging Sumatran gangsters—are used to describe a trauma, the genocide of 1965. However, at the end of the film, Oppenheimer films Anwar Congo alone on a rooftop to interrogate him—and Congo in turn is traumatized by this filming, which forces him to confront former acts of violence, cruelty, and murder.

Thus, even as Mead's film was credited to Bateson as well, and Oppenheimer's gave codirector credits to an anonymous Indonesian filmmaker (titled Anonymous) and Christine Cynn, their films were seen as being of the voice of one auteur (literally, too, with Mead's authoritative voice-over, and Oppenheimer's voice heard in the background in several scenes) without their faces ever being shown in the film. This auteur effect was upheld by the ways the discourse about the films, including marketing, interviews, and film reviews, revolved around the words and images of Mead and Oppenheimer. Visual biopolitics supports the network of power that determines who shoots (who is in the line of recoil) and who gets shot (by the gun/camera).[55]

The role of women in the macho, violent world of *The Act of Killing* is the same as in the Suharto government's official depiction of progressive women in national culture. In *The Act of Killing*, the men all insult women sexually: when the head of the Pancasila Youth group is shown playing golf, he talks to the caddy, who is a young woman, ridiculing her that she has a mole on her vagina. Gangster Herman Koto talks about raping fourteen-year-olds as "hell for them, heaven for us." Women are either sexualized or idealized as Kartini (the nineteenth-century Javanese writer who was held up during and after the Suharto regime as the idealized Indonesian woman). Oppenheimer is well aware and critical of the violent sexism of his subjects. So is Oppenheimer simply reproducing the violence or revealing it to subject it to critical scrutiny? I argue that this is another instance of fascinating cannibalism: giving the floor to such representations, which are already part of the iconography of the conscious and unconscious minds of US and European viewers, without crucial balance, including explaining and implicating the United States' own involvement in the crimes. But Oppenheimer is also engaging in another crucial aspect of visual biopolitics: hypervisibility. Without context, a viewer does not understand why Herman Koto is cross-dressing and eating a human liver, or who the Gerwani were, and thus they become completely invisible to a mainstream North American or European audience. The women become invisible because the men become hypervisible (figure 2.7).

In Mead and Bateson's *Trance and Dance in Bali*, the political structure underlying the film—colonialism—is elided. As Rachmi Diyah Larasati states, what becomes "timeless" and "ancient" is actually what also bears Dutch influence.[56] In *The Act of Killing*, the hold is the hidden structure—global neoliberal capitalism—underlying the killings: that is to say, the US support and

FIGURE 2.7 Herman Koto as Aminah eats the liver of a headless corpse, played by Anwar Congo. Still from *The Act of Killing* (Joshua Oppenheimer, 2012).

funding of the administration of Major General Suharto, who ruled with an iron fist until the economic crisis helped drive him from power in 1998. In essence, Oppenheimer's film recuperates US visual biopolitics—the power differential of the Civilized versus the Savage, the erasure of American participation in what led to the killings of 1965—while purporting to expose the visual biopolitics of Indonesia as a corrupt, evil, aberrant regime. Under the guise of being a film about the making of a film about the killings, Oppenheimer fails to inform Western viewers, notwithstanding a short title at the beginning of the film, of the full extent of complicity by a United States paranoid and fearful of any country leaning left or flirting with communism, which helped actualize the coup that put Suharto in power in 1965 and continued to bolster his military state that ruled by intimidation and murder.

As Geoffrey Robinson writes, "The mass killing and arrest of hundreds of thousands of people was a small price to pay for the destruction of one of the world's largest and most successful Communist parties."[57] The killings were concentrated in Bali but also took place in Aceh, Central Java, East Java, North Sumatra, and other parts of the eastern islands of Nusa Tenggara. There was a specific pattern to the violence led by "vigilantes or death squads," like the protagonists in *The Act of Killing*, leading Robinson to describe its matrix: hatred against Others due to social, ethnic, cultural, and religious difference was inflamed, and the most common modes of violence were "disappearance, bodily mutilation, corpse display, and sexual violence."[58] On the other side is Oppenheimer, who has declared that he is not interested in explaining history. Even though he had interviewed American CIA agents and Indonesian army generals, he chose not to use the footage: "The reason is that the film would inevitably become a historical film about the mechanics of what happened, and this is primarily a film about the miscarriage of the collective imagination that underpins this condition of impunity and open celebration. And it's about these very thorny issues: what does it mean to take joy in reenacting mass murder?"[59] But it is precisely the need to understand this matrix—the use of visual biopolitics to discipline and justify the disappearance of certain Others—that *The Act of Killing* ignores. Oppenheimer blames Indonesian society for what he decries as "the miscarriage of the collective imagination" without elucidating that it is the North American audience who is being entertained and, in a sense, getting off on this pornography of bodies of the Savage, the re-creation of mass murder by brown men, an entertainment of violated boundaries that is the essence of the history of ethnographic cinema. And this support for the Suharto regime continued into the 1970s, 1980s, and 1990s. Even as Indonesia continued its military abuses of power, US presidents continued to funnel billions of dollars in aid to Suharto. This was not just one-time support for atrocity but continued, systematic legitimization and aid.[60]

The final scene of *The Act of Killing* brings us fully into the cinematic dream that purportedly Anwar Congo and Herman Koto have conjured up for us and that Oppenheimer has placed his full auteurist art film stamp on, and it involves a chorus line of young, slim, beautiful, black-haired female dancers in shimmering strapless gold gowns, undulating along the stunning backdrop of Lake Toba. It is powerful and dreamlike, and it underlines how the dancing woman is used as sexual allure, as replica, to use Rachmi Diyah Larasati's formulation, and as an ornament of exoticism.

WHAT MAKES YOU VANISH

As in the Mead and Bateson film, trance also plays a role in Oppenheimer's film: Indonesians whose families have suffered from the trauma of genocide are forced to watch reenactments of such violence and sometimes fall into trance. The sadism of the auteur director—Alfred Hitchcock, Quentin Tarantino—is only now being acknowledged by film historians. Auteur documentarians like Oppenheimer also use force, which becomes voyeuristic force that we as the audience view, and, in Oppenheimer's case, the use of Sumatrans as performers for filming evokes traumas in locals that becomes trance. As I have explained, Mead enlisted young women who had never performed trance before (instead of the older men who normally danced) and filmed in the daylight (instead of at night). Her film is, therefore, a kind of reenactment of trance for scientific and pedagogical purposes, an image of exoticism dressed in the guise of anthropology. In *The Act of Killing*, Oppenheimer shoots a filmed reenactment of a massacre and the burning of a village, edited along with a shot of Anwar Congo dreaming in bed, as if the reenactment is issuing from Anwar Congo's mind. During the reenacted massacre, a woman appears to faint. In an interview, Oppenheimer explains, "Indonesians don't say, 'she's passed out,' they say she's *kesurupan*, which means 'possessed'" (figure 2.8).[61] And the fact that this person in trance is a woman, surrounded by crying, also traumatized children, reveals the gendered and racialized biopolitics of documentary film. To a non-Indonesian audience, she is just a native woman "freaking out," so the stereotype goes, one long entrenched with the visualization of the native Indonesian woman that we saw in Mead's film. This filmed trance was not planned; it is a consequence of a filmmaker who allowed subjects to suffer from the reenactments, many of whom did not realize that the scenes were fiction and thus were overcome by the trauma of the experience.

But even more perversely, what most viewers do not understand is that the trauma these villagers are going through is happening in the present and the recent past: local people were and are often victims of extortion, driven off their land, blackmailed, or harassed regularly.[62] They are in the hold of a system of visual biopolitics that predetermines their fate and circumscribes their freedom. In *The Act of Killing*, the torture is inverted: we are witnessing subjects being tortured by torturers reenacting what's really an ongoing torture. In a market, a Chinese Indonesian man shakes with fear as he is filmed being extorted by a local paramilitary leader; another man, Suryono, whose stepfather was taken away and disappeared during the 1965 killings, breaks down in sobs during a reenactment scene in which an actor playing his stepfather is blindfolded and tortured; children cry uncontrollably during the filming when adults play at murdering their parents. As Rachmi Diyah Larasati has pointed out, Indonesians are scared and going into trance not because they were there during the 1965–66 killings, but because violence by military-backed local militias has been commonplace.[63]

Trance is relevant, then, to both Mead and Oppenheimer because the concern is to get to what is authentic, the truly Real. It is that acting out, that resistance, that play of being in the Cut, to paraphrase Pandolfo again, that is also common to the subjects of both films, if a reader is sensitive to

FIGURE 2.8 The village burning scene. Still from the *The Act of Killing* (Joshua Oppenheimer, 2012).

both the visual biopolitics of documentary and the political and historical experience of Indonesian culture and language. British filmmaker and critic Nick Fraser has critiqued Oppenheimer's use of what he describes as getting "killers to script and restage their murders for the benefit of a cinema or television audience," and he likens it to sending filmmakers to rural Argentina in the 1950s, rounding up a bunch of aging Nazis, and getting them to make a film about it.[64] I would go further and suggest that the equivalent would be if Oppenheimer had gone to Alabama, lived there for several years, and invited a group of poor and/or working-class, aging white Ku Klux Klan members to make a film reenacting their murdering and lynching of African Americans, in the community where people's fathers and sons had been lynched, in the style of an art film that was inspired by *The Birth of a Nation*. The outrage that this would create among US viewers is clear. Violence that implicates whites would upset the visual biopolitics of Mead and Bateson's and Oppenheimer's films. Some of the elements necessary, then, for the visual biopolitics of documentary to work are distance (geographical and colonial distance), which creates a different subjectivity for the audience watching Anwar Congo or Herman Koto from a distance; and the authorial voice of the filmmaker (not necessarily in the form of voice-over but in the auteurist hand of the director), which can explain away the violence of brown men performing violence on other brown men and brown women or, in the case of trance, on themselves.

Thus, in many ways, *The Act of Killing* actually reveals how film creates powerful fantasies of violence that erect and legitimize the divide between those who are allowed to live and those who are allowed to die. Unlike the Mead films that attempted to reinforce categories of real versus performed, *The Act of Killing* shifts into a new configuration, one that upsets the cognitive categories of what is real and what is performed, what is authentic and what is faked. This is the reason for the prizes and awards and glowing reviews the film received: it reveals, to these viewers, a radical new form of ethnographic subjectivity, whereby they can really get into the heads and the fantasies of killers brought up on fantasies of killing. What we see is what Oppenheimer knew would be more entertaining, a "majestic" artistic vision of killing with artful mise-en-scène, sound, scoring, and editing, not what would be closer to Anwar Congo and Herman Koto's vision, more like *Pengkhianatan G30S/ PKI*, which Oppenheimer says would look more like a tawdry karaoke video. In an interview, Oppenheimer describes how he directed the mise-en-scène that was supposedly the work of the gangster filmmakers:

> I think it was really important to try and make those scenes as undeniably majestic as possible, as beautiful as possible, as profound as possible— just as Anwar would wish them to be. We could have made the musical numbers look like cheap Southeast Asian karaoke videos, but to do so would be sneering at them and it is very important that we enter Anwar's nightmare or his fantasies and [that] we enjoy them or are afraid of them—just as he is. Although the waterfall scene is kitschy, crazy, tacky, and ridiculous, it is also beautiful and heart-stirring. That is what allows the fiction scenes to take over the film's form and what allows the scenes they are making and the film that we are watching to melt together into a kind of fever dream. I think that would not have been possible if we didn't do everything we could to make those scenes as powerful as possible.[65]

Here, we are offered a good example of how the documentarian directs. Both awareness and intentional nonawareness of the camera are performances, so that it is usually our desire to see "realness" that gives the representational the valence of the real. Oppenheimer presumes that Anwar's vision, closer to that of Southeast Asian karaoke, would appear "tacky." The fevered dream is that of Oppenheimer, who is the film's auteur. With a documentary film, especially one by outsiders about Indonesia, directing is on the level not only of choosing the mise-en-scène, what gets placed in front of the camera, or what gets shot, but also how it is edited, produced, and ultimately shown to audiences. Visual biopolitics also determines which films get seen and which do not, what gets heard and what is not explained. To return again to Rangan's question, what does endangered humanity do for documentary, *The Act of Killing* provides the following answer: endangered humanity constitutes the very function of documentary, providing material that entertains, and that reassures, and in its overpresence as the savior film about the Indonesian genocide, it takes the place of actual films by Indonesians that have been made on the subject.

Several voices have taken issue with the use of fascinating cannibalism and the aging *preman* (low-level gangster killers) in *The Act of Killing*. Anwar Congo and Herman Koto (these are their gang names, which would not be apparent to a non-Indonesian viewer), along with the other crony gangster murderers we see throughout the film, were only hired killers, uneducated gangsters from the ghetto. Yet in the marketing of the film, in reviews, and on the internet, they are portrayed as mastermind killers, rather than petty lackeys. Historian Robert Cribb attacks the film for continuing Orientalist stereotypes of Indonesians casually killing without regard to life, and he also points out that the film's thesis appears to be that the killings had to do with "the work of civilian criminal psychopaths" rather than a political and systemic government campaign of execution.[66] Scholar Dag Yngvesson points out that structurally there is no position for Indonesians to inhabit other than as objects or as the "ghost" that is the camera.[67] The film, he argues, actually causes Indonesians to disappear (ironic for a film whose theme is the disappearance of a million Indonesians), because of the way it patronizes Indonesians as being "not yet enlightened" and "in need of a caring outsider to help guide them."[68] Indonesian literature scholar Viola Lasmana and US anthropologist Janet Hoskins are also skeptical of the authorial hand of Oppenheimer and question whether it is ethical to push Anwar Congo to "a real or sham catharsis for the purpose of making a documentary."[69] To Cribb, Yngvesson, Hoskins, and Lasmana, the director is posing as the guide who will lead the Indonesian viewer to enlightenment, yet traumatizing Indonesians in the meantime in an unethical way.

Oppenheimer represents a continuation of Robert Flaherty and Margaret Mead, and thus, because of its flexibility and changeability, visual biopolitics is perpetuated. Like Flaherty, who created the Real by casting the actor Akalariallak as the character Nanook, in what is considered by many the first classic documentary, *Nanook of the North* (1922), Anwar Congo and Herman Koto are set up as the metonyms for the face of the killing; this belies US and foreign involvement, like Mead and Flaherty bely history. The gruesome and gigantic human flesh–devouring Aminah, played by the cross-dressing Herman Koto, in her tight scarlet dress, echoes the razor-slashing red kebaya murderess in *Pengkhianatan G30S/PKI*, a representation that both satirizes and continues (in classic fascinating cannibalism) the representation of the evil progressive female dancer. Like *Trance and Dance in Bali*, it purports to root out the truth, and instead sets up the auteur as the teller of the truth. To the West, this film becomes the image of the truth and of history uncovered, in part because it dismisses the need for historical specificity. American talking heads such as US generals and others who could have contextualized the killings would have confounded the pleasure of the cool beauty of the gold-laméd dancing girls shimmering by the giant wood fish perched at the edge of Lake Toba, on the island of Sumatra (figure 2.2).

It is a film that makes you vanish.

OTHER MEDIA

Like Mead, Oppenheimer has mined several years of footage to produce more than one film. *The Look of Silence* (2014) is Oppenheimer's follow-up, and in its exquisitely composed and color-saturated tableaus exploring human cruelty we can see clearly Oppenheimer's style of filmmaking, one that was purported to be that of the aging gangsters in *The Act of Killing*, but is clearly Oppenheimer's hand. *The Look of Silence* follows Adi Rukun, a humble optometrist, as he confronts the men who viciously killed his older brother Ramli in 1965, many of whom still live in his community. Adi's gaze at his brother's torturing murderers, who deflect, deny, and diminish the killings, becomes the eye of the storm, similar to that of Jewish Holocaust survivor Simon Srebnik, who confronts the Polish villagers from Chelmno who had lived near the concentration camp which he survived, in Claude Lanzmann's documentary *Shoah* (1985). *The Look of Silence*, carried by the conviction and determination of Adi to do the seemingly impossible and find answers to his brother's death, is an impressive film.

However, long before *The Act of Killing* appeared on the festival circuit, Indonesians were making films that confront the genocide that occurred in 1965. These films do not receive visibility. Biopolitics is also present in whose films get to be screened and whose do not. To present himself as an American savior who speaks truth to power in Indonesia would obfuscate the many other Indonesians exploring their own history.[70]

What else gets disappeared in the wake of the singular attention focused on *The Act of Killing* as the pioneering voice of truth about the killings of the Suharto regime? One answer is all the many Indonesian films and videos that attempt to speak to and even dismantle the realism and truth status of *Pengkhianatan G30S/PKI* resisting visual biopolitics.

As Katinka van Heeren explains, the Suharto government's production of *Pengkhianatan G30S/PKI* was presented as the truth, as a documentary film, part of a four-part government film series. During Reformasi, the Reformation period following Suharto's stepping down in 1998, Indonesian filmmakers began to redefine exactly what was documentary. A generation felt courageous enough to speak out about the truth of 1965, and the ur-film that they all had to challenge was *Pengkhianatan G30S/PKI*. Van Heeren describes and analyzes many of these documentary films, including Lexy Rambadata's *Mass Grave* (2001), which is about the exhumation of the dead in Wonosobo, Java, recalling the ending of *Pengkhianatan G30S/PKI* in which Suharto talks over the exhumation of bones; and Lasia Fauzia Susatyo and Abduh Aziz's *Tjidurian 19* (2008), which addresses the history of LEKRA, the vilified arts organization accused of communism during the Suharto era. Narrative fiction films have also been made including *Sang Penari* (2011), directed by Ifa Ifansyah and produced by Shanty Harmayn, about a poor Javanese dancer who, like her fellow villagers, becomes involved in communism. She is eventually arrested and tortured, and perhaps disappeared, only to appear in the last scene, dancing with a fellow villager, ten years later, on a lone dirt road. The dead refuse to vanish, their traces return to haunt, in these films that resist visual biopolitics.

Indonesians have been and are working with media and creating archives of disappeared histories to explore and record testimonies of 1965. For example, the 2006 documentary film directed by I. G. P. Wiranegara, *Menyemai Terang Dalam Kelam* (Sow light in the darkness), discussed in my introduction, opens with one of the survivors, Putu Oka, a writer whose words, commentary, and interview provide a structure for the film, visiting the PKI monument at Lubang Buaya, with its engraved bas relief images of the government version of the killings of the generals. As a former prisoner condemned as a PKI traitor, he stands silently watching, as scores of schoolchildren on class trips to the monument are regaled with the official propaganda history. The film takes a third-eye perspective, providing us with an active spectator to identify with, who watches the visual biopolitics of the state that were and are used to condemn scores of people to inferior status.

These films by Indonesians about the killings of 1965 are never shown in the West and are intended for Indonesian audiences. Many are grassroots activist media, not to be considered art films. Scholar Ariel Heryanto describes three categories of these films: first, documentary films by LKK (Lembaga Kreativitas Kemanusiaan or the Institute of Creative Humanity), such as the aforementioned I. G. P. Wiranegara's *Menyemai Terang Dalam Kelam*, and *Plantungan: Potret Derita dan Kekuatan Perempuan* by Fadillah Vamp Saleh and Putu Oka Sukanta, made in 2011 about the women's prison camp, and the struggles and strengths of the women prisoners. The second category Heryanto describes encompasses documentary films by nongovernmental organizations, including a remarkable series of films interrogating official history by interviewing former political prisoners, produced and directed by young high school students, called *Putih Abu-Abu: Masa Lalu Perempuan* (Gray white: women's past), with Syarikat Indonesia and Komnas Perempuan (National Commission on Violence against Women). Finally, there are independent films such as Garin Nugroho's *Puisi yang Tak Terkuburkan* (Poetry that cannot be buried) from 2000, starring Ibrahim Kadir, playing himself, a former political prisoner and poet, as he is falsely imprisoned for twenty-two days and witnesses the murders and false arrests of others who go to their graves. Here I would add a fourth category of online media. In 2013 a group called Engage Media invited filmmakers to make video-essay commentaries on the film *Pengkhianatan G30S/PKI*. Like Rachmi Diyah Larasati, many of them had grown up watching the film in school, so they reworked and reedited the footage to comment on the disappearance of history, a form of resisting visual biopolitics that I discuss along with editing in chapter 3. As short videos they play back, rewind, and deconstruct the history of the nation that the Suharto regime wrote as Real.

As I described in my introduction, in Wiranegara's *Menyemai Terang Dalam Kelam*, a former female prisoner, the dancer Jumilah, explains how she was caught and tortured after attending a conference of Gerwani (figure 2.9). The torturers made her confess that her name was Atikah Jamilah (not her name), and that she danced naked and plucked out the eyeballs of the generals. As she recounts her story, we see the engraved bas relief of the PKI monument at Lubang Buaya of the evil dancing women that so many Indonesians have believed are the true killers for so many years. Through cutting to newspaper stories and close-ups of the monument, Wiranegara reveals how Jumilah was visualized and forced into the role of the murderous sexual traitor, and thus he creates a film that resists visual biopolitics. The "evil, murderous, sexually voracious female dancer" speaks back, but only forty years later, in a film that has never been shown on screens in the United States.

THE DANCER AND THE REPLICA: FORCES OF RESISTANCE

More than a million people were imprisoned or killed in 1965, and subsequent generations were deeply affected by this trauma. Tragically, the vilification of communism continues to the present day. Anyone seen as being

Jumilah
Eks Tapol. Ibu Rumah Tangga
Former Political Prisoner, Home maker
I was taken to KOTI and I was tortured like an animal.

FIGURE 2.9 Jumilah
speaks in a scene from
*Menyemai Terang
Dalam Kerang* (I. G. P.
Wiranegara, 2006).

somehow disagreeable to the police or the local governments can be labeled
PKI and denied human rights. Those whose parents had links with any left-
leaning organizations, such as LEKRA, were labeled communist, including
many Chinese Indonesians, as well as women who were working in the arts.
At the center of the question of fascinating cannibalism, even though she is
much maligned, is the Indonesian woman who had a particular place in the
history of the killings and the Orde Baru government, as the story of Jumilah above is testament.[71] Among those deeply affected and seen as tainted
were the children of victims. Rachmi Diyah Larasati is one of those children;
her mother, a dancer, went missing. In her stunning and brave book, which
painstakingly outlines visual biopolitics and its effects, *The Dance That Makes
You Vanish: Cultural Reconstruction in Post-genocide Indonesia*, published the
same year that *The Act of Killing* was released, Rachmi Diyah Larasati provides a first-person scholarly account, using historical research, memory, and
corporeal experience as a dancer who was trained and supported by the Indonesian government to represent Indonesia all over the world (figure 2.3).

Larasati takes aim at the visual biopolitical nature of exoticism: "Exoticism, with its emphasis on spirituality and religiosity, indirectly nurtures the
colonial fantasy of the West toward Indonesia (and much of the rest of the
East and Africa) and successfully legitimizes the new cultural representations
that Indonesia's New Order regime reconstructed; it simultaneously erases
the violence perpetrated against historical Indonesian bodies, and in particular Indonesian women's bodies."[72] In that statement she excoriates the representation of the Indonesian female dancer we have seen from the World's
Fair to the art documentary, and explains its function. What Larasati grew to

realize was how she had become a replica replacing the real, vanished bodies of the large number of Indonesian women dancers and artists who had been members of progressive arts groups and who, during the 1965 massacre, were murdered or were required to report to local authorities in a weekly cleansing, which meant submitting to rape and sexual abuse. This is a strong statement: it is the dancer read in the context of exoticism who is used to erase the crimes of thousands murdered during periods of violent resistance to Dutch colonialism or the 1965 killings. Rachmi Diyah Larasati examines her own positioning as a state dancer and as a scholar working in the United States: "Thus, I trace the history of the female dancing body that vanishes and is then 'replaced,' its experience and the fact of disappearance erased from view by new, highly indoctrinated, strictly trained female bodies—not unlike the idealized Indonesian citizen that lives within myself."[73] "Replica" is the word she holds onto to reveal how the holes in the cloth of history are sewn shut by the simulacra of "new, historically, politically 'clean' dancers," even as that cleanliness comes at the price of the murder of her mother and other family members, and sexual abuse and torture of women accused of being leftists.

The narrative that the Indonesian state created was that the Communist Party (or PKI) and other leftist organizations such as the arts organization LEKRA were havens for insidious, evil, murderous, and sexually deviant female dancers. The pathology here is that of women's sexuality. The visual biopolitics of colonialism lent itself well to the totalitarian government of Suharto's military dictatorship, and at the center of the assemblage of the communist was the image of the naked, sexual, castrating, penis-devouring female dancer.

In addition to hypervisibility, visual biopolitics functions with hyperaudibility and silence. The Suharto regime ensured closed mouths on the part of Indonesians who would speak against injustice and violence, and question the propaganda of national history. The power delineated here was that of Suharto and of surviving generations who were part of the Reformation, in which talking was perhaps the greatest crime. Even more chilling was what Larasati learned from women in Bali whose husbands or who themselves were accused of being part of the Communist Party or leftist organizations like Gerwani. They were forced to report regularly to the local authorities for *wajib lapor* (mandatory self-reporting) and were sexually abused and raped as a form of placation.

> The bodies of the accused women, considered a threat to the purity of the rituals, were instead sent as "offerings" to the local authorities so that they might be "cleansed" within the walls of the regional military or village

headman's house. Thus the female body performs the continuous function of mediating the transition from violence and chaos to state reidentification; whether as sublimated dancer, as a means of sexual placation, or as aesthetic adornment, the moving, performing female body represents the promise of recovery for a nation-state that is nonetheless always necessarily in the process of cultural and political reinvention.[74]

It is the dancer that mediates the violence necessary to create the state; she is in the hold of the syncretic accretions of power from colonialism, anthropology, the new state, and globalization.

It is with Larasati's description of the Barong dancing in Bali that we see what Mead and Bateson could not see: "Performed for tourists, their dance is meant to take on the aura of an unbroken continuum of spiritual practice, which the purchase of a ticket will help to preserve. Yet in the context of the Balinese village where it is performed, it serves as a coded reminder of the violence that took place and that threatens to return if anyone deigns to disturb the ruling order."[75] The performed dance is thus a form of biopolitical control. What she describes as "the flashy, action-filled 'stabbing' dance" that was the subject of Mead's film is now a global commodity through tourism. The body of the dancer becomes "tourist attraction and signifier of order." She continues in her description of a seller, who was one of the women raped during the mandatory reporting sessions, who now has a food stall near the Barong dance for tourists: "Thus, the woman I spoke with who was repeatedly raped during her state-ordered wajib lapor visits after 1965, and who owns a small warung behind the performance space, now receives regular business because of the Barong. Yet the 'ordered' reality presided over by the female dancing body remains tenuous, fragile, and threatened by embodied memory, waiting for the chance to show itself, to respond to the violent scene replayed daily in the backyard of its victims and their children."[76]

The dancers are in the hold of national propaganda that disciplines and controls the bodies dancing, but what Larasati reveals is how to perform or give witness and show the wounds of colonial or state violence as well. In other words, how to be, as Pandolfo terms it, in the Cut. Larasati unravels the weft of the social imagery, but quietly, for her book does not have international capital distributing it or the flash that would attract anything like the audience for The Act of Killing. The book itself and the performances Larasati has staged, directing herself and others, provide a critique that is both inside and outside.

What is also unique about Larasati's account is her acute awareness of how history is using her as a replica. She names other masters as well: those who are entranced by the dancer's exotic docile beauty, such as the Western Indonesianists who fetishize the cultures of Java and Bali. Unlike Oppenheimer, who was lauded as a salvation filmmaker, purporting to get to the truth that the Indonesian government refuses to uncover, Larasati is aware of how her positioning makes her complicit, as a scholar now working in the United States, struggling to put together the pieces of a fractured whole, but still compromised by using academic language. That is why her concept of a third body is so important, as a postnationalist dancing body, who carries within her the memory of what the murdered ones taught her, who dances between the extremes of past and present. With a third eye the dancer sees the past murders of the other dancers, and becomes a force of resistance.

That haunting can be revealed in a trembling middle finger as resistance that will not stay still in the choreography of the dancer Setyastuti.[77] In 2008 in Yogyakarta, Rachmi Diyah Larasati collaborated with the dancer and choreographer Setyastuti, whose dance in their collaboration *Talk to the Wall* (*Tembok Mari Bicara*; her own translation) betrays in her pose what is unsaid and unheard. Unlike the deathlike immobility usually required of the slow court Javanese dances like *bedhaya*, which the government favored in artistic missions abroad, Setyastuti (in particular her middle fingers) willfully will not remain still. They exceed what is required:

> While her expression and the pose of her head and limbs were the picture of formal perfection, the middle fingers of her outstretched hand—which was itself held, true to form, at an impossibly obtuse angle to her arm—betrayed the tiny signs of restlessness, moving apart and then together again as if in time to some unseen rhythm pulsing from within. It was here, watching a seemingly endless—yet always strangely fascinating—repetition of the most official and sublimated of dances, that I first began to read, and to feel, the presence of that which "exceeds," if only slightly, even the most hegemonic and deterministic of embodied national representations.[78]

Unlike the Mead and Bateson film, or the Oppenheimer film, Larasati's book reveals a collective sense of identity, of those who must always view with a third eye. It is also one that we can find implicitly in the found-footage film *Mother Dao* and the omnibus films produced by Nia Dinata, which I discuss in chapters 3 and 4.

At present, the specter of the communist demon in the form of the female dancer endures and continues to be used politically as a scapegoat figure, much in the way Willie Horton figured in George W. Bush's campaign and the "Mexican rapist" figured in Donald Trump's. In this chapter we have excavated the foundation of Indonesian visual biopolitics in the figure of the dancer, which we can trace from the 1893 painting of Annah la Javanaise by Gauguin to the art documentary *The Act of Killing*. Time and history are ongoing; time is not asynchronous. There is an alternate space beyond the archive and its silences, the government and its propaganda history, and the need to reproduce with fidelity. What the next examples that I examine in chapters 3 and 4 transcend are the boundaries of identity between those whose egos align with an individual subjectivity versus those who must always view with a third eye and thus whose identity is a collective subjectivity.

The tiny dancer is murdered; let us show it, even though she will never be brought back whole. In the replica dancer that takes her place beats the heart of the murdered one, in the trembling of her body that refuses to remain still.

THE DRESSING DOWN

The Mother blew in one afternoon, like a sudden draft of wind. There she was, her snotty-nosed two-year-old in tow. Around her neck was a tape measure, as if she had just found out from street gossip where to find the Man and left behind her sewing, grabbing the child from under the table to carry along as collateral. She called out the Man's name and roamed restlessly about the studio looking for him. I kept silent.

I am small, and, sitting still in the armchair, she did not notice me. Perhaps she thought I was just another ethnographic statue or a pet monkey.

Finally, she came upon me, and her eyes narrowed. She hissed with disgust, like a snake startled upon a path. Thanks to the first Madame I understood all the bad words that the Mother hurled at me. She was spitting with fury. If her goal was to get back with the Man, I'm sure that if he heard her from outside the door he would have stayed away.

When she had just about run out of breath, I finally, calmly, looked at her, and asked, "Are you done?" The Mother's jaw dropped.

Nobody thinks that I speak French. I ate her tongue and she could say nothing further.

When I had to face the French public, I dressed up. I was already a woman, so the short dress, like the kind the Girl wore, seemed inappropriate. I preferred long gowns and long gloves. I would pull my hair up like Madame, with my hat cocked just so. I had it made from the plaited straw the Man had given me, and I wore it like a crown. I liked to walk the streets of Paris this way. Let them stare. I was a lady.

It ended one day when we went to the countryside. They called me a Witch and threw stones. The Man himself got hurt and took months to recover.

So I got him to send me back to Paris alone, since he was too injured to move. When I arrived, I thought about how I had cleaned his house, cooked his meals, and was forced to lie with him. He had never paid me. He had only hurt me.

And so I looted his studio, and took the portrait he had done of me, which was not really me. I was about to walk out the door of the studio, when I decided to torch the place.

Nobody was home. I lit the match, and I watched the fire burn. I wanted it all destroyed. The bed, the chairs, the sculptures, the woodwork, the whole dead Museum. The flame smelt dry and acrid and pure. I did not stay to see what happened.

I no longer cared. I had my image. It was not me. But it was mine.

3

MOTHER DAO

In a video I found on YouTube, "Genjer-Genjer—Lilis Suryani [PKI-Song],"
posted in 2012, a photomontage of images from the history of the PKI is set
to Indonesian pop singer Lilis Suryani's rendition of "Genjer Genjer," the
song that we hear the women and men singing in the orgiastic killing scenes
of *Pengkhianatan G30S/PKI*, discussed in chapter 2.[1] The history of this song
reflects the history of the left and the killings. During Japanese occupation
and Dutch colonialism, people were so poor that they were forced to eat anything, including weeds that grew along the river. In 1943 Muhammed Arif
wrote a sad song about a mother who picks the weeds (the *genjer*) to cook
and to sell in the market, reflecting the conditions of starvation and despera-
tion under Japanese occupation. Later, two major stars recorded it. One was
Bing Slamet. The other was Lilis Suryani, a beautiful young pop singer with
the short mod haircut and A-line dresses of a French Ya-Ya singer. During Sukarno's reign, the PKI adapted "Genjer Genjer" as a kind of popular song for
the party, in the way that "Bella Ciao" became a song for the Italian partisans
of the Resistance in World War II (and now used in the popular Netflix series

La casa de papel or *Money Heist*). After 1965, Suharto's government spread the rumor that it was a song sung by the Gerwani women as they were sexually torturing the male generals, and the song was banned. Muhammed Arif, who had first recorded the song in 1942, was accused of being a member of the PKI and was killed. After Suharto's downfall and the Reformasi at the turn of the twenty-first century, young activist musicians began to sing "Genjer Genjer" in their shows, in a brave act of defiance. And what became apparent was that the song was not a scary ideological song about murder, castration, and armed uprising, but a blues song—Javanese style—about fortitude despite being young, poor, and female.

Suryani's version of "Genjer Genjer" is a gorgeous pop song that opens with lush string instruments. Her clear, smooth voice is evocative of a golden era, with the silky sound of a Rosemary Clooney or a Doris Day. But the photomontage that accompanies this long-banned song is chilling and incongruous. They are shocking, censored images, all black and white, of men tied together by their necks by a rope, walking into a mass grave. There is a photograph of a stadium with huge posters of Marx and Lenin and Stalin, a *becak* (bicycle rickshaw) driver in the right foreground. Another photograph in the montage of dissolves is a medium shot of a dead man, newly tortured and killed, naked to the torso. We see portraits of Aidit, the leader of the Indonesian Communist Party, handsome, charismatic, and young—an activist and political leader who was also a jazz musician. There is another image of a man, his hands up behind his neck, being interrogated by soldiers (figure 3.1).

When I saw the video it made me shiver, because I had never seen such images before, and because the golden-brandy-like voice of Lilis Suryani is in sharp contrast to the images of the killings. But it was precisely her song that was banned by the Suharto regime (figure 3.2).[2] Video interventions like these show us that the sound- and mediascape of the killings is not a straight road of revelation. Visual biopolitics harnesses images and sound, yes, but it also becomes subverted by them, in this song about a poor woman, written during World War II, sung by a pop singer in 1965, and recomposed thirty-seven years later, in the broad daylight of a twenty-first-century platform.

Subjectivity for colonized or formerly colonized subjects, in moments of states of exception, require a different kind of subjectivity from that of the posited Western rational Self. As I explain in chapter 2, inspired by what author Driss Chraïbi describes as the thin line of modernity, Stefania Pandolfo posits Moroccan thought within the Cut or the wound, which allows the patient to withstand the lived and metaphorical possession of colonial culture and language. Springboarding from Pandolfo's conception of living

FIGURE 3.1 Still from "Genjer-Genjer—Lilis Suryani [PKI-Song]" (Mister Gaje, posted 2012), YouTube video.

FIGURE 3.2 Album by Lilis Suryani, *Selamat Tinggal*.

in the Cut, I will focus on how one can resist visual biopolitics' use of the photographic and film archive, in particular through recontextualization and unsettling juxtaposition. What would it be like to live within that thin line of modernity, to acknowledge rather than hide the colonial wounds of cultural, linguistic, and medical possession? By drawing from a family photograph of a Batak (Sumatra) village chief, taken in 1863, and *Mother Dao, the Turtlelike*, a found-footage film of 1995 that raids films from the archives of the Dutch colonial era, I will dwell on photography's specific relationship to time, lying in the Cut between linear, regulated, modern time and circular, uncanny, supernatural time.

THE PHOTOGRAPHIC PRINCIPLE OF SURREALISM

The art of raiding the archive and creating new juxtapositions—whether it be the archive of the ethnographic museum, the bin of old Hollywood film footage, or a colonial art collection—was made famous by surrealism, the French avant-garde art and literary movement of the 1920s to early '30s. Critics have expanded the definition of surrealism as a praxis, as historian James Clifford put it, a way of thinking, a modernist aesthetic that could subvert or parody the West's way of stumbling into world wars and colonizing others.[3] Clifford opened up a debate on what he called ethnographic surrealism. He points to the connections between ethnography and surrealism in France of the 1920s and '30s. The worlds of both are exotic, and make the familiar strange, highlighting collecting and how cultural reality is composed of artificial codes, thus calling all hierarchies into question. He argues for a different kind of ethnography, one that uses the metaphor of collage to see the constructedness of the writing.[4] Surrealism is, therefore, "an aesthetic that values fragments, curious collections, unexpected juxtapositions—that works to provoke the manifestation of extraordinary realities drawn from the domains of the erotic, the exotic, and the unconscious."[5] Recontextualized footage—photographic or film—unsettles.

Many scholars—Alan Trachtenberg, Christopher Pinney, Elizabeth Edwards, Malek Alloula, Ann Stoler, and myself included in *The Third Eye*—have written about biopolitics' use of photography during the nineteenth and twentieth centuries as a surveillance technology used to classify and delimit subjugated peoples into categories of type—race, ethnicity, class, gender, sexuality—in particular colonized and enslaved bodies (racial typing of different ethnic groups, for example). During colonial times, photography was used by scientists and medical researchers to create an archive around the physical attributes of race (this was true of Mead and Bateson's planned archive on Balinese movement, discussed in their book *Balinese Character*). This generalized form of knowledge falls into Roland Barthes's studium category of photography, what was seen as known and common, general and informative.

The other aspect of photography pointed out by Barthes, and one that I would like to develop in the context of resisting visual biopolitics, is the punctum. Barthes famously wrote that film could not compare to the photograph because the time of looking at a film was shared and regulated, whereas the time of the photograph is akin to the dream and private, the punctum. The photograph stops time. There is something unique to photography, for it, above all other media, has the capacity to shock with subjective meaning. Photography has pathos and desire embedded into it, that quality of the private moment that cinema is deprived of, since it is edited and experienced through a controlled time.[6] André Bazin, the champion of anti-Hollywood realism and one of the founders of the *Cahiers du Cinéma* in the 1950s, describes the photograph and the object photographed as sharing a common being, like a fingerprint. Bazin continues, "the surrealist does not consider his aesthetic purpose and the mechanical effect of the image on our imaginations as things apart. For him, the logical distinction between what is imaginary and what is real tends to disappear. Every image is to be seen as an object and every object as an image. Hence photography ranks high in the order of surrealist creativity because it produces an image that is a reality of nature, namely, an hallucination that is also a fact."[7]

Photography is closer to surrealism than film because it is an index, like a fingerprint, and hence it destroys the boundaries between the real and the imaginary, the object depicted and the representation. It is a trace, like Veronica's veil, the imprint of Jesus's face on a cloth taken from his corpse, and Bazin argues that it liberates painting from man's desire to embalm time. Bazin notes that man's great desire is for a "mummy complex," for an art that would serve as "a defense against the passage of time. . . . To preserve, artificially, his bodily appearance is to snatch it from the flow of time, to stow it away neatly, so to speak, in the hold of life."[8] This control over time is part of the shock that photography brings. Hence the charm, Bazin presents, of family albums: "Those grey or sepia shadows, phantomlike and almost undecipherable, are no longer traditional family portraits but rather the disturbing presence of lives halted at a set moment in their duration, freed from their destiny; not, however, by the prestige of art but by the power of an impassive mechanical process: for photography does not create eternity, as art does, it embalms time, rescuing it simply from its proper corruption."[9] The phantom aspect of photography is the beating heart in the representation, the replica that Rachmi Diyah Larasati theorizes and that I discussed in chapter 2, and one that I want to explore further in the medium of photography.

Ann Stoler's works on the nonbinary intricacies of power as it inheres in class, ethnicity, and gender in colonial societies in Indonesia are groundbreaking, as is Karen Strassler's book *Refracted Visions: Popular Photography and Natural Modernity in Java*.[10] Both Stoler and Strassler challenge Western notions of photography by looking at how different genres of photography are used or, to use Strassler's term, refracted in Javanese subjects. Their co-written essay on reading Dutch colonial photographs taken of Indonesian servants and Dutch colonialists, "Memory-Work in Java: A Cautionary Tale," finds that the way the Javanese use and regard photographic remnants of the colonial past can be at odds with tidy narratives of either colonial nostalgia (found in Dutch accounts) or in postcolonial readings of resistance.[11] At the end of their essay, they take a surprising rhetorical tactic: they explain that the interview subject, the former maid Ibu Darmo, was a very resistant subject indeed. Stoler and Strassler had hoped Ibu Darmo could speak back to the archives, but she resists their interview, refusing to speak to Stoler and Strassler. The writers explain that she only speaks to the Indonesian interviewers, Nita and Didi, "as if we were not there," the "we" being presumably Strassler and Stoler, a noninclusive "us."[12] What is radical is not only that Stoler and Strassler reject easy, tidy readings of the relationships of Indonesian servants to Dutch colonialists, but that they also acknowledge the rebellious subject, the maid who refuses to address or even view the white interviewers, an act of acknowledgment normally omitted or smoothed over in scholarly accounts or in ethnographic film. I would like to offer a third but related kind of reading, not of the sympathetic but foreign interviewer or of the subject who was photographed, but that of the viewer who is tied to the photograph by kinship.

Kinship is not necessarily based on blood. When I first saw the photographs of Annah la Javanaise, this girl with the impossibly fierce and startled eyes among all the louche, white men playing dress-up, in a tableau set up as a joke, I saw the disturbing presence of a life halted at a set moment in her duration. Because I saw the way that time was halted, I resisted the joke. (I had to because if I did not resist the joke, I would be the joke too.)

I have discussed photography's biopolitical uses during colonialism in *The Third Eye*, and how the photograph is utilized to categorize and racialize people. Biopolitics has famously used photography as a means to classify and categorize colonized natives into ethnic groups and as a means to survey and discipline subjugated peoples: criminals, hysterics, and natives.[13] Missionaries also took photographs to lay claim to those they converted to Christianity and to raise and justify further funding for missions. By converting colonized peoples from their animist beliefs, they helped lay the ground for colonial exploitation. Visual biopolitics, such as is seen in the early colonial and missionary photography and film, circumscribed, legitimized, indoctrinated (informed), and entertained Dutch audiences back in the metropoles.

The unconscious, however, is also present in visual biopolitics. Colonial footage will have a different relationship to an audience who was not intended to be the viewer, those who see with a third eye—say the natives themselves, or a native's great-great-granddaughter. Here theories of surrealism bring some force to bear, in the sense of witnessing time both in and out of sync.

Cultural critic Susan Sontag writes eloquently on the surrealism of photography. Ironically, she notes, it is not the rayographs of Man Ray or the photomontages of John Heartfield that exploited this principle, but photography itself: "Surrealism has always courted accidents, welcomed the uninvited, flattered disorderly presences. What could be more surreal than an object that virtually produces itself, and with a minimum of effort? An object whose beauty, fantastic disclosures, emotional weight is likely to be further enhanced by any accidents that might befall it? It is photography that has best shown how to juxtapose the sewing machine and the umbrella, whose fortuitous encounter was hailed by a great Surrealist poet as an epitome of the beautiful."[14]

Sontag argues it is not the photographs typically seen as surrealist, those abstract photos using superimposition, underprinting, and solarization that are the most surreal, but street photographs from the 1850s of unposed slices of life. The most surreal photographs are those that, to use Bazin's expression, embalm time; depict the local, the regional, the particular, and class. The most surreal element of all was the "most brutally moving, irrational, unassimilable, mysterious—time itself. What renders a photograph surreal is its irrefutable pathos as a message from time past, and the concreteness of its intimations about social class."[15] To the local, the regional, and the particular in relation to class, I would like to add another category: the ethnographic. Here I would like to spend some time looking at an image of the ethnographic Savage. By the ethnographic I am not referring to the Hollywood romanticized version of the East Indies, ironically seen in *Rose Hobart*, the first film by surrealist Joseph Cornell, which raided the archive of Hollywood exoticism. Instead I will be raiding the missionary archive of the Lutheran mission found in Wuppertal, Germany, and turn to a photograph of the first Batak raja to convert to Christianity. Unlike Roland Barthes, who spent an entire book talking about finding his mother's essence in a family photograph, those of us descended from colonial subjects find our family portraits in wide circulation. It is to reclaim the private moments and the nontidy narratives in such photographs that I turn to my great-great-grandfather's photograph.

"Isn't it true that the Dutch East Indies Company ordered you to subjugate
us so that we will be forced to work for you? Aren't you planning to send our
children abroad if they come to study with you?"

With clarity, Nommensen explained that he was not from the Company,
but was a minister, so that they shouldn't be afraid. Hearing that, one of the
village chiefs said, "Yes, indeed his words sound great, but we will lose our
children, because our children will become his children."
—From the biography of Ingwer Ludwig Nommensen
(DeWaard, *Pioneer in Sumatra*)

In the nineteenth century, a little boy is born in the Batak region of North
Sumatra, Indonesia. A soothsayer warns the uncle of the boy, the great King
Si Singamangaraja X, that it is destined that this boy will one day grow up
to destroy him. In an attempt to thwart the prophecy, the king places the
boy in a wooden chest and throws him into Lake Toba, the largest volcanic
crater lake in the world. But the baby miraculously survives and grows up in
the Muslim region of west Sumatra. He becomes a leader of Muslims and
bears the title Tuanku Rau. When he reaches adulthood, Tuanku Rau is
determined to return to Batak land and forcibly convert the Batak to Islam,
thus starting what historians later refer to as the Bonjol War. After leaving in
his wake a bloody swath of thousands of dead bodies and burned villages,
Tuanku Rau finally meets the person face to face who cast him out into
the lake—the king, his uncle. In rage and for revenge, Tuanku Rau cuts the
king's head off. But the head whirls around in the air only to disappear. It is
never found. Only then is Tuanku Rau struck by remorse for the crime he
has just committed.

So many Batak were killed or died of disease in the Bonjol War that the
Batak became extremely suspicious of all foreigners. A pact is made by all
the Batak village chiefs to destroy any outsider who tries to bring change to
Batak land. If some of these outsiders, including Christian missionaries, were
killed, it is because the outsiders were seen as harbingers of death.
—A story told to me by my Ompung (grandparent) Sinambela

I met my grandfather's grandfather in a photograph hung prominently on a
wall of my grandmother's front room in her house in the village of Pearaja,
in North Sumatra, Indonesia.[16] In the same room, his portrait was also

emblazoned on a hanging wall calendar produced by the local church, the Huria Kristen Batak Protestan (HKBP), whose broken clock tower (forever set on ten minutes to six), perched high on a hill, dominates the landscape of that part of the Silindung Valley (figure 3.3). It was this man in the calendar, Raja Pontas Obaja Mandailing Lumban Tobing (known locally simply as Raja Pontas), who was said to be the first well-known Toba Batak to convert to Christianity and who allowed his land to be leased in 1873 to the German Lutheran missionary Ingwer Ludwig Nommensen to build the HKBP church.

Stories are believable. Stories inscribed in texts are believable. And images need to be talked about. The missionaries brought cameras along with their hymnals, Bibles, and European medicine, and so not only was my grandfather's grandfather one of the first village chiefs to convert, he was also one of the first to be photographed. The photograph itself was a conversion. The microsecond in which light entered the aperture of the missionary's camera left a trace on the emulsion of the film inside, to be printed upon specially treated paper (figure 3.3).

Raja Pontas was a village chief. His face was strongly chiseled in the way of people who constantly countenance the sun, the land, and the jungle. He was said to be strong and courageous. One of the stories my grandmother told about him is that he captured a wildly charging buffalo by looking it square in the eyes, and with one motion grabbed it by the horns and flipped it over. This was a man who left his father's village at a young age and founded his own village in a rocky, mountainous land with deep green valleys, blazing hot sun, and cool night air. It was a land of all the blues and all the greens of the imagination: according to the time of the day and the intensity of the sun, the sky and the river transform from midnight blue to aquamarine, the verdant green of the fields and the hills now emerald, now jade, now almost yellow green.

I looked to the black-and-white photograph in order to solve a mystery that had plagued me. I asked Raja Pontas, my Ompung, one very simple question: Why did you convert to Christianity? But the man in the photograph remained obstinately silent.

Until the generation of Raja Pontas, the Batak successfully fought back outsiders' attempts to convert them to anything. The Batak do not have religion but have their own way of being: beginning with a belief in one supreme power, Debata Mula Jadi Na Bulon, and the three worlds of the underground, the earth, and the sky. It was a culture intensely centered on the ties of family and the attendant obligations, manifested in the exchange of specific gifts including rice, meat, carp, and multipatterned *ulos* (woven cloth). In the indigo-blue-dyed ulos wrapped around Raja Pontas's waist and head, and

FIGURE 3.3 Photograph of Raja Pontas, owned by the author.

draped long across his shoulders, was a history of family and ancestors. The ulos was woven, exchanged, and worn for every significant occasion: hung around the shoulders of a woman who is expecting a baby, wrapped around a baby and its parents; draped around the shoulders of a nervous bride and groom; placed as a covering over the body of a person who has left for the next world; and set carefully over the dug-up bones of the beloved dead in order to ask for their blessings. The history was written in the cloth, not the archives.

In the late nineteenth century, the Dutch, who had successfully colonized Java in the early 1600s, had not yet attempted to convert the Batak of Sumatra into loyal colonial subjects. The Dutch colonialists were more interested in establishing coffee, tea, tobacco, sugar, and rubber plantations in lowlands to the north near Medan and Siantar. The Muslims had not succeeded in converting the Batak either, despite the bloody Bonjol War that left many dead bodies but few conversions. Upon meeting the Englishmen Burton and Ward, the first missionaries to come to Batak land, Raja Pontas's own grandfather was reported to have told them, "In my opinion, our traditions and customs are very good, and do not need to be changed further. However, if you gentlemen know of a way to achieve prosperity and well, show it to us."

And so I was especially curious about this photograph of Raja Pontas. The photograph was probably taken by Ingwer Ludwig Nommensen, the German Lutheran missionary who finally succeeded in converting the Toba Batak (figure 3.4). Nommensen was very patient. He was clever at pitting village chief against village chief; he carried a big stick, which he waved at dogs and people; he wooed them with the music of his harmonica and viola; at other times, he threatened people, explaining that he would write into a very large book the names of any village chiefs who did not accede to his wishes and report them to authorities in the city; many of those who converted worked for him and were given money and clothes sent from Europe. Was Raja Pontas impressed by the medicine that Nommensen brought? By the fact that Nommensen, unlike the Muslims who preceded him, did not use guns to convert? By Nommensen's ability to speak Batak?

Travelers, scientists, and missionary accounts about the Batak all agree upon one thing: that the Batak were cannibals. Because of these accounts, Sumatra holds a particular mythology in the Western imagination. Just as Skull Island, of Ernest Schoedsack and Merian Cooper's 1933 film *King Kong*, was set off the coast of Sumatra, so was Jonathan Swift's Lilliput of the 1726 novel *Gulliver's Travels*. Andrew Causey writes that cannibalism was believed

FIGURE 3.4
Ingwer Ludwig
Nommensen, slide
6002-410, Copy-
right Archiv- und
Museumsstiftung
der VEM.

to be a thing of the past, and so when William Marsden, an East India Company employee, wrote his tome *History of Sumatra*, it set off a debate due to
the incongruity of its tales of barbarous cannibalism in a culture that was also
known for "a well-established system of law, complex architecture, and most
important, a writing system based on ancient Sanskrit. These were institutions that many post-Enlightenment westerners felt were the essential marks
of 'civilized' humans, not cannibals."[17] Causey explained that after 1865, the
date when Nommensen began to convert hundreds of Toba Batak, and even
after 1907, after the Dutch killed the great Batak resistance leader and king Si
Singamangaraja XII, the myth of the Batak as "lettered cannibals" continues
to this day in travel books and tourist guides. What is known is that Dutch
colonialism and missionary work on the part of Nommensen and the Rheinische Mission, according to Causey, "worked in tandem."[18]

And yet none of the accounts by travelers and missionaries of the nineteenth century yield any acts of cannibalism that were actually witnessed. They are all hearsay. The authority of verbal hearsay stands for what is actually seen. Palpable in all of them is a desire to be the first person to see these cannibals, and also to convince the reader that the accounts that they hear about are incontestably true. A German traveler, Ida Pfeiffer, despite hearing accounts of four men being killed and eaten by the Batak, wrote, "All this did not deter me from my purpose; I was determined to penetrate if possible, through the great valley of *Silingdon*, as far as the lake *Eier Pau* (Great Water), which no European had hitherto seen, and of whose existence there was not other testimony than the stories of the natives."[19] John Anderson regaled readers with stories about cannibalism in his book *Mission to the East Coast of Sumatra in 1823*. One chief confided in him that the flesh of young men was "soft" and "watery" and the best flesh "was that of a man whose hair had begun to turn grey."[20] Anderson felt the need to justify why accounts of cannibalism were true, even though he had not seen it with his own eyes: "I determined I should omit no opportunity of arriving at the truth. I am fully justified then, not only from what I witnessed, and the proofs now in my possession, but from the concurring testimony of the most respectable and intelligent natives whom I met, in asserting, that cannibalism prevails."[21]

Conversion was never simple. After Burton and Ward, missionaries from the United States, Samuel Munson and Henry Lyman arrived to convert the Batak. Munson and Lyman had studied Chinese and Malay for three months. Such languages were as incomprehensible to a Batak as, for example, Russian and Basque would be to a native Swede. Naturally there was great cultural miscommunication. A marker was erected to commemorate the deaths of the missionaries, stating, "here lie Munson and Lyman, eaten by Batak, 1834." The truth is unknown, but the marker reflects how the Batak's purported cannibalism inspired fear or at least reluctance on the part of outsiders to establish contact with them. But were the Batak cannibals? Scholarship has suggested that there is no proof of cannibalism by non-Western peoples that can be verified, but the tenacity of the image of cannibalism—the classic image of Savages dancing around a great vat on an open fire in which could be glimpsed the flailing legs of some unfortunate white man—grips young missionaries dreaming of great conquests of conversion like no other image.[22]

It certainly inspired the childhood dreams of Ingwer Ludwig Nommensen, born of a peasant family on the tiny North Sea island of Noordstrand, who at age thirteen promised the Lord that if his diseased leg were healed, he would go and convert the heathens. His leg healed.

"To convert to Christianity" in Indonesian is to "*masuk* Kristen" (literally, to "enter Christianity"), and this word "masuk" is also the root word of *kemasukan* (spirit possession). The photograph of my Ompung itself is one in which he appears to have entered the space; it is a photograph of emergence: the background is so washed out, so overexposed, that one is forced to focus on the figure of Raja Pontas as if he is the only defined being in a space of brilliant but unfocused light. I wonder, Ompung, if you would see how your power to control your image is diminished in the moment that the camera clicks, making your face accessible to a circulating network of books of anthropology, missionary newsletters, colonial documents, and church calendars. The camera is a time machine that stops and documents the flow of a calculable, linear time, metamorphosing you, with the aid of a caption, into a type: the Batak chief. A French anthropologist in Paris, never having set foot in North Sumatra, would study missionary photographs of the Batak, marveling at the ease of a Batak's ability to squat, and theorize that the Batak, like the Wolof or the Samoan, was a Savage, and that Savages naturally squat, whereas the Civilized man sits. But you choose to do neither, Ompung. You stand next to the chair; you do not sit in it. And it is because of this photograph that I was able to meet you, even though it was from none other than the Germans who banned ancestor worship when they converted us.

Scholars such as Vicente L. Rafael and Gauri Viswanathan moved away from a view of religious conversion as totalizing. Viswanathan points to the nineteenth-century Indian nationalist figure Tilak, whose conversion to Christianity, but subsequent desire for Christianity to syncretize with Hinduism, she sees as containing "an implicit critique of the alienating effects of British colonialism."[23] Syncretism is also seen in the Spanish attempt to convert the Tagalog in the Philippines, according to Rafael, since the need to keep the vernacular meant that translation could "cast intentions adrift, now laying, now subverting the ideological grounds of colonial hegemony."[24] What both Rafael and Viswanathan are suggesting is that conversion is contained within the seeds of itself, in its use of translation and its syncretism, the possibility of subversion, or, I would add, a form of resisting visual biopolitics.

Conversion therefore, once translated into the vernacular, or applied to a syncretic form, resists visual biopolitics. Determined, as his biography puts it, to bring light to a land of darkness, Nommensen sailed from Germany to North Sumatra. In 1863, the year that slavery was abolished in the United States, Raja Pontas and Nommensen met for the first time. Nommensen and the other German missionaries imported an evolutionary ideology that saw indigenous non-Christian peoples as illiterate, man-eating, polygamous

Savages. The Savage is a projection, embodying the attributes that the white man is said not to possess. There is no Civilized if there is no Savage.

According to missionary accounts, the Batak armed themselves on November 23, 1864, and gathered to decide Nommensen's fate. Missionary Nellie DeWaard wrote that although he was denounced by a priest who demanded that he be killed to satisfy the spirits, Nommensen overcame their doubts by telling them that the priest was actually speaking the words of Satan. Because of a sudden storm, the people were so impressed "that they said, 'The magic of the white man is greater than that of our priests.'"[25] According to this account, Raja Pontas willingly allowed Nommensen to move his church to his land, on the top of a hill, saying it was healthier for him and his family than where they had settled in Hoeta Dame, where it often flooded. "Tuan, you must move up higher."[26]

According to my Ompung Hutauruk, the German missionaries burned three symbols of the raja's power: the *pustaha* or holy books of the *datu* or healer (the Batak had developed their own systems of writing); the sacred *tunggal panaluan* or elaborately carved wooden staff; and the *gondang*, or Batak musical instrument ensemble of gongs, drums, and string and reed instruments. When a loved one dies, the gondang is played, and often the child or grandchild of the beloved dead will begin to walk, and talk, and sing, and *manortor* (dance), and demand the favorite foods of the departed one, and this the Germans labeled trance. (Music is so much a part of being Batak that my Ompung Sinambela explains that even a child born in Jakarta who has never heard the gondang will, upon arriving in Batak land and hearing it for the first time, immediately dance like those who are already Batak. In their body and soul, he concludes, Batak children of diaspora are always Batak.) The trance that the gondang induces is a means for the living to communicate with the ancestors. This music frightened the missionaries, and Nommensen swiftly translated Lutheran church hymns into Batak and introduced the accordion and oompah music.

But the Christianity that the German Lutheran missionary envisioned, and the Christianity of the Batak, are never exactly the same. Michel de Certeau's insight into the Spanish colonialization of indigenous Indians applies to the Toba Batak as well:

> The Indians often used the laws, practices, and representations that were imposed on them by force or by fascination to ends other than those of their conquerors; they made something else out of them; they subverted them from within—not by rejecting them or by transforming them

(though that occurred as well), but by many different ways of using them in the service of rules, customs or convictions foreign to the colonization which they could not escape. They metaphorized the dominant order; they made it function in another register. They remained other within the system which they assimilated and which assimilated them externally. They diverted it without leaving it.[27]

Rituals were banned by the missionaries, but then permutated into other forms. The translation of terms missed; meaning never found a simple conversion. The ulos that Raja Pontas wore contains the *tondi*. The German missionaries translated "tondi" as "spirit" to explain the concept of resurrection and afterlife, but the tondi, in truth, are spirits that are everywhere, in ulos, in the trees, in the river, in Lake Toba, in the mountains, protecting the living and hovering over the yet to be born. When my grandmother left this world, she was wrapped in a beautiful *ulos saput*, the ulos of love. For two days and nights we danced or manortor around her body, to oompah music, asking for her blessings. A large photograph of her was propped prominently on the headboard of the bed in which she lay. With my aunt once I attended a *mangokkal holi* ceremony in which the Lord's Prayer was intoned as ancestors' bones were dug up to be celebrated in a great ritual feast with music and dancing—not a ceremony that would be condoned, one imagines, in nineteenth-century Lutheran Germany.

Conversion was, therefore, always twisted. In legal terms, "conversion" meant theft. Not all the pustaha, tunggal panaluan, and gondang were burned. One day, I visited the Metropolitan Museum of Art in New York City to visit a display of Batak art on exhibition. The pamphlet for the show referred to the Batak in the past tense, as if we were a vanished race, the first ones to go. Instead of being housed in the dazzling new Southeast Asia wing, I was told by a guard that the Batak show was "in Africa," which turned out to be the Michael Rockefeller wing, the Primitive Art wing, established by the Rockefellers for their son, who was killed, purportedly, in New Guinea on an anthropological expedition. There I found, sandwiched between material culture exhibits of the Dogon of Mali and the Aztecs, the Batak exhibit.[28] For me, to see the ulos not draped around a person's shoulders but hung straight on a museum wall, to see the pustaha propped open on wire racks, and the wondrously carved tunggal panaluan displayed inside glass cases was to realize how the museum yanks away sacred objects and entombs them in a sterile ahistorical dimension: I collect the authentic, therefore I am; I collect you, the Primitive, because I have banned these objects and decide to keep them for myself. Isolated elaborate red-and-black carvings torn from the great swoop-backed, ship-like Batak houses, houses that are now rare but still stand, hang upon the walls of the museum like the dismembered limbs of a culture.

I see the tunggal panaluan again this time, banalized in a Hollywood movie. They painted "my Ompung" with painted slash marks and wigged him in a great Afro, and he points his carved wooden staff to summon the greatest Sumatran Savage of all time, King Kong. So, you see, they did not burn the tunggal panaluan but kept it in circulation in museums and in the cinematic dreams of children.

Intertwined in the history of my grandfather's grandfather was that of the great king Raja Si Singamangaraja XII, who in 1877 declared his intention to kill all white men and Christians in Batak land. His war against the Dutch lasted until his defeat in 1907. His wife and children were brought by the Dutch to Pearaja, the village of Raja Pontas, and they converted to Christianity. Thinking that my Ompung Sinambela, a direct descendant of Singamangaraja, would perceive Raja Pontas's conversion as akin to collaboration, the opposite to Raja Si Singamangaraja's revolution, I asked him to tell me about the history of his family and mine. The answer that I received was not what I expected. "Don't you know," he replied almost reproachfully, "that Raja Si Singamangaraja XII's sister married Raja Pontas's son?" His reply challenged me to reconsider my definition of history: history is, most importantly, the history of family. I am descended from both in the family: those who converted and those who rebelled.

I had never encountered a historian like Ompung Sinambela before, who told me miraculous stories about flying, disappearing heads as well as great battles and the machinations of contemporary Indonesian politics. The *ajaib* (magical) was part of the political.

In many Batak minds, the German missionaries and the Dutch colonialists were one and the same people. For conversion paved the way for Dutch colonialism, and colonialism for all that followed: capitalist wage labor, and later Japanese occupation, the war for Indonesian independence, Sukarno's taunt to the UN, "to hell with your aid," the great massacre of 1965 following the coup, and the rise of the US-supported Suharto government. All these histories, Ompung, and yet in this photograph I find the simplest history of all: I trace my uncle A.'s and my cousin Tota's faces in yours. Ompung Sinambela reminded me of the story of Raja Pontas's grandson, my grandfather Dr. Gerhard Lumban Tobing, a great surgeon and a hero in the revolutionary struggle against the Dutch for independence. After the Japanese surrender, the Dutch returned, thinking that the archipelago was still their colonial possession. What they did not understand was that these educated natives, such as Sukarno and my grandfather, had imagined and were constructing an independent nation called Indonesia. Some identities were stronger than the affiliations of religion.

The Dutch were desperate to regain their colony, and an extremely bloody and bitter war broke out. My grandfather sat in a Red Cross van returning from the front lines of a battle. And so, even though it was illegal under international law to fire at a Red Cross van, the Dutch soldiers gunned my grandfather down. A hospital in Tanjung Morawa, North Sumatra, was named after him.

Now that they were fatherless, my mother's and uncle's dreams of higher education were shattered. Several years later, however, a geographer, Professor Karl Pelzer, came to North Sumatra to study the Batak and searched for a "native informant." He hired my mother's older brother, my Tulang, or Uncle A. (My mother also later worked as a research assistant for anthropologist Edward Bruner.) When the geographer's fieldwork was almost finished, he offered my uncle a scholarship to come to the United States and study at the university. With great trepidation, my grandmother reluctantly gave my uncle permission to go. And thus, we all came to the United States, for after my uncle came, so did my mother, followed by my grandmother. I was born here, Ompung, your first American great-great-grandchild.

There remains a dissonance in the competing cultural logics of the Batak and the German missionary. Who was converting whom? The boundary between tradition and true believer, or tradition and modernity, was never absolute, and even for the educated true believer, such as my grandmother and Ompung Sinambela, change did not take the form of homogeneous rationalization or Westernization. Nommensen, who died in Batak land at the age of eighty, was also, in a sense, converted, incorporated into Batak culture and made into a special ancestor, Ompu i. My grandmother and Ompung Sinambela were as fiercely Christian as they were Batak; in fact, the two identities are inextricably intertwined.

The mystery was never solved. The photograph of my grandfather's grandfather only provoked a feeling in me that exceeds words. This feeling was perhaps what Ompung Sinambela, often asked to explain the history of the Toba Batak to German tourists, visiting Lutheran officials, and anthropologists, is hinting at when he tells me how troubled he is by Western writings about Batak history and culture: "We can't fault the Westerners for their great storehouses of knowledge, their libraries. We can't compete with them on that level. But what strikes me is that no matter how long they come to study the Batak—these Western anthropologists, historians, etc.—they never fully understand us. What is missing from their treatises about us is the real soul and philosophy—the feeling—of the Batak. That they have never been able to understand."[29]

What we have then is a portal. The missionary photograph provoked a reconfigured notion of time that is no longer linear, ordered, but instead what Dipesh Chakrabarty calls supernatural time.[30] Historians and anthropologists have traditionally seen the history of the subaltern, who spoke of the subjectivity of the gods or of spirits, as resisting the rationality of modern society. If the subaltern or the medieval were people who refused to distinguish between what is visible and invisible, which we moderns must invoke, then certainly photography, and in particular ethnographic photography, invites us to inhabit the fragments of a subaltern past, even as we, to paraphrase Chakrabarty, "classify ourselves as modern and secular."[31] It is our portal to madness, to another notion of time, and even, ultimately, to our own selves. In the missionary archives of Wuppertal, what I saw after looking at images of German missionaries who had settled in Batak land was a new society of Germans who dressed in sarongs, had children who played with Batak children, and who fell in love with Batak land and culture. Nommensen is described as a Batak ancestor not just because he converted so many to Christianity, but because he also became Batak. And the colored slide of Raja Pontas that I found in the missionary archive in Wuppertal, Germany, revealed a man in a blue suit jacket, his head still covered by a tied cloth (figure 3.5). He was still not smiling. But the photograph, framed in medium shot, looked more like a photograph of identification, by the medium shot and the Western-style blue jacket he is wearing. He is a revenant.

The photograph is thus a shimmering through time. It also sits across the thin line of modernity, between two chairs, as an emanation of the referent, as the unruly detail needing to be tamed by stories and the archive, of a time out of joint. You, my beloved Ompung, chose neither to squat or sit, but stand by the chair. I had wanted to understand that moment right before first contact. My first desire, a great longing to go back in time and capture that microsecond when you stood in front of the missionary's camera, was, I realize, a false one. I had thought that in that moment you gave birth to me, my sisters and brothers, wherever they are, scattered across several archipelagoes, all across the globe. In truth, there is not only measurable, historical time, but also the time in which you and I now live.

Can that wound, that prick, that cut, be experienced in film as well?

FIGURE 3.5 Raja Pontas, slide 6002-411, Copyright Archiv- und Museumsstiftung der VEM.

SHARED VIOLENCE AS PERFORMANCE: THE FOUND-FOOTAGE FILMS OF CORNELL AND MONNIKENDAM

In 1906, nearly eleven years after the birth of cinema, some thirty years before Margaret Mead and Gregory Bateson would set out to create their archive of the Balinese body, and some sixty years before the genocide of Indonesians by the Suharto regime, there is another incident of traumatic mass killing. The colonizers of what was then known as the Dutch East Indies conquer southern Bali. The Dutch colonial soldiers, after storming the gates of the palace of the raja of Badung, are astonished to discover that the raja and his court, dressed in royal white finery and numbering in the hundreds, are waiting to greet them. The court of Badung refuses to submit. The scene turns red with their blood. In a puputan (finishing or ritual suicide), some of the people stab themselves, some stab each other, and some march forward toward the Dutch colonial army, which guns them down. The soldiers later loot the raja's palace. A photographer is there to document the events.[32]

Although at the time the press carried stories about the siege of Badung, photographs of puputan, which depicted the extreme violence of the Dutch colonialists against the Indonesian natives, were not distributed or exhibited.

Instead Bali and Java were portrayed as ahistorical pathological kingdoms, as we have seen in the previous chapter with the 1889 Javanese village at the Exposition Universelle and Mead and Bateson's film *Trance and Dance in Bali*. Long before Mead and Bateson filmed in Bali, there were Dutch colonial films with scenes of natives laboring in such activities as mining, train building, plantation life, factory work, and cotton processing; prison life; scenes of travel from the point of view of pith-helmeted Dutch traveling by train or boat or horse; scenes of conversion of natives to Christianity and Catholicism; volcanoes exploding and great trees being felled; picturesque tropical beach landscapes; plantation workers toiling in the fields; natives dying in hospitals, lepers left alone in asylums; and smiling Dutch families in their gleaming white cotton suits and beribboned dresses holding their goblets of wine aloft as they toast the camera and their fellow citizens back home. All of these were accompanied with great fanfare in lectures about colonial life, later to be stored in archives in national libraries, art museums, colonial institutes, and churches, as well as tobacco propaganda agencies, the sugar industry headquarters, and natural history museums in the Netherlands. A second kind of film about Indonesia, then the Dutch East Indies, burgeoned in the 1920s and '30s, the fantastic adventure film, including *King Kong* and *Goona-goona*, that were set in a mythic Indonesia. If Annah la Javanaise was conceived of as a creature from an exotic sexual kingdom, la java, this Indonesia, including images of Sumatra, Borneo, and Bali, was conceived of as an exotic fairy-tale spectacle with brown princes (*East of Borneo*) or giant apes (*King Kong*) who lusted after white women. In both types of film—the colonial/ethnographic/missionary and the narrative spectacle—Indonesians were conceived of as subhuman and animal; these were, to again use Weheliye's term, "racializing assemblages" of the colonial native.

In *East of Borneo*, a 1931 Universal Pictures jungle melodrama directed by George Melford, the beautiful Linda, played by the actress Rose Hobart, travels alone to Marudu, a fictional island in the East Indies, to track down her husband, who left her because he mistakenly believed that she was unfaithful to him. Her husband has become court physician to the raja of Marudu, a Sorbonne-educated prince whose fate is mysteriously tied to the island volcano. As Hollywood Indonesian princes are wont to do, the suave raja attempts to seduce Linda, who shoots and wounds him. Linda escapes from the island after quickly reconciling with her husband as the volcano of Marudu suddenly and violently erupts. Joseph Cornell, an American artist deeply influenced at the time by surrealism, collected the film, which he reedited and titled *Rose Hobart*, making what is often pointed to as the first-found footage film. The year is 1936.

Some sixty years later, exactly one hundred years after the birth of cinema, a filmmaker decides to use this method of found footage first discovered by Cornell. But instead of creating a deeply meditative piece about obsession and fetishism of a female icon, Dutch filmmaker Vincent Monnikendam uses found footage to create films using archival colonial footage from the time of the Lumières up to the 1920s. Instead of searching the collectors' cache of old Hollywood films, as Cornell had done, Monnikendam raided the drawers of art museums, national libraries, colonial institutes, and natural history museums. He produced *Mother Dao, the Turtlelike*, incorporating salvage ethnography, that is, made from the kind of archival footage that repudiated native peoples—without history, without writing, without a voice. It is a film that reconfigures cinema's function in visual biopolitics.

Mother Dao is a fantastic dreamscape of Dutch colonial documentary footage of Indonesia, which actually transforms the found footage genre that began with Cornell's blue-tinted meditation on the actress Rose Hobart and resists the urge to "tidy" (to use Stoler and Strassler's term) the narrative to explain the disciplining and regulation of native bodies found in colonial propaganda and memoir. These are films that give us a glimmer of what surrealist writer Robert Desnos thought was impossible to find in cinema: "the unexpected, the dream, the surprise, the lyricism that erases the baseness in souls and hurls them enthusiastically over the barricades and into adventure; what we ask of the cinema is what love and life have refused us—it is mystery, it is the miracle."[33] André Breton, the surrealist poet, loved the following subtitle from F. W. Murnau's 1919 film *Nosferatu*: "When he was on the other side of the bridge, the phantoms came to meet him." Or to paraphrase James Baldwin, here we have the phenomenon of corpses beginning to speak, just as Rachmi Diyah Larasati refers to the replica that contains within it the traces of those murdered and disappeared.

Thus it is not the canonical surrealistic *Rose Hobart* but the film *Mother Dao* that best exploits surrealist properties of the photograph to shock, to provoke, to disrupt. In this film, the phantoms finally rush over the bridge, as Breton so wished. Using footage of films shot in the Dutch East Indies between 1912 and 1933 recovered from the archives of the Dutch Colonial Institute, the Tobacco Bureau of Amsterdam, the Dutch offices industry, and the Catholic Church, *Mother Dao* reveals to us an aspect of cinema that Barthes and Rosen attribute more to photography: its oneiric quality, or what according to Barthes is like a prick or a wound—its punctum. Here, there is no narrator, no braggadocio, either in the marketing or in the film's sound itself. The footage is divided into three categories—natural decor, such as ethnic groups, dance, and sacrifice; colonial exploitation, such as harvest, factories, and machines; and the colonial European presence, such as education and medicine. Each, although not explicitly linked to each other, flows imperceptibly into the next.[34] The film is one of the greatest dream voyages ever made.

Like *Rose Hobart*, *Mother Dao* has the classic properties of interruption of a found-footage film, as outlined by William Wees. It lifts the travelogue and colonial documentary out of its original context, and thus exposes its ideological meanings; and it interrupts the narrative flow visually, aurally, and in terms of film speed.[35] As Wees explains about found-footage films, "Whether they preserve the footage in its original form or present it in new and different ways, they invite us to recognize it *as* found footage, *as* recycled images, and due to that self-referentiality, they encourage a more analytical reading (which does not necessarily exclude a greater aesthetic appreciation) than the footage originally received."[36]

Monnikendam goes further; he transcends all of the collage aspects of found-footage film by bringing the punctum—the prick, the private moment, the wound—back into film. The film is fragmented, but it is a fragmented phantom that achieves the startling juxtapositions of life and death through sound and editing. Uncharacteristically, for a film using documentary archival footage, Monnikendam does not use an authoritative voice-over, which would have ordered the film into a historical survey. Nor does he use gamelan music, which he felt would be too stereotypical, exploiting the preconceived notions of Java, Bali, and the other Indonesian islands.

Instead, Monnikendam chooses to use a mix of unexpected kinds of sound. He layers sound that is diegetic, that is, the sounds of synchronous reality: the ambient sounds of water, a train, a factory pounding out metal boxes—an effect that immediately lends to the footage a sense of immediacy and present-day-ness. He also uses the sounds of poetry: the origin story of the Nias, contemporary Indonesian protest poetry by authors such as Rendra, and startlingly revolutionary Javanese songs called *tembang*, traditionally associated with picturesque dance but here shown to have tremendous revolutionary potential. This is truly the coupling of two realities, the Lautréamont moment, the surrealist ideal of the fabled dissecting table, "as handsome . . . as the fortuitous encounter upon a dissecting table of a sewing machine and an umbrella."[37] And it is present even in the opening poem that describes how the world was formed by Mother Dao, the turtlelike. This mixture of reality and dream, poetry and atmospheric effects takes us on a voyage into the past, certainly embalmed in time, in which we see on a scale never shown before how much colonialism used the bodies of native peoples to exploit them for capitalist gain. toddlers collect caterpillars from tobacco plants, men become human mules to a mill, women winnow kapok (cotton stuffing) by hurling their bodies up and down in the suffocating air of cotton to provide beds for their colonial masters. This is a film about what is most surreal, according to Sontag: labor, class, and time.

What is so compelling about the images is the mixture of the obscure and the precise: the often scratchy texture of the film and the use of horrific deep focus that orthochromatic film provides, accompanied with Foley sound (that is, recorded sound effects) and ambience, creating a ghostlike world from the past. The camera movements and compositions are as architectural and well composed as one would expect of a filmmaker from the land of Vermeer and Rembrandt. Like the work of his late Dutch colleague Johan van der Keuken, Monnikendam's documentary does not immediately pitch an understandable narrative to the viewer. One must follow along and piece together the story or meaning, stitching it, as it were, with the textiles from one's own attic trunk of the unconscious. Moreover, Monnikendam's transitions act as an undertow; they do not state the obvious but lurk just below the surface. Nothing is ever explained. *Mother Dao* has the most exquisite order wrought from the logical flow of a dream and the visual shock of the nightmare.

Mother Dao compels the viewer to question the hierarchy in film and media studies where ethnographic film and found-footage film are marginal. This black-and-white film exposes how cinema can be the site for subjective private moments that spill over into the boundaries of the oneiric and the subjective. The apartheid of the archive, so necessary for bolstering the strategies of visual biopolitics, is destroyed here. Previously, scholars had to go to archives in Europe to see old colonial and ethnographic film. They were stored in short pieces, not edited into long-form films. Monnikendam calls our attention to these vestiges of early cinema; he brings them to us.

Mother Dao realizes cinema's truly surrealist potential. In Monnikendam's Frankenstein of a film, the viewer becomes viewed by ghosts from the past. Life is violently arrested, and the dead are brought back to life. The normal necropolitical segregation captured on film, where the dead are on the other side, behind the fence, is reversed; through editing the viewer becomes the object of the gaze. *Mother Dao* provokes in two ways: in its surrealist time travel as a crossing over via the portal of time and memory, and as a manifestation of resistance to the visual biopolitics of the colonial archive. Monnikendam reveals how cinema can resist through visual and sound editing, while at the same time clarifying the two tenets of visual biopolitics: the body as a machine that must be regulated (scenes of disciplined and imprisoned bodies), and the body as part of the human species (scenes of adults and, horrifically, children and babies dying from smallpox).[38] *Mother Dao* lays bare what is significant about film, demonstrating how visual biopolitics creates its vocabularies of justification and allowing us to inhabit the death worlds of the past, present, and future by addressing a viewer who is forced to question the images that are re-presented.

RAIDING THE FILM ARCHIVES FOR THE DEAD:
MOTHER DAO'S RESISTANCE OF VISUAL BIOPOLITICS

Anthropologists, in their zeal to discover the mystery of race, used calipers, photography, and then film as tools of inscription. Anthropologists, including Margaret Mead, considered ethnographic film to be the scientific mode of inscription par excellence. After all, Mead's ideal for capturing history was "a camera running on its own steam."[39] As an inscription, film was necessarily accompanied by the words of the ethnographer/scientist: there was a tension that the image of the ethnographic might not be easily contained or comprehended as intended, and thus the scientist must always speak for what is represented.[40] The problem that Mead and other anthropologists faced was what to do with the boxes and boxes of footage of the archive. Without editing and the concurrent voice-over of the narrator, nobody watches. There is, as we have seen with the modes of framing of Annah la Javanaise by Gauguin, or the ethnographic and documentary films of Mead and Oppenheimer, an ideology that creates the notion of the primacy of the individual subjectivity of the artist or filmmaker—the light, as Foucault would put it. What is remarkable about Monnikendam's film is that the filmmaker disappears and yet his hand is everywhere present, in the constructedness of the work. There are hardly any interviews with Monnikendam, no fanfare, and we never hear his voice on the soundtrack or as a voice-over; instead, we are compelled to hear the sounds and see the images of the film and make sense of them on our own.

Born in 1936 in The Hague, the Netherlands, Monnikendam spent most of his early career directing, editing, and producing documentary films for Netherlands television (NOS-TV and NPS-TV). In 1995 he became an independent documentary filmmaker with *Mother Dao*, which took six years to make.[41] Monnikendam turned the archive on its head by taking from it. There is an active and invested sense of raiding the archive, which should be distinguished from the purportedly more passive and accidental designation of the found-footage film. The notion of the collection, so important to surrealism—think, for example, of Cornell's collection of films and film stills—is revealed here to be linked to questions of power and privilege: Who gets to collect? And who collects what? Populations can be colonized and decimated for the gaze of the viewer of the archive, for gazes that are bolstered by and justify visual biopolitics.

The archive justifies the annihilation of people and culture for the needs of capitalism and colonialism. The 1904 St. Louis World's Fair, with its native villages (the Philippine village alone took up forty-two acres), was intended to be "an elaborate scaffolding whose aim was to prove the thesis of racial difference."[42] Johannes Fabian notes that archives are not just innocent depositories but "institutions, which make possible the [politically charged] circulation of information."[43] In other words, while the ethnographic film archive purports to be nothing more than a collection of visual documents from a diverse array of cultures—the anthropologist-filmmaker merely goes out into the world, objectively captures life on celluloid, and brings it home for storage—the circulation of images presupposed by the archive implicates social, historical, and political relations of dominance. The archive is a technology that scans the species body, makes visible and classifies the norm, justifying colonial violence and regulatory control, and sets up the visual vocabularies of culture that continue to the present day.

During the colonial period, it was common for lantern slides and then film to be brought back to metropole cities in North America and Europe. These films would be shown in lectures, always accompanied by a speaker: the footage attested to the veracity of the speaker's voyage and also set up a condition of the ethnographic present, in which the history of that encounter was erased and the people would be spoken of in metonymic terms. The travelogue genre emerged from these films, often including the point of view of the settler surveying the landscape from boat or train, with picturesque views of the natives' customs and manners including dance, food preparation, labor, and close-ups in anthropological fashion of physiognomic types. Often the lecture was comedic, emphasizing the Savagery of the people who were encountered, or, if in the interests of science, dry and authoritative.

I am not going to dwell further on the history of the colonial film and the colonial film archive, since I wrote extensively about this genre in *The Third Eye*, as have Alison Griffiths and Jennifer Peterson.[44] Instead I focus on *Mother Dao* for the way that it loots the colonial archives for films shot in Bali, Sumatra, Flores, Kalimantan, and East Timor between 1912 and 1933, reacquainting the viewer with the many travelogue films that showed the colonizer in his and her white cotton attire traveling by train, boat, or horse through the terrain of what was then known as the Dutch East Indies. In these films we also see what they see: toddlers held in slings smoking cigarettes; laborers moving like bees or ants building the infrastructure needed for that beautiful white attire, harvesting rows upon rows of crops and pounding cotton with their bodies; smallpox victims suffering in a hospital.

Racism, Foucault wrote, is "the break between what must live and what must die."[45] In *Mother Dao*, racism is the break between who gets to smile and who does not. The particular period of *Mother Dao* coincides with the height of colonialism and the use of film as a form of evidence for the travelogue speaker ("I was there"), and the evidence of colonial glory and justification for colonial dominion is present in the actual scenes shown: the white people find being filmed a hoot, while the indigenous people filmed in various modes of bare life—hurling their bodies to pound kapok, pounding metal, carrying loads from the mines—are not privy to the comedy, a situation we saw as well in the photographs of Annah la Javanaise. If Foucault locates the disciplinary and the regulatory as the means of controlling populations biopolitically, *Mother Dao* is a portal into the origin of the modern state as a colonizing force. Although the film begins with a close-up shot of a young boy wearing a hat and looking at the camera (figure 3.6), smiling and then bowing his head in shyness, as well as powerful images of the volcano Krakatoa exploding, and other haunting landscapes surveying volcanic fire, there is a female voice-over in Indonesian telling the origin tale of Earth as Mother Dao, or Mother Earth, as a turtle, her progeny—man and woman—born from her dirt. Unlike *Trance and Dance in Bali*, which essentially used Margaret Mead's dry and dispassionate voice-over to unify the material, *Mother Dao* is about poetry, mythology, and the indexical, what Roland Barthes called the "that has been."[46] Immediately, then, the film is transformed using the Indonesian voice. Slowly it dawns on the viewer that all of the people filmed are now dead.

COLONIAL BIOPOLITICS AND THE BEGINNING OF TIME

Mother Dao allows for a new form of conversion involving visual biopolitics, which operates in two ways in this film: power as a disciplinary and regulatory phenomenon on spectacular display—the power of film to scan, shoot, archive, and represent the lives of natives who are barely holding on to life— and finally, the power of editing to unsettle the archive by questioning the discourses of authenticity and empiricism that these films and the ways they were used purport to uphold.

FIGURE 3.6 Young boy in a scene from *Mother Dao, the Turtlelike* (Vincent Monnikendam, 1995).

Monnikendam provides us with the origin of the colonial biopolitical world, the disciplinary gaze of the schools, prisons, and medical establishment firmly linked with death and the regulation of bodies. If the film begins with the explosion of Krakatoa, we are then led to the power of stoking coal and the steam of the ship and the force of the train. More than any other film that I have seen, *Mother Dao* explicates in no uncertain terms the way that native bodies turn into machines, or really cogs of machines, parts of the whole machinery of the colonial industry's roar to power. In a sense, the notion of brown bodies as machines unites three themes of Foucault's theories of biopolitics: sex, death, and race. So the content of the film is historical evidence, but the film also comments upon the cinema machine. We can see with the eyes of the colonizer and the audience of the colonizers, experiencing the Dutch East Indies as a possession (figure 3.7). But we also view as a time traveler, watching the colonizers watch the colonized. Thus, the beginning of the film marks other beginnings: the beginning of the word, but it is also the beginning of cinema (made in 1995, *Mother Dao* marks the one-hundred-year anniversary of the birth of cinema), the beginning of biopolitics and colonialism, and the beginning of the archive.

We see from the point of view of the apparatus (the camera), the point of view of the spectator (the colonizer), and thus we see the imaging created

FIGURE 3.7 Conver-
sion scene in *Mother
Dao, the Turtlelike*
(Vincent Monniken-
dam, 1995).

by the apparatus and the point of view. Visual biopolitics is the imagining of certain populations as Savage and thus less worthy of life, while at the same time, as Pooja Rangan has explained, it forces this other to prove its worthiness of life. In the hierarchy of both the colonial film and the travelogue film, as I delineated in *The Third Eye*, the native is set up as a contrast to the white person, there as a signifier of authenticity or Savagery, and sometimes as little more than landscape. But in this found-footage film the silent native regains subjectivity. By juxtaposing different scenes, by allowing the film to have a kind of ghostlike quality with its sepia tones and scratched surfaces, by scoring the film with music and an often eerie soundscape, along with poems and Javanese tembang songs, as well as adding Foley to create a present soundscape with diegetic sound, the native's silence is actually made to say something and to be more and more deafening and disturbing. If in watching a normal travelogue we become used to seeing the native as the landscape or the comedic element (think of Nanook biting the record in Flaherty's 1922 classic *Nanook of the North*), this silence, taken with the words said by the narrator, becomes a reproach, a reproach to the smiling, laughing Dutchmen hamming it up for the camera. Just like Ibu Darmo, who refuses to look at her US interviewers, Stoler and Strassler, these Indonesian subjects look down or away, or, when they do look into the camera, it is without humor.

Sound becomes the cure for the ways we as spectators have become inured to the scenes. Sound is the resistance, to the point where a song like "Genjer Genjer" has to be banned. But also, when there is no dialogue we hear the machines, which underscore how the bodies have become voiceless and machinelike.

It is worth describing a few scenes at length in order to illustrate this. In one section, we are at a river where a man is paddling a canoe, accompanied by the rhythmic sound of paddling. It's as if we are on a journey to another dimension. As the paddling sound fades, the sound of crickets gets louder as a woman's voice recites a poem by contemporary poet Sitor Sitomorang:

I am the fish from the primeval sea
stranded on the rocks of Parangtritus
gasping for water.
I am the poet
all but bereft of language who can discern no sense.
Inner wind which can make stone sing.
I am the mystical bird
feathered with the wind.
The fish from the world's beginning
whose fins are the sea.

After a few street scenes, we find ourselves in a factory where men are cutting metal rectangles, and then we realize that they are making shiny tin boxes, probably for oil. A man in a coolie hat cuts a sheet and looks up for a moment. Noncommittal, his regard is that of a ghost: to paraphrase Barthes, he is becoming a specter. And then one realizes that the subject of this scene is not only about tin box making, but also about bodies, about human hands and human feet that operate the machines through sheer human power.

The presence of the colonialist is at first seemingly harmless, if not comic. First, we see a Dutchman in a pith helmet followed by a coolie, then an abrupt cut to a shot of the water of a river in which he has fallen; three Indonesian men are rescuing him while at the same time holding his bags. The sound lulls, the sound of crickets, river water, and bird calls.

Then, slowly, Monnikendam pulls us into deeper waters. A colonizer in a pith helmet and white suit climbs a menhir or huge stone sarcophagus to talk to a *dukun* (wise man or healer) wearing a head wrap. We hear birds, and then an eerie sound of Muslim and Christian religious chanting. A white European priest with a beard and long robe sits with brown-skinned children and women, natives from one of the eastern islands. He is teaching them to pray and gesture in the sign of the cross. Water is poured on their upturned faces, blending with the scratches on the film. Nobody smiles. It is a pure moment of conversion: the Indonesians convert to Christianity, and they also convert into an image for the white man, as they are blessed by the priest. They convert into spectrality.

We are still in the realm of religion with the next two scenes: a white man in a pith helmet paints a large Jesus icon, and a priest teaches an orchestra of Indonesian children how to play music, his arms wildly gesticulating and overacting in a comedic fashion for the camera. For one of the first things that Christianity in this part of the world must do is destroy indigenous music (particularly the drums, which invoke the dead) and destroy their religious art, to be replaced by Christian music and art. Here the film is silent, and one is left to imagine what kind of oompah music the children are being taught with the tuba, cymbals, and so on. Again, nobody except for the priest, who is clearly mugging for the camera, smiles. What jars is how often the priest stops the children and tries to correct the performance of the child pounding the band drum. The priest is the only one laughing.

The most horrific footage is yet to appear. To the sound of belabored breathing and the ambient track of something high-pitched like birds or crickets, we dolly down an outside corridor where doctors and nurses wrapped in gowns wearing masks are pounding with a hammer the open body of a native man on an operating table. We then cut to shots of children with smallpox wounds, naked children who are so sick that their eyes are shut from the pustules covering them, a young boy whose body is totally covered with sores, a leper who stares into the camera.

It is then that we realize that this is a film about perishing and death. These babies and children are dying even as their images are being taken. This is not what Barthes calls the noeme of photography, the "that has been."[47] This is "the that is being done." The natives are not just rendered into specters because they are being photographed, as Barthes suggested, but because their bodies are being colonized. We experience another lull. What follows is the bathing of a body for a funeral. It is raining. A woman sings a tembang from the mid-nineteenth century, as the body is laid out:

> The bats hang under the branches
> Fluttering their wings
> The bats are likewise sorrowful
> If they could, they would have said:
> "But why do Pandhoe's sons not journey
> with him, asking for their realm?"
> The blossom of the Tanjung trees
> Lies scattered over the ground
> The Tanjungs are likewise sorrowful

The animals and the flora are sorrowful, but the colonizer is not sorrowful. We then cut to an astonishing scene. A lone native woman stands in profile in a sea of white clouds (figure 3.8). There is no perspective, no more achingly deep

FIGURE 3.8 Woman worker in a sea of kapok cotton in a scene from *Mother Dao, the Turtlelike* (Vincent Monnikendam, 1995).

space here. The clouds of white look like sky, as we see many men and women throwing up kapok cotton that sticks in their hair and mouths. They use their bodies to pound the cotton, jumping up and then disappearing as they sink down. Four native men walk around and around on a platform of cotton that looks like a gallows, the light from above illuminating this theater of torture.

Monnikendam transforms the colonial archive by sound editing, by adding ambient sound—the sound of lapping water, the buzz of tin-can machinery; contemporary poetry of protest; and an asynchronous score, not the gamelan that one would expect, but the drone of an ominous tone. Like the surrealist found-footage filmmakers before him, he juxtaposes scenes to create new connections: the dreamscape of kapok relates to the bright white garments of the grinning Dutch family and the cotton used to stuff the corpse of the native.

The colonized natives are essentially the cogs of the machines harnessed for power. *Mother Dao* is one of the greatest instances of clarifying visual biopolitics while at the same time resisting it, in the ways it reveals how biopower is an inextricable component of colonialism, indentured labor, and the development of capitalism. As Foucault describes it, "The latter would not have been possible without the controlled insertion of bodies into the machinery of production and the adjustment of the phenomena of population to economic processes. But this was not all that it required; it also needed the growth of both of these factors, their reinforcement as well as their availability and docility; it had to have methods of power capable of optimizing forces, aptitudes, and life in general without at the same time making them more difficult to govern."[48]

When we see the footage that follows of a Dutch colonial family, a colluding Javanese official, and the Dutchmen who mug for the camera as they try to dance like Javanese women, what we realize is this: the beautiful white linen, the crisp bows in a Dutch daughter's blonde hair, the tennis whites, the white shoes, the lawns, the tea sets, the horse races, the goblets of wine, the gorgeous hats and gowns and gloves, the beautiful colonial verandas and houses, and the enormous expanse of servants come at a great cost. The colonizers no longer look nostalgic, picturesque, or glamorous: they look like cruel crows. That is because through the edited structure, the subtle use of ambient sounds, sound effects, and haunting music, Monnikendam has led us into the world of those colonized, and their gaze pricks us with their pain.

The irrefutable knowledge of the "that has been" is transposed and converted into the beauty of a wonder world created through music, verse, and the shock of new contrasts and associations through montage: from the elegant dolly movements down a colonial hospital corridor, to the horrific pounding of doctors, to the smallpoxed faces of children and babies with the white-masked nurses, to the use of kapok in the ear of a dead woman whose corpse is being prepared, to the snowy unreal world of the natives in the kapok/cotton landscape, and then ending with a smiling, waving Dutch family sitting in an interior listening to a record player and wearing crisp ironed whites. We are in the realm of an aesthetic death world. This is what film can do that other media cannot: we are within and without the death world, facing the eyes of the already dead that are still living. This is visual biopolitics: we see how the relentlessly aesthetic camera of the Dutch colonialist is marshaled to convert bodies just surviving in necropolitical worlds into documents for archives in metropoles in the West, or as illustrations for a live show of educational value for the institutions that profit from the propaganda. The images have not changed, but the meter and the movement of the presentation has. The surrealism, I would argue, is what artist Pat Ward Williams was to describe as the shock of "WHO took this picture?"[49] It is the hubris of the gaze of power that thought that these images were so pure they could never be used against them.

It is precisely film's indexicality that provides the final shudders of this experience because the "that has been" is turned around against itself. What Monnikendam accomplishes in his film, just as Achille Mbembe does in his essay "Necropolitics," is to reveal how the colonies were and are an extension of terror formations that existed with colonialization and slavery.[50] Because the colonized are considered Savage and not human, the state of exception is permanent, "the zone where the violence of the state of exception is deemed to operate in the service of 'civilization.'"[51] Moreover, because the colonized are seen as another form of animal life, and thus are seen to "behave like a part of nature," in the words of Hannah Arendt, it is clear that the footage that the Dutch cameramen produced was intended to document the civilizing force of the Dutch colonial regime.[52] What found-footage editing accomplishes, however, is to reveal the presence of these ghostly figures in a death world, and we see how this world was a controlled, delimited space. The colonizers wear white jackets and pith helmets. They sit on chairs or horses. Everything is ordered; the camera placement is precise and follows the action of machines and people in machines smoothly, whether it's the naked prisoners who are lined up and physically examined, the naked dying children covered with smallpox boils, or the river boat that surveys the houses on shore. Within this ordered death world, the native subjects are not seen as human. Cinema creates a form of visualization that underscores, becomes its own form of visual biopolitics.

Mbembe quotes Paul Gilroy in *The Black Atlantic*, who explained that death for the slave or the colonized can be a release from terror, and so therefore death can be represented as agency. "For death is precisely that from and over which I have power. But it is also that space where freedom and negation operate."[53] In theories of the suicide bomber, scholars Talal Asad, Achille Mbembe, and Stefania Pandolfo have argued that death is a form of agency in a necropolitical society that leaves one's self, family, and community vulnerable to premature death and violence. One can determine one's life by determining one's death. Death can be a form of agency in the figure of the suicide bomber, and instead of being just a figure of horror, the suicide bomber is an essentially active agent. In *Mother Dao* these disciplined regulated bodies have agency: their looks, recontextualized with radical poetry, sound, and music, speak to us and comment upon their placement as mere cogs in the visual biopolitical machine of colonialism.

Through editing and sound, and through adding a three-dimensional presence, the articulation of the colony as a death world is created in Monnikendam's film. Film and photography were intended as tools to measure time, but it is precisely their closeness to time that accounts for its closeness to the oneiric. As Barthes says, "I am looking at the eyes of someone who is now dead, or who is about to be hanged."[54] When we look at Monnikendam's film—the gaze back of the factory tin cutter, the smallpox boy who won't live another day, the coal miners, the converted, the men walking as light pours down, as upon Christ, in a circle to process the cotton, and countless others—we are looking at the eyes of those who are condemned to eternal hell. The horror slowly dawns that this is a world in which humans are the slaves of a nightmarish assortment of machines, factories, plantations, and mines that use human bodies as their fuel. The life moments of birth, marriage, and death—so beloved by anthropologists and travelogues—take on a new meaning: the images were meant to entertain, inform, and classify native inhabitants for purposes of the picturesque and the travelogue, but the images recontextualized and reedited now have an affect that exceeds their original intent. The children who smoke while suckling at their mother's breast, of men and women who marry but break their backs cutting stone, the deaths of those disfigured by smallpox, all point to a fact, which Sontag understood: surrealism lies not in surrealist photography, but in the eyes of the poor and the agency of the dead. In these films, the horror of reality is an unreal prick. It is like a hot desert wind slicing the nape of your neck. The silence of the subjects deafens into a roar.

The film evokes the voices and the presence of the dead. Monnikendam reveals the clash of, on the one hand, a society in which the spirits of the ancestors are notably present and, on the other hand, a society that strongly disbelieves in spirits. We as viewers are positioned along what Pandolfo calls the thin line of modernity: we are in the Cut, the gap, the aporia, where we understand the past with its wounds still visible and uncovered. In order to show the gap between the Indonesian and the Dutch, Monnikendam used the poem and the song to implicitly critique the relentless objectivity of the Dutch camera gaze. He explains, "It's not explicit, but implicit, I thought that the effect on the viewer would be more strong if they said nothing. One feels an emotion. That works better."[55]

Hence, finally, *Mother Dao* allows us to see the agency of the dead. At the end of the film, the origin myth of Mother Dao continues. In this story from the Nias, the myth went that the creator goddess of the Indonesian island of Nias created the Earth by collecting all the dirt of her body and kneading it into a small ball on her knee. She became pregnant and gave birth to a man and a woman, and they became the first people and lived in the fertile world. Mother Dao is called "the turtlelike" because the inhabitants of Nias perceive the horizon from the beach as half-curved, reminding them of the shell of a turtle. The English subtitles read:

> There came a time when hence from our Mother Dao
> The ever-rejuvenating the turtlelike
> Fled her life spirit, hence like the wind
> Her soul receded like mist
> She died and was turned into earth

Dead she became dust
Her earthly remains filled the chasms
Her ashes filled the earth where it was cleft.
Her progeny on earth
Her issue in the world
Became as abundant as dust and sand
Became myriad as dust and grains of sand
But they were not aware that they are family
That they are brothers and sisters.

In the last few minutes of *Mother Dao*, we see young girl dancers, wearing feathers, their faces powdered, who flit across the screen and look sideways and then at the camera. They pass the camera in medium shot and look right, and then right back at us. These tiny dancers, with their glance at the camera at the end of the film, powerfully suggest a message, like the story told of Wakiem, Seriem, Taminah, and Soekia in 1889, an exotic image and narrative placed upon the child maid/sex worker Annah la Javanaise, and those who came later, including the young girls drafted to do older men's trance dances by Mead and Bateson, and the dancers like Rachmi Diyah Larasati who were hired to cover over the dead bodies of the women slaughtered and raped in 1965 and later, and the dancers in gold lamé shimmering in the Savage pornography of *The Act of Killing*. But of what? The end of time, the beginning of cinema, the cinematic visualizing of colonialism, and the impossibility of understanding that lacuna, that gap, that aporia, and the agency of the dead.

In photomontage, an individual can loot the archive of banned images of violence from Indonesia's past, the photographs unfolding like a slide show, set to the haunting strains of "Genjer Genjer," as I have shown in the You-Tube video example discussed earlier. Similarly, Monnikendam plunders the colonial archives in 1993 for his film *Mother Dao* but recontextualizes them by giving them a presence and a subjectivity. The found-footage genre of *Mother Dao* goes further than *Rose Hobart* by incorporating the voice of the native in surrealist praxis: both use disjunction, sound, and editing to question the authority of art. This kind of cinema collapses the parameters normally set by visual biopolitics: that certain people are subhuman or nonhuman, justifying the ways that they are allowed to let die.

It also transcends the boundaries of identity between those whose egos align with an individual subjectivity versus those who must always view with a third eye, and thus whose identity is a collective subjectivity. This works in multiple ways: there are many authors, since this is found footage; Foley sound provides presence and fullness to the image that in an earlier colonial context would have had the voice-over of the colonizer (or anthropologist as in the case of Mead) bringing back the footage; sound effects with music and poetry provide emotional affect, if not implied commentary, so that the viewer is invited in to contemplate and recontextualize the footage; the editing juxtaposes unlikely voices and images together; and finally, the looks of the natives back at the viewer provide a spectral presence. We are forced to hear them breathe through sound and often through their looks. In *Mother Dao* the subjects of the film from the past plainly ask the viewer, "How do we look?" Not in the sense of the women in *Trance and Dance in Bali*, but making us question how we as viewers look and how the dead look back at us. *Mother Dao*, through its use of recontextualizing archival footage and principles of surrealism, is an indictment of visual biopolitics; it is a portal into the birth of colonial visual biopolitics and cinema; it is a means through which to trouble the norm from its category of the empirical.

Near the beginning of the film, we are on a boat going down the river, and we hear these words: "I am the poet all bereft of language/who can discern no sense." Poet Tracy K. Smith talks about how poetry unsettles: "You want a poem to unsettle something. . . . There's a deep and interesting kind of troubling that poems do, which is to say: 'This is what you think you're certain of, and I'm going to show you how that's not enough. There's something more that might be even more rewarding if you're willing to let go of what you already know.'"[56] The found-footage film has that quality of unsettling, and what it troubles is visual biopolitics and the archiving of life.

A coolie looks into the camera. An older man looks into the camera. And then a little boy, whom we saw in the very opening of the film, looks shyly into the camera: and suddenly the viewer is quite naked. The final look back is of the young boy, but now we see him differently. Monnikendam troubles the normalizing of the native as the dysselected, as the Savage. He and she are given agency in death. The narrator goes back to the idea of genesis: "In the beginning was the word. The world has been made of words. And behind them only empty space and wind . . . that is why I hide behind words and let myself sink without a trace."

We realize that there are films, as there are photographs (like that of my great-great-grandfather) in which the relations of viewer/viewed are reversed: we are being watched with the eyes of those who are now dead. Cinema has achieved its true status as time machine in perhaps its most sublime moment of surrealism.

Do we have the strength to resist?

FLIGHT

At first, I didn't recognize the Girl.

I was working as a model, and she was back in Paris after a long stint abroad. She had become a painter, and so invited me to her place, so that I could sit for her. Afterward we ate dinner there together.

We never spoke of what really happened. Instead we drank.

When I woke up she was already gone. Her maid let me out into the morning light.

As for me, I am going home soon. I didn't tell her. My mind is often whirling too much. The drink does that to you.

In the next life, I will be free. And I will collect all these memories, the comb in my mother's hand, the falling snowflakes at the harbor, the blue peonies of the ivory white vase, the straw hat that I wore on my plaited hair, the Girl's brown eyes watching me as I slept, the smell of the fire that I started and put out, and they will become part of somebody else's dream, a long time later. A small daughter will be visited one night with my dreams and not understand why.

But I know why. And I will protect her.

We die and are born again. And then we die. And are born. Again.

4

NIA DINATA

What will happen to all that beauty?
—JAMES BALDWIN, *The Fire Next Time*

Darol Mahmada is a young Indonesian woman, a mother in fact, and an activist, seeking answers as to why female circumcision (a taboo topic on the national level) is somehow compatible with Islam. In the documentary feature film *Pertaruhan* (*At Stake*, 2008), with her young daughter in hand, Darol Mahmada visits her father, a *kyai* or religious leader of a school to ask him why he thinks female circumcision is necessary for Islam. If we think about how Muslim women are usually portrayed, as oppressed, exploited, and suffering, representations used to justify Western military interventions in Afghanistan and other parts of the Muslim world, it is then surprising to watch the complexity in the relation between this father, who believes in female circumcision, and his daughter, Darol.[1] In a sense, a simple scene of Darol and her father, talking to each other on the family couch, about a private matter that still traumatizes her, and that he was directly responsible for, is a radical moment for documentary. It is the cinematic representation of these kinds of profound interactions that resist visual biopolitics: instead of tidy condemnation, we see something involving agency that is more than individual but is collective: a father, a daughter, and a granddaughter, confronting collectively how their sexuality and identity are determined by religion, culture, and family.

The producer of *Pertaruhan* is Nia Dinata. Recent films by Indonesian directors, such as this one produced by Dinata, provide a different way of filmmaking that challenges the representation of the Indonesian as ethnographic or ethnographiable, that topples the idea of the auteur, and that provides novel forms of exhibition and distribution.[2] Dinata's practice as producer, filmmaker, director, writer, teacher, and political activist contextualizes biopolitics in visual media and reconfigures the norm, in her use of the subgenre of the omnibus film, a feature film made up of several short films that share a theme or location, often by different directors.

How does Dinata's work reflect and resist visual biopolitics? To find the answer, I first historicize her films within Indonesian cinema, and then I examine closely her important feature narrative *Berbagi Suami* (*Love for Share*, 2006), and two of her omnibus feature films, the fiction film *Perempuan Punya Cerita* (*Chants of Lotus*, 2007) and the documentary *Pertaruhan* films that go beyond the normal collaboration required to produce a feature film. Dinata moves us beyond the subject/object dichotomy in the representation of the Indonesian woman found in ethnographic film, colonial footage, and Western documentary film, with their histories of exoticizing representations in photography, painting, and world's fairs. She destroys the norm of binary opposition by foregrounding differing forms of subjectivity in three ways: (1) in the content of her films; (2) in the ways that the viewer is addressed; and (3) in their actual production, distribution, and exhibition. Dinata's work challenges the label of auteur film that so suits the ideology of homo economicus and instead resists visual biopolitics through the network structure of narrative and through her radical modes of distribution and exhibition. Moreover Dinata and others during the Reformasi period reformulated the standards of what is fiction and what is documentary, particularly by conducting extensive field research.

Dinata's collective filmmaking is a form of production of which I have some firsthand knowledge. In his groundbreaking book *Production Culture*, scholar and filmmaker John Caldwell argues that film studies should look beyond a textual analysis of films that often leads to a kind of hagiography of the male auteur; instead, we should see how those narratives reconfigure and conceal power relations. It is not enough to just examine the finished text of the film to understand the production of it. If we follow the money, if we theorize production as culture, we can see that the narratives told by those below the line (the gaffers, the makeup artists, the painters) are as pertinent and valid from a theoretical and economic point of view as those above the line (the so-called creatives, the directors, producers, screenwriters, headlining actors).

The methods Caldwell uses in studying the production culture of the film industry—interviews, analyzing trade and worker artifacts, ethnographic field-work and observation, and economic industrial analysis—are detailed and systematic. In discussing the work of Nia Dinata, I draw from my own interviews with her, but also from my experience as a director working with her as my producer, and watching her direct, produce, and run her production company. I was in Jakarta, at the Kalyana Shira office, for the making and touring (the term used in Indonesian is *roadshow*) of several of her films, including *Berbagi Suami*, her short documentary *Batik Our Love Story* (2011), and *Pertaruhan*. I am not offering a production studies analysis per se, but a description of major aspects that I observed of this do-it-yourself Indonesian film production company, in which the emphasis is not on the auteur but on the collective subjectivity of a community or a nation.

Filmmaking was an occasion for a great adventure.[3]

INDONESIAN CINEMA, FEMINISM, AND THE ROLE
OF WOMEN DIRECTORS AND PRODUCERS

During the period of *Reformasi*, Indonesian cinema, whether narrative or documentary, was in a very tenuous position altogether. Popular in the 1970s and 1980s, Indonesian cinema declined in the early 1990s with the advent of cable television, the telenovela, and the Indonesian version of the tele-novela, *sinetron*.[4] Many local cinemas closed down; currently there are no distribution networks and only four exhibition chains in Indonesia.[5] Late in Suharto's tenure, quotas for imported films were loosened, and thus for-eign films, particularly Hollywood films, began to flood the market. Suharto also, in 1992, instituted a film law that allowed more censorship of domestic Indonesian films. The tanking of the economy in 1998 and the subsequent political unrest that led to Suharto's eventual eviction from his post as presi-dent meant that the Indonesian film industry also ground to a halt. In 1999, only three feature films were released.[6] The three most famous film produc-ers who came into prominence in the early 2000s were all young women: Mira Lesmana, Shanty Harmayn, and Nia Dinata (Dinata had a background in television), all of whom are still active and successful producers, making narrative features set all over Indonesia, across ethnicities and historical pe-riods, often with strong women protagonists.

Thus, women's current prominence in the Indonesian film industry was brought on by several factors that led to the demise of the male-dominated film industry. One factor was the loosening of quotas for Hollywood film. The second major factor was the great financial crisis in Indonesia of 1998, in a country that had been led by a military dictatorship for thirty-three years. The severe economic crisis caused violent political chaos: the military dictator, Suharto, was forced out of power, but it also meant that the Indonesian film industry was decimated. The economic recession of 1998 that led to Suharto's downfall allowed for strong, independent, progressive filmmaking on rather small budgets of $200,000 or so, and about subjects never before shown in film, such as women, gays, and Chinese Indonesians.

The struggle for women's rights and the women's movement is still ongoing in Indonesia. Under the oppressive, authoritarian New Order regime of Suharto, who was president from 1965 until 1998, the icon of Kartini, the famous nineteenth-century female writer and activist who fought for education and the rights of women, discussed in chapter 2, was used to construct an ideology of the perfect woman as the patient, sweet, refined wife and mother. The regime pressured women to join conservative women's organizations such as Dharma Wanita, Dharma Pertiwi, and PKK (Family Empowerment and Welfare Movement), which channeled women into cooking, fashion, and household areas. The New Order's conception of wifeliness, based on a patriarchal and one-sided interpretation of the writer Kartini, was articulated in the five precepts for women, which were prominently displayed on posters in village and city offices: "A wife is to (1) support her husband's career and duties; (2) provide offspring; (3) care for and rear the children; (4) be a good housekeeper; and (5) be a guardian of the community."[7] As scholar Silvia Tiwon delineates, on the other end of the spectrum from Kartini were the members of the Gerwani (Gerakan Wanita Indonesia), who were vilified as communist, castrating whores, as we saw so graphically in chapter 2. Tiwon writes, "Kartini and Gerwani are both fictions, both shape the reality that Indonesian women live."[8] Kartini is the ideal of the perfect wife; Gerwani is the demon of the hypersexual female political activist: these are the opposing norms of Indonesia's gendered visual politics.

Suharto stepped down during the economic crisis of 1998, ushering in the present period known as Reformasi, the more open and liberal period following Suharto's fall from power. Yet the specter of these New Order models of womanhood continues to have a strong hold. One would expect that due to the tenure of a female president, Megawati Sukarnoputri, from 2001 to 2004, the rights of women in Indonesia would have been improved. This has not been the case. One setback for women is the Pornography Law passed in 2008, which allows the government to jail anyone for up to twelve years for any "sexually suggestive performance."[9] The law bans any human-made creation or activity that can incite sexual desire, including writings, drawings, voice, sound, moving pictures, conversation, and even gestures. Dinata described the Pornography Law as an invasion of privacy, because it is not truly aimed at stopping the distribution of pornography (she cited the fact that anyone can purchase pirated pornographic DVDs in the markets of Indonesia).[10] On another occasion, she explained, "The anti-porn law is quite broad and vague and can be interpreted in many different ways. Pornography is in the eyes of the beholder and it's hard to measure whether conveying facts in film about women can be sexually arousing. Some religious conservatives may consider the topics in our film too provocative and this new law empowers them."[11] This law is seen as a kowtowing to Islamic fundamentalists on the part of former President Susilo Bambang Yudhoyono, the man who defeated Megawati in 2004. Such conservative religious blocs have pressured governments to pass laws that discriminate against women. As Katinka van Heeren argues in her comprehensive and astute book *Indonesian Contemporary Cinema*, Islam has become a political tool in the hands of political parties, and other mass and local movements, as a rallying cry for increased conservatism, but also to invoke a countervailing fear of domination by radical Islam.[12] Politicians in recent local and national presidential campaigns in Indonesia have exploited religious divisions for their own gain.

Another major setback was the enactment of the Health Law in 2009. This law was intended to help prevent the thousands of deaths from illegal abortions, which are mainly provided to married women, not unmarried teenagers. In its original form it was supposed to be passed by the legislature in the last few days of Megawati Sukarnoputri's presidency, but she did not sign it before leaving office. As it was then amended, the Health Law reflected the growing influence of conservative Muslim forces in Indonesian politics under President Yudhoyono. The law also exacerbates the problem of deaths from illegal abortions, because of its highly stringent rules: the fetus can be no older than six weeks at the time of abortion, before many women even know they are pregnant, and the woman must get the approval of her husband, except in cases of rape. What is worse, a woman can be jailed for up to ten years and is subject to a $100,000 fine for having an illegal abortion.[13]

The Health Law and the Pornography Law reinforce a kind of shame culture, as the former makes it unlawful to provide sexual and reproductive health services to unmarried women and girls, and the latter limits the ability to educate them about such issues. Women trying to fight against recent setbacks such as the Pornography Law or the Health Law are seen as being "immoral," and as "girls who are out of control," explains Mariana Amiruddin, director of the Jurnal Perempuan Foundation.[14] Even under the more progressive current president, Joko Widodo, laws that curtail free speech, which include the antipornography law but also civil defamation laws, mean that citizens may be arrested even for singing old antimilitary songs or sending WhatsApp messages.[15] It is against this political and religious backdrop that we must contextualize the films produced by Nia Dinata.

DIVERSITY IN PEOPLE, DIVERSITY IN FILM:
NIA DINATA AND *KALYANA SHIRA*

A forceful and brilliant filmmaker, Nia Dinata started the production company Kalyana Shira in 2000 with her husband, Constantin Papadimitriou (Kiki). Dinata is tellingly called Teteh by everyone (the Sundanese word for "older sister"), and the world of the production house of Kalyana Shira takes on an almost familial subjectivity. Through her work with Kalyana Shira, Dinata has produced the first films of directors such as Sekar Ayu Asmara (*Biola Tak Berdawai*, 2003), Joko Anwar (*Janji Joni*, 2005), and Lucky Kuswandi (*Madame X*, 2010, a film about a transgender superhero).[16]

Dinata's production company, located for fifteen years in a residential house in Cipete, South Jakarta (it has now moved to another location, in Kemang, South Jakarta), is known among Indonesian production houses for its diversity in terms of the sexuality and ethnicity of crew members, actors, staff, writers, directors, marketing, and public relations. Dinata explains, "For me, film is a description of social reality. In my social realm, there are homosexuals, there are Indonesian Chinese, Indonesian Indian. I meet a mix of people. Why should I only tell a story about mainstream people, mainstream religion, mainstream sexual preference?"[17] But the diverse labor force and controversial content—gay sexuality, male gigolos, transgender superheroes, polygamy, teenage sex, overseas lesbian communities, inadequate health care for women, female circumcision, AIDS, and trafficking—are not the only unique things about Dinata's work. Her collaborations reconfigure, translate, and convert the commercial feature documentary and feature narrative genres, overturning certain conventions regarding the authorial voice and subjectivity of the filmmaker and his or her relation to the audience. Among the many genres Dinata has directed and/or produced in feature film form are comedies, an animated film for children, a musical that was inspired by a popular Indonesian film from 1957, and a sex comedy with male gigolos; other formats include documentaries, numerous shorts, many television shows, and narrative content for web streaming services like VIU, an entertainment streaming site targeting viewers in Southeast Asia. Multiple voices and viewpoints, the treatment of the transnational and globalized subject matter of Indonesian women and sexuality, and the divergence from the traditional forms of film authorship, production, distribution, and exhibition are the hallmarks of Dinata's cinema.

One defining characteristic of Dinata's work is diversity along several different axes, from the directors she supports (male, female, and transgender) to the subject matter of her own films; all of Dinata's films take on images of women and sexuality never before seen on screen in Indonesia. Her first film from 2002, *Ca-bau-kan*, based on a novel set in 1930s–50s Java by Remy Sylado, focuses on the Chinese Indonesian heroine Tinung (Lola Amaria), a Ca-bau-kan, or courtesan, who entertains Chinese Indonesian men during the colonial era, and who becomes involved with a successful tobacco businessman named Peng Liang (Ferry Salim). Just by having a Chinese Indonesian story, Dinata was flouting decades of convention, since Chinese Indonesian representation had essentially been banned during the Suharto regime. Her second film also spurned New Order mores. *Arisan!* (2003) was a film with gay characters, written with Joko Anwar, who was then a film critic. In this hit film about a straight woman whose best friend is gay, Dinata deftly used comedy to deflect the weightiness of making the first Indonesian feature film with gay subject matter.

Berbagi Suami (*Love for Share*, 2006) was another original foray: a tripartite story that threads together three women from different ethnicities, classes, and religious backgrounds. In many ways, it works as an omnibus film of three short films about polygamy helmed by one director. The theme of community, the complexity of narrative structure, the explorations of sexuality, class, gender, and race, the focus on women's health and women's oppression that are so much the center of her later films are uniquely explored in *Berbagi Suami*, and it is for this reason that I would like to describe this 2005 film in some detail. The film reveals how polygamy and women's oppression affect the whole structure of a family, across generations.

With bold camera work, saturated colors, striking performances, and vivid characters, Dinata provides us with a portrait of what it is like to share husbands, per the Indonesian title, *Berbagi Suami*. Salma (Jajang C. Noer) learns to accept that her husband has a second wife for the sake of keeping the

FIGURE 4.1 Salma (Jajang S. Noer) speaks to her husband's other wives, Ima (Atiqah Hasiholan) and Indri (Nungki Kusumastuti), in a scene from *Berbagi Suami* (Nia Dinata, 2006).

peace for her son, Nadim (Wingky Wirawan), but after her husband has a stroke, more wives come out of the woodwork (figure 4.1). Comedy ensues when all the wives are forced to meet each other at the hospital for the first time. In one funny and moving scene, we see Pak Haji recovering at home, visited by his beautiful young third wife, Ima (Atiqah Hasiholan), who, like his son Nadim, is a college student. In the foreground we see Ima first looking at Nadim, then looking away; then a cut to Nadim looking at Ima rather curiously, followed by a cut to Pak Haji noticing his son's gaze, followed by a cut showing Salma looking at her son looking at the third wife, Ima. Salma's wealth and education do not make her immune from the pain of being betrayed by a husband who lusts after other women.

Unlike the male gaze that Laura Mulvey delineates as a major underpinning of Western cinema—the woman's to-be-looked-at-ness—the gazes in the societies that Dinata depicts are not binary oppositions but complex networks involving both men and women.[18] Following a master shot, the shots are not from a godlike position looking down at the scene (the man looking at the woman and vice versa), but of a whole communitarian view of the scene with each person looking at all points of perspective. It is a viewing structure that one finds in all of Dinata's films.

In the second story, a poor village girl, Siti (Shanty), is tricked into becoming a third wife. At the time Shanty was a singer and former VH1 announcer known for her sexy, brash personality and fluent English. By casting Shanty, Dinata presents a stark contrast to Siti, a character who is demure and quiet, poor and uneducated, and the direct opposite of Shanty's star persona.

Like Annah la Javanaise, Siti is brought to a new place to service the household and sexual needs of the man of the house, Pak Lik (Lukman Sardi), but she also finds a way to break away from her situation, through conspiring collectively with the women of the household (think of the contrast of Zhang Yimou's *Raise the Red Lantern* [1991] or the HBO television show *Big Love* to see how polygamy is usually represented in cinema, as a den of viperous women fighting over the husband). When Pak Lik comes home from Aceh with a fourth wife, Siti decides she has had enough. But because Siti has fallen in love unexpectedly with Dwi (Rieke Diah Pitaloka), the second wife, she schemes to run away with Dwi and her kids, but not without first getting medical care for the first wife Sri (Ria Irawan), who is suffering from an infection (figure 4.2). The doctor who treats Sri is Salma, the protagonist of the first story in this tripartite, three-narrative, film. Finally, early one morning, Sri flags down a taxicab to escape with Dwi and her kids. Exiting the cab before them is the main character of the third story of the film, the beautiful and very young Ming (Dominique Agisca Diyose), a Chinese Indonesian waitress, coming back to the *kampung*, newly independent, after being dumped by her husband.

In the third story, Ming is enamored by the new apartment and money that being a common-law second wife to the rather coarse Koh Abun (Tio Pakusudewo), owner of a roast-duck restaurant, provides. All that changes the day Koh Abun's first wife and Ming's former boss, Cik Linda (Ira Maya Sopha), and her two girls barge into Ming's apartment to punish her. When Ming faints from the force of the confrontation, Cik Linda, who up until this time has been screaming at her, all of a sudden gets worried and tries to revive the unconscious Ming, much to the chagrin of the daughters. "She is someone's daughter too," Cik Linda explains as she cries out to Ming to wake up. Here Cik Linda's identity as a mother trumps her jealousy as a wife.

This web of identification, in which one switches from seeing the other as husband stealer to daughter, forms the basis of *Berbagi Suami*. It is this scanning, filmmaking eye that provides another model for independent film-

FIGURE 4.2 Siti (Shanty) and Dwi (Rieke Diah Pitaloka) in a scene from *Berbagi Suami* (Nia Dinata, 2006).

making, worlds apart from the North American ideal of the independent male auteur of the likes of Quentin Tarantino and Christopher Nolan. The camera and editing catch these switches in apparent identities: Cik Linda the jilted wife facing her competition becomes Cik Linda the mother nurturing a young woman, her former employee, who has just collapsed.

In the second story, it is the care of the children and the health of the household that is important to Siti: sexuality is intimately tied to a woman's health and a woman's sense of worth, and this is a major theme throughout Dinata's work, as is the sense of self that comes from the "we" or *kami* (inclusive we, the us) and *kita* (you and I) versus the I. If Dinata focuses on the third wife—one could argue, why not the first wife, Sri, who loves sex, or the second wife, Dwi, the mysterious one—it is to focus not on individual protagonists but on how all women's subjectivities are affected by each other: the I is the we.

In *Berbagi Suami*, the narrative complexity of the film allows for identity changes, according to the structure of the groups in which the character finds herself, and is subject to change when the function of a member of the group changes or when a new person enters the web. In her three omnibus films, including the four-segment narrative film *Perempuan Punya Cerita* (*Chants of Lotus*) of 2008, the four-segment documentary *Pertaruhan*, also of 2008, and another omnibus documentary, *Working Girls* (2010), Dinata continues her resistance of visual biopolitics by producing diverse content relating to women and sexuality, new patterns of spectator and audience identification in the narrative form of the films, and by bringing uncensored copies of her films into communities for public discussion.

THE OMNIBUS FILM: MULTIPLE GAZES AND TRANSFIGURED GENRES

In the 1990s, US and European independent film embraced forms of narrative that wove several stories within a story, such as Quentin Tarantino's *Pulp Fiction* (1994), and these films, "network narratives" to use David Bordwell's term, also inspired a generation of Indonesian filmmakers, including Dinata.[19] The rise of independent film heralded by the incredible success of *Pulp Fiction* shook up cinema around the world. Other independent films foregrounded intricate narrative, including Robert Altman's *Short Cuts* (1993), Tom Tykwer's *Run Lola Run* (1998), and Christopher Nolan's *Memento* (2000). In the independent film world of the United States and Europe, multilayered narrative films have been the domain of young, male, maverick auteurs whose films often featured tortured male individuals and sexual femmes fatales. In contrast, Nia Dinata and other feminist women directors in Asia created, as noted by film historian and theorist Patricia White, collaborative films that respond to multiple audiences with a more networked subjectivity. It is this kind of group subjectivity that White redefines as "network."[20]

Bordwell's idea of network cinema was that of indie films that began in the 1990s to tout clever but often weak links between characters and narrative events, featuring ensemble casts. Discomfited by using "network" to describe male auteur films that conclude their narratives with prescribed racial, gender, and class determinations, White suggests a more radical possibility for the network film: "In contrast, I want to suggest that network narratives function as open structures in women's film texts and that these in turn link to the feminist and related cultural networks that sustain a growing number of women film practitioners."[21]

Nia Dinata is one of the women filmmakers that White analyzes from this point of view. Dinata radicalizes filmmaking in three ways. First she films Indonesian women as complex, sexual beings with multiple roles and responsibilities across classes and ethnicities, thus intervening in the categories of pure woman/Ibu Kartini versus castrating Gerwani killer that serve the visual biopolitics of Suharto's regime up to the present day. Second, as director/ producer, activist, collaborator, and educator, she transgresses boundaries normally held by auteur cinema. Throughout her career, she has made it her mission to redefine and topple the categories of national cinema versus transnational cinema, documentary versus fiction. Thus she is a filmmaker who engages in the discourse of the nation (literally in her fight as a member of Masyarakat Film Indonesia to expand upon cinematic and creative freedoms) as well as in the ways that her films are shown and studied transnationally in international film festivals and academic film studies. Dinata's eye crosses genders, sexualities, classes, and ethnicities: characters look at each other and look at the camera in multiple ways; filmmakers collaborate to make omnibus film; and exhibition and distribution are changed, through roadshowing films to discussion groups all over Indonesia, allowing for a long tail for her films that goes beyond theatrical exhibition. In collaborating with others, Dinata creates new forms of production, exhibition, and distribution, and consequently new forms of subjectivity and audience.

In the wake of the severe economic crisis, political unrest, and uncertainty of Reformasi in the late 1990s, packing several stories into one was also a good way to make a feature film less expensively. When Reformasi arrived in 1998, the film industry was already much weakened by the new Century 24 Group, allied to Suharto's family, which allowed a heretofore protected market to be flooded by Hollywood films. Four years after the release of *Pulp Fiction*, a group of Indonesian filmmakers produced and directed *Kuldesak* (1998). Arguably the first independent film produced after the economic crisis, this omnibus film was directed by several Indonesians including Riri Reza, Nan Achnas, Mira Lesmana, and Rizal Mantovani, all of whom went on to have respected careers as filmmakers.

As a feature film comprising several short films, the omnibus film usually engages different directors and often is yoked to a provocative theme or a centralized subject or place. Paris, in essence, is the star of *Paris, je t'aime* (2006). Historian Shekhar Deshpande refers to the genre as the anthology film, and he draws upon the musings of French omnibus film producer Emmanuel Benbihy. To Benbihy, the omnibus film promotes the short film form and elevates it out of its marginalized position. *Paris, je t'aime* was produced by Benbihy, who invited several famous auteurs to make individual segments. The tension in the omnibus film, according to Benbihy, is in creating unity out of diversity.[22] Different internationally renowned filmmakers, many of whom had already made network feature films, such as the Coen brothers, Tom Tykwer, Gus Van Sant, Olivier Assayas, Alexander Payne, and Isabel Coixet, directed individual films, each set in a different Paris arrondissement. Another marketing tool was the billing of major international stars such as Juliette Binoche, Gérard Depardieu, Willem Dafoe, and Natalie Portman.

Because it is made by various film directors who direct different short films within the longer feature format, the omnibus film always has the potential to lose an audience groomed to follow a narrative held together by a three-act structure that ends in closure. The viewer created by the omnibus film engages with a feature film put together by theme and not by linear action or prolonged spectator identification, and thus this genre requires a different kind of spectatorship. Every time a film segment ends and a new one begins, one is in a sense made aware of watching a film, and thus there is a kind of self-reflexivity in the omnibus film not found in a traditional three-act feature film.

As Deshpande explains, by its nature the omnibus film's production demands a creative producer who makes sure that all the stories have an organic collaborative theme. When it comes to creative producing, the genre found a brilliant match in Nia Dinata.

THE OMNIBUS NARRATIVE:
PEREMPUAN PUNYA CERITA (CHANTS OF LOTUS)

In *Berbagi Suami*, we saw how Dinata disturbs the state's representation of the Indonesian woman as either the good wife or the leftist whore. There is no implied omnipresent godlike male viewer, but a series of shifting viewers fluctuating between different alliances and identities. The film consists of three stories from vastly different classes and ethnicities, yet because Dinata is the one director and writer of all three of the films, they all share the look, the signature, of one auteur. Her touch—sudden swings from comedy to tragedy, the investigation of networks of women who must support each other under the gaze of one man, elegant camera work and saturated color and production design—unites three very disparate stories. Just as the taxi driver who delivers Ming back to her little apartment in the kampong picks up Siti, Sri, and her children, as they flee their life with Pak Lik, occasionally the characters of each of the three stories bump or pass by each other, in an attenuated relationship.

In *Berbagi Suami*, the complexity of her female protagonists, her extensively field-researched stories of women and sexuality, and her innovative and intricate narratives replete with multiple gazes and viewing structures are forms of resisting visual biopolitics, and these modes of resisting continue in her subsequent omnibus films. The first omnibus production, *Perempuan Punya Cerita*, placed four female directors together to make one film. Each director was tasked to put to the screen one story, and it was Dinata as producer who became the overseeing eye of the whole production. The film could easily have turned into a willful four-headed beast. Instead Dinata produced a film that cohered in vision even as the stories, characters, and directors diverged. Centered on stories about women's sexuality and women's health, Dinata's omnibus films continued the themes of the intertwined gazes of a female-dominated community and an emphasis on community narrative interconnectedness. But she also took her collaborative practice of filmmaking to another level. Here I open up my analysis of Dinata's work to discuss her intervention into filmmaking praxis in terms of collaborative production.

One of Dinata's missions is to build up the Indonesian film industry, and she has produced and encouraged many filmmakers and screenwriters. Although filmmaking is of course a collaborative endeavor, and others like Indonesian auteur Garin Nugroho have set up workshops such as SET to help other filmmakers, arguably no Indonesian filmmaker has so generously and consistently tried to help and launch the careers of other directors and writers (as well as actors and crew). Absolutely essential to her production of the omnibus film is Dinata's consistent love and desire to nurture the Indonesian film industry, which emerges from her conviction that a great Indonesia is a creative Indonesia with freedom of expression, and in fact that such a vision of the country has already been present since the founding of the nation in 1949. The omnibus film under Dinata was an important training ground for emerging filmmakers as well as a networking tool for established filmmakers. Like Mohsen Makhmalbaf's film school in Iran, Kalyana Shira trains people in all aspects of making a film: acting, directing, writing, producing, and so on.

Dinata's films are intended for an Indonesian audience, not a foreign audience: we see this in her films' content, point of view, extensive use of dialogue in Indonesian and other ethnic languages, and lack of exoticism or sexual exploitation. Yet because of her unique style and status, Dinata's films are often shown on the international film festival circuit or get distributed by foreign distributors like Netflix.[23]

After making *Berbagi Suami*, Dinata founded the Kalyana Shira Foundation in 2006, which raised funds for *Perempuan Punya Cerita* (*Chants of Lotus*), *Pertaruhan* (*At Stake*), and later short films like *Batik Our Love Story*.

Perempuan Punya Cerita, Dinata's first omnibus film, is a fiction film with four directors that deals with women and sexuality—in particular, abortion, teen sex, child trafficking, and HIV/AIDS. Dinata chose the other three directors—Upi Avianto, Lasja Fauzia Susatyo, and myself—and the film was released theatrically in 2008.

If melodrama jerks tears from the body, *Perempuan Punya Cerita* evokes heart-wrenching sobs. The film begins with an abortion and cancer; moves on to group sex, thwarted abortion, and then betrayal; then on to child trafficking; and ends with a mother, discovered to be HIV-positive, traveling at night alone on a bus, with the rain on the window pouring down like her tears, after having to give up her daughter. The four protagonists of the film were Sumantri (Rieke Diah Pitaloka), a midwife on a remote island who conducted abortions; Safina (Kirana Larasati), a tough teenager observing all her friends around her having sex in the university town of Yogyakarta; Esi (Shanty), a naive bathroom cleaner of a *dangdut* dance club in West Java whose daughter is sexually abused and then sold to traffickers; and Lakshmi (Susan Bachtiar), a beautiful Chinese Indonesian widow whose life unravels when her heroin-addicted husband dies from an overdose and his family tries to take away her only child, Belinda.

PREPRODUCTION: COLLABORATIVE MONTAGE

Dinata approached me in December 2006 to come on board as one of the directors. In April 2007 I joined the preproduction team and participated with writers, producers, assistant directors, directors, and public relations on the feature film as a whole. The two screenwriters were at the time new to the field, revealing Dinata's mission to develop the Indonesian film industry and encourage women: Melissa Karim, a television personality who has since acted in, written for, worked for, and produced many Kalyana Shira productions; and Vivian Idris, a marketing director for Aksara bookstore in Jakarta, who is now a documentary filmmaker and film producer. At that point the stories had not been assigned. I gave my feedback to the writers and Dinata on all four stories themselves, and then as a group we conducted several extensive on-site research trips in Jakarta, to HIV/AIDS centers and support groups, to hospitals to meet students studying midwifery, and to various cities in Java, meeting with locals whose lives were similar to those of the characters in our stories. If radical filmmaker Dziga Vertov defines montage as more than just editing, but also the preproduction process involving the selection of what is filmed, then a Kalyana Shira production involves extensive montage before shooting: considerable travel, research, and a kind of camaraderie one can only find on a trip in a van riding the roads in various regions of Java.

On one trip to Indramayu, a port city in West Java with a reputation for child trafficking, Dinata and her producing team stopped at a café and pretended to be clients seeking a baby to buy. On another research trip to Yogyakarta, the Kalyana producing team gathered a large group of teenagers in one room and asked them if they had sex and how they did it; it was from these teenagers that we learned that sex was common, done blatantly in bedrooms at home, with classmates, not prostitutes. One teenage boy recounted an incident where a girl had had sex with many partners who were all friends, and so when she got pregnant it was impossible to know who the true father was, so the boys drew numbers from a Sprite can to determine who would marry her. This story became a pivotal incident in the film. Based on our meeting with midwifery students, and in particular with one student named Reni Septiani, we decided to locate the story about a midwife who performs an abortion on Reni's island of Pulau Kelapa, about three hours by boat from Jakarta, a poor island in the Pulau Seribu area that provides many of the laborers for the local tourist industry. We also conducted research at a dangdut club (the dance music featured in another story).

In May 2007 the four filmmakers sat around a table with writers Melissa Karim (who was also second assistant director) and Vivian Idris (who was also coproducer), and assistant director Cinzia Puspita Rini; we discussed the stories, provided feedback, and decided who would direct what. Lasja Fauzia Susatyo was slotted to do the film set in Jakarta because she was eight months pregnant, so if she went into labor, she could get to a hospital quickly. Upi, known as the rock-and-roll director and whose feature films had starred young people, chose the story on teenagers having sex in Jogja. Nia Dinata directed the sequence on child trafficking that was set in the dangdut club, and I directed the story about an older midwife who is the only medical practitioner on an island. As a result of the research we conducted before directors were assigned, the stories were modified to incorporate ethnographic details we had discovered, and at the directors' and writers' meeting, stories became even more refined with the directors' input.

In *Cerita Pulau (Tale from an Island)*, the first story, written by Vivian Idris, the island midwife Sumantri has a special motherly relationship with her neighbor's granddaughter, Wulan (Rachel Mariam), an autistic, nonverbal young woman (figure 4.3). When Wulan is raped by a visiting rich boy, Tommy (Edo Borne Putra), who is passing through the islands of Pulau

FIGURE 4.3 Wulan (Rachel Maryam) and Sumantri (Rieke Diah Pitaloka) in a scene from *Cerita Pulau* (*Tale from an Island*), directed by Fatimah Tobing Rony, from the omnibus film *Perempuan Punya Cerita* (*Chants of Lotus*, 2007), produced by Nia Dinata. Still by Dianti Andajani. Cinematography by Teoh Gay Hian.

Seribu, it is Sumantri who takes her to the police station, only to find that the police refuse to deal with her rape, in an illustration of biopolitics at work. When Wulan becomes pregnant, Sumantri decides to perform an abortion, which is forbidden by the community and the state, even as her husband is pressuring her to leave for Jakarta to get treatment for her stage 4 breast cancer. For this character I chose more static shots with great depth of field, rather than quick cutting, because I wanted to frame the networks between people within one tableau.

The next story, directed by Upi Avianto and written by Vivian Idris, set in the lively city of Yogyakarta (Jogja), *Cerita Yogyakarta (Tale from Yogyakarta)* focuses on Safina (Kirana Larasati), who is seduced by Jay Anwar (Fauzi Baadila), an undercover reporter from Jakarta. At the end of the story, she lambastes him on television for taking her virginity. The film opens with Safina confronting the boys who got her friend pregnant (figure 4.4). The boys are unfeeling, coarse, and rude, and they explain to the visiting journalist that they only sleep with good girls, not with prostitutes, and in their homes, not in hotels. For the most part the main characters in the film were found in auditions, since almost all of them were teens, and a few of them had never acted before. Unlike the fluid, long takes used in my previous story to reflect the turbulence and the grace of Sumantri's life, Upi used a handheld camera for a faster *Kids*, documentary-like style, with quick editing.

In another horrifying story, *Cerita Cibinong (Tale from Cibinong)*, written by Melissa Karim, naive Esi (Shanty), the bathroom cleaner for a dangdut music club, comes home from work to discover her daughter Maesaroh being sexually abused by her boyfriend. She and Maesaroh run away and end up staying with her friend Cicih, a local dangdut singer, played by Sarah Sechan.

FIGURE 4.4 Schoolgirl Safina (Kirana Larasati) stands up for her pregnant friend in a scene from *Cerita Yogyakarta* (*Tale from Yogyakarta*), directed by Upi Avianto, from the omnibus film *Perempuan Punya Cerita* (*Chants of Lotus*, 2007), produced by Nia Dinata. Still by Dianti Andajani. Cinematography by Teoh Gay Hian.

When asked about the abuse, Maesaroh explains, "I didn't have sex with him, I just sucked him." The horror of these words devastates Esi. Worse, Cicih betrays Esi by colluding to traffic Maesaroh. The lush production design and murky melancholy colors of the nightclub and night prostitution reveal the distinct style of Dinata's directorial hand.[24]

The final story, *Cerita Jakarta* (*Tale from Jakarta*), written by Vivian Idris, opens with a heroin addict, Reno (Winky Wiryawan), plunging a needle in his arm as his eyes roll in ecstasy and then in death. Because he has AIDS, his widow, Lakshmi (Susan Bachtiar), a Chinese Indonesian woman, is kicked out of the family house and wrongly accused by her husband's wealthy family of giving her husband the disease (figure 4.5). The story follows her and her daughter, Belinda, as they run from place to place to find shelter, until finally, after having gotten medical treatment, Lakshmi gives up her daughter to be raised by her late husband's family. For this film, Lasja Fauzia Susatyo directed in a very assured, well-lit, smooth and precise style, combined with strong storytelling and subtle acting.

FIGURE 4.5 Lakshmi (Susan Bachtiar) prays in a scene from *Cerita Jakarta* (*Tale from Jakarta*), directed by Lasja Fauzia Susatyo, from the omnibus film *Perempuan Punya Cerita* (*Chants of Lotus*, 2007), produced by Nia Dinata. Cinematography by Ical Tanjung.

MULTIPLE STORIES, MULTIPLE WRITERS, MULTIPLE CREW

Let me now elaborate on the production history of *Cerita Dari Pulau* to show what the actual network of production was, and how the divide between reality and fiction, documentary and narrative was blurred in this film's production. Screenwriter Vivian Idris had written the script for the film I directed, and it was an extremely harsh tale in which Sumantri must sell her house and move to Jakarta to get treatment, abandoning her livelihood and the autistic neighbor Wulan, upon whom she doted. In the first iteration of the script by Vivian Idris, Wulan is repeatedly raped brutally by local men, and she becomes pregnant, forcing Sumantri to give her an abortion. Later we see Sumantri dying in the hospital in Jakarta with Wulan by her side. After meeting with the midwife student Reni from the island of Pulau Kelapa, and after visiting the island for our first research visit, I could not see how Wulan would have been brutalized by her own kampung in such a manner. I proposed to Vivian the idea that the rapist was an outsider, a rich boy from Jakarta. Effectively, Dinata as producer pointed out, that would change the story: in real life the boy would pay off the parents of the girl, here her grandmother, for the crime. In the final version of the film, the grandmother apologizes to Sumantri when she accepts the boy's money. I also proposed an ending in which we do not see Sumantri dying in a Jakarta hospital. Instead we see Sumantri leaving the island, at a moment when Wulan is nowhere to be found. Then as the boat sails off to the horizon, we see Wulan running to the pier, too late to say goodbye to Sumantri. The writer creates the story, and the director gives input, but the final approval rests with the producer.[25] And the story itself reflects the visual biopolitics of real life rather than a happy ending: power is reflected in those with money to buy complicity and silence.

As I explained above, we conducted initial research in Jakarta at a midwifery school, and then went to research Reni's island twice: first to scout locations in order to prepare for shooting there, and then to do *reki*, or reconnaissance, with the director of photography, Teoh Gay Hian; the sound recordist, Suhadi; the art director, Wencislaus, and the assistant director, Cinzia Puspita Rini. Reni took us to Pulau Kelapa and introduced us to the midwife there, who allowed us to use her own house as the set for Sumantri's house. From the midwife we learned that women on the island often died of complications if she happened to be away during their labor. Indonesia has a high mortality rate for pregnant women, at the time of filming the highest in Southeast Asia. Because the lack of sufficient medical care affects women so deeply, we included a scene where the local women Yanti and Susiana talk about these issues; I asked Vivian to write the scene, but then with the input of several women from Pulau Kelapa we modified the dialogue further. In addition, Rachel Maryam and I went to several schools for autistic children in Jakarta, and Rachel immersed herself in research to shape her performance as the nonverbal autistic Wulan.

Production, therefore, has a complex interface. We begin with the writers, Melissa Karim and Vivian Idris, and the characters they've created, but then through research, travel, and interviews, these stories are molded and changed to resemble the stories of these characters' real-life counterparts. Moreover, the directors, producers, assistant directors, and PR also change the stories. During reki, new insights can emerge: on my first trip to Pulau Kelapa, I heard a local music group and asked that they perform in the film. And then there is the actual shoot itself. Costumes by Isabelle Patrice, makeup by Yoga Septa, and production design and art by Wencislaus decide the overall look, but it is the actual moment when you are on set that things get put together and decisions get made. At that point, the director, in collaboration with the director of photography, almost always makes the final decisions, quickly, to beat the movement of the sun, the relentless heat, and time.

Diverse casting was another unusual tactic of this film. I decided to budget payment for professional actors for the three principal parts. Ahmad Rokim, the husband, was played by theater actor Arswendi Nasution. For Wulan, I cast Rachel Maryam, an extremely talented movie actor and the star of Riri Reza's *Eliana, Eliana* (2002). For the main character, Sumantri, I cast Rieke Diah Pitaloka, who had played the second wife, Dwi, who had run away with Siti in *Berbagi Suami*, because at the time she was a famous comedic celebrity. My hope was that audiences would come to see Rieke Diah Pitaloka and stay for the story of Sumantri. The rest who were not crew

FIGURE 4.6 Sumantri (Rieke Diah Pitaloka) has a question for Mak Tua (Sana'ah), in a scene from *Cerita Pulau* (*Tale from an Island*), directed by Fatimah Tobing Rony, from the omnibus film *Perempuan Punya Cerita* (*Chants of Lotus*, 2007), produced by Nia Dinata. Still by Syamsul Hadi. Cinematography by Teoh Gay Hian.

were locals from Pulau Kelapa. For example, the grandmother or Mak Tua was played by Sana'ah, a neighbor, and Wulan's sister Sari was played by a local girl, Zakiya (figure 4.6).

The divide between actor, nonactor, crew, and local is very fluid in these productions, thus breaking down the hierarchy normally found in Hollywood films. The rapist Tommy's bodyguard was the director of photography in other segments of *Chants of Lotus*, Ical Tanjung. The menacing Pak Lurah (village chief), who tries to investigate Sumantri's clinic, was the film's still photographer, Syamsul Hadi. Tommy's friend, the despicable Nanda, was our supremely competent location manager, Ferry Ardyan. The midwife-in-training, Yani, was played by Nina Desilina, our unit production manager. The character who buys the house from Ahmad Rokim so that he can take Sumantri to Jakarta to get treatment was played by Barlan, the husband of Pulau Kelapa's midwife, whose house we used; we also used her midwifery equipment as props. Although there were only three professional actors, with the rest of the cast being either crew members or local island people, this made artistic sense. Sana'ah, a local woman, was better able to play Mak Tuo, Wulan's grandmother, than anyone I could have cast from Jakarta: the lines on her face and the way she held her body could not be embodied by a professional actor. I could frame the story in such a way that her presence was more important than a skilled delivery of lines. For example, in the scene where Sumantri tells Mak Tuo that Wulan has been raped, I asked Teoh Gay Hian, the director of photography, to frame Sana'ah in the extreme right foreground: the camera could focus on Rieke's face and her reaction to the rape. It was not uncommon for the real-life counterpart to be included in a scene, or for crew to change jobs and be actors or extras during a scene.[26]

Postproduction involved a talented team of specialists. Once we were picture locked in terms of editing, we could build sound. I met with the music composing team of Aghi Narottama, Bemby Gusti, and Ramondo Gascaro and explained to them I wanted a bluesy sound that was also indigenous; they created a beautiful score similar to West Javanese *kecapi suling* and brought in the singer Tika, who was also there for the recording of the score for my story. I also worked with Satrio Budiono on the final sound mix of *Cerita Dari Pulau*. Finally, although I watched the dailies, transcribed them, and worked closely with the editor, Wawan I Wibowo, ultimately Dinata decided the order of the films within the feature, and it was the postproduction supervisor Tia Hasibuan who directed the color timing in Chennai, India. I could suggest things for the final postproduction, but these were taken as suggestions: the creative producer, as Deshpande explained, is the ultimate arbiter of the omnibus film, who makes the final decisions generally and who ensures the organic wholeness of tying together four disparate films.

REGULATING BODIES, REGULATING STORIES:
CENSORSHIP AND ACTIVISM

Filmmaking then under Dinata's omnibus rubric was a process of collaboration, research, and exploration. It was an incredible feeling to make these films, to collaborate with filmmakers and with communities, but it was a sinking feeling to find out that *Perempuan Punya Cerita* would be heavily censored by the Lembaga Sensor Film (Indonesian Censorship Board).

All of Dinata's films in some ways explore, in varying ways, the diversity of ethnicity, religion, race, sexuality, and class, and *Perempuan Punya Cerita* is perhaps one of the most hard-hitting of her films.[27] The censors felt the film had "sexually suggestive performances" that would incite sexual desire, a charge also held up by the Pornography Law. For example, the scene where a naked Wulan is bathed by Sumantri was cited for being sexually suggestive, but the producers successfully argued that there was nothing sexually suggestive about a girl being bathed after being violently raped: the scene was one of the rare moments in the film left uncut. *Perempuan Punya Cerita* is a film par excellence of how female bodies are regulated and thus vulnerable to sexual abuse, exploitation, and early death, and yet the producer's version of the film was prohibited by the Censorship Board, causing the body of the film itself to be destroyed by cuts.

The cuts transformed the meaning of the stories. For example, there is a scene in which a teenage girl is forced to have sex with several boys, but the censor's cut made it look like the girl is having sex with only one boy. The wifely ideal of the Suharto regime still manifests itself in the film: teen sex between two people is better than teen group sex. This of course changes the meaning of the story, and the plot itself, as to who must marry her to save the family's honor.

As a producer, Dinata did not stifle us directors because of worries about censorship or fear of the Pornography Law, but we were unprepared for the extensive censorship cuts made to the film. Why? This is a film with true stories, dominated by female protagonists who were working class, that touched on the taboo issues of abortion, teenage sex, child trafficking, and AIDS, and that did not use ambiguity or metaphor as might have been the case in other films. The women and girls were neither the wifely ideal of Ibu Kartini nor its counterpart, the dancing, sexual military killers. They are sexual without being evil. And perhaps what was worse, and starkly opposite to the kind of films passed by the Censorship Board, good never triumphed over evil in the film. As van Heeren explains, the Censorship Board maintains a code of ethics in which Indonesian films can be seen as traditional morality tales.[28] This is not true of *Perempuan Punya Cerita*, where the endings are ambiguous.

Sex comedies about men who are gigolos, arguably more sexually provocative than *Perempuan Punya Cerita*, are not censored. The title of the extremely funny sex comedy that Dinata produced the same year is sexually suggestive: *Quickie Express* (2007), a film directed by Dimas Djayadiningrat. Comedy juxtaposes opposites together that are startling and make you laugh: it can provoke a trauma, nervous laughter inciting humor. It can disguise subversive, gay humor, sexual older women, dominatrixes flourishing whips, and men in drag, in a way that drama about resisting the regulation of women's bodies cannot. *Perempuan Punya Cerita* is not a funny film; it was meant to draw attention to aspects of sexuality that directly affect Indonesian women's lives, and this was seen as threatening, requiring censorship. The genre of melodrama—that which draws tears and moves people—is potentially more subversive. Melodrama about women having sex can be threatening, where comedy about men having sex is not. Both films explored sexuality, but the censors ignored *Quickie*, perhaps because they did not get the joke. Men in drag are funny; women taking charge of their lives are threatening. In truth, the sex portrayed in *Perempuan Punya Cerita* is meant not to arouse the viewer, but to pain the viewer.

When the heavily censored cut of *Perempuan Punya Cerita* was released in major theaters all across Indonesia in January 2008, Dinata likened it to a rape; indeed, seeing one's film cut does feel like a violation, because the scenes are literally cut out. Ironically, that experience made her want to do an even more serious film. She explained:

> You know when PPC [*Perempuan Punya Cerita*] got all the censorship cuts and got all the protest, then that's like the momentum for me to really do something. . . . It's the momentum for, "Yes I have to do something that is even more daring and more touching than anticipated." It has to be documented. So that they know that these things happen. And then why do you have to close your eyes and close your ears. . . . Because otherwise if you ignore these things, then you know . . . there will be more and more violations in human rights, right?[29]

State censorship is a form of visual biopolitics, a way of derailing and curbing stories about the physical oppression and subjection to risk of death of Indonesian women. Here Dinata took on another role highly unlikely for her counterpart in the West: as a political activist and leader, Dinata helped form a coalition of film artists, Masyarakat Film Indonesia, in December 2006, who brought their case to the Supreme Court to argue that Film Law no. 8/1992 passed by the former president, Suharto, which in essence allowed for the kind of film censorship that *Perempuan Punya Cerita* was subject to, was unconstitutional. Masyarakat Film Indonesia was made up of filmmakers like Dinata, Joko Anwar, and Riri Reza, film producers like Shanty Harmayn and Mira Lesmana, film activists, actors like Shanty, and crew members, who wanted to promote change in government legislation affecting the film industry and to protest the draconian closed-door policies of the Film Censorship Board.

During Reformasi, most of the restrictive New Order film regulations could be ignored, but not, unfortunately, the Lembaga Sensor Film, to whose scrutiny all films to be projected in theaters had to be subjected. Under President

Suharto, films could be censored for touching on issues of SARA, an acronym for Suku Bangsa (ethnic group), Agama (religion), Ras (race), and Antar-Golongan (class), and the Censorship Board still enforces this mandate down to the present day. Lembaga Sensor Film is made up of members with positions in government and the military, and representatives from various religious groups including the Indonesian Ulama Council, Nahdlatul Ulama, Muhammadiyah, Dewan Gereja-Gereja di Indonesia (Council of Churches in Indonesia), Konferensi Wali Gereja Indonesia (Bishops' Conference of Indonesia), and Parisada Hindu Dharma Indonesia (Hinduism Society). Van Heeren details how religion, in particular Islam, has been used to apply political pressure since the period after Suharto's fall. One example is how the vastly influential paramilitary organization Front Pembela Islam, which is often marshaled to put political pressure on the government or on voters, supports Lembaga Sensor Film.[30]

In particular, Masyarakat Film Indonesia fought against Film Law no. 8/1992, set up by then President Suharto, which they argued suppressed freedom of speech.[31] Van Heeren and Intan Paramaditha note that Dinata and her allies were not antination or antigovernment, quite the contrary. They upheld the nation and in fact brought their case in 2008 using an article from the Indonesian Constitution of 1945: "Everyone is entitled to communicate and obtain information for their personal development and that of their social environment, and the right to seek, obtain, possess, store, process and convey information using all types of channels available."[32] As Paramaditha explains, the filmmakers embraced the idea of freedom of expression as essential to Indonesian nationalism, which was an important tenet of transnational film festivals and distribution.[33] In opposition, conservative artists such as renowned poet Taufiq Ismail argued that there must always be a fence or *layar tancep* against controversial representations that could be obscene.[34] Masyarakat Film Indonesia did not argue against the nation of Indonesia and its government, but fought for what they believed was inherently Indonesian: to protect diversity of opinion and free speech. This young generation, which was derided by the conservatives as being like monkeys suddenly let free, was a more transnational generation, promoting ideas like creativity and autonomy.[35] The upshot of their court fights was a new Film Law in 2009 that filmmakers felt was progressive in its terms concerning cinema monopoly and the film business, but which in effect had censorship points that were worse than the 1992 law, including expanding its domain into provincial capitals.[36]

Reacting to the repression of the censorship by Lembaga Sensor Film in 2007, Dinata decided to embark on another omnibus film project, *Pertaruhan (At Stake)*. Because she had come to the conclusion that the level of training in documentary film was not high enough, she decided to found Project Change!, a workshop for thirty-two documentary filmmakers from all over Indonesia. To the general public and beginning in the twentieth century, as Van Heeren points out, the Indonesian public equated documentary with national propaganda films or historical docudramas, produced by the government in the late 1970s and early 1980s, like *Pengkhianatan G30S/ PKI*, discussed in chapter 2. This film was compulsory annual viewing for schoolchildren, and all commercial broadcasters were required to broadcast it once a year. Thus, ironically, before Reformasi, state propaganda films that described the history of the rise of the Suharto government like *Pengkhianatan G30S/PKI* were called documentaries: fiction films appeared to be more objective.[37] Later, TVRI, the national television station, also broadcast propaganda films that were labeled documentaries.[38]

Van Heeren details how independent documentary filmmakers like Aryo Danusiri and Lexi Rambadata began to flourish during the Reformasi period with projects that, like *Perempuan Punya Cerita*, were funded by nongovernmental organizations like the Ford Foundation.[39] Dinata wanted to spread documentary storytelling further to the nontrained through education, telling them, "If you want to be a real documentary filmmaker, you have to take sides, choose daring issues."[40] After Reformasi, Dinata explained that most of what passed for documentary was similar to a television news show. She wanted to expand the idea of documentary beyond government propaganda and television news spots. Women activists came to the workshop to discuss gender and sexuality. Five of those filmmakers went on to direct Dinata's next film, *Pertaruhan*.

In comparing the three-story structure of *Berbagi Suami*, the narrative film, to *Perempuan Punya Cerita*, an omnibus narrative film inspired by documentary research, to *Pertaruhan*, an omnibus documentary film, we can see that ironically, melodrama is also in the documentary, although to a lesser extent. Like *Perempuan Punya Cerita*, *Pertaruhan* is structured around four stories. *Perempuan Punya Cerita* tells stories of great tragedy. *Pertaruhan* also has melodramatic moments, but because it focuses on several Indonesian women and girls, it has less opportunity to function as melodrama. Instead we see Indonesian women undergoing travails that are normally never discussed, much less put on screen, almost all of which interrogate and deconstruct the myths of the wifely ideal or the communist whore that are used by religion, medicine, culture, and commerce to repress and physically harm women and girls.

While film representing the indigenous became the genre of ethnographic film, representations of the poor, the urban, and the marginal classes became the genre of the documentary film.[41] Documentary in North America and Europe has often taken the underclass and the marginalized as its subject matter, including the poor, women, ethnic minorities, and so forth.[42] Intimate confessions, crying monologues, wrenching scenes of family dissolution, and heartfelt moments of human understanding all form part of the documentary film's generic convention of portraying marginalized subjects, sometimes to the brink of voyeurism or exploitation, as we saw in the work of Mead and Bateson, and Oppenheimer. Media scholar Brian Winston, who has spent a career exploring the creative treatment of actuality, to use pioneer John Grierson's definition for documentary, points out the unequal power relation created by the filmmaker, with his or her technology and use of marginal subjects for the entertainment of outsiders, "the tradition of the victim."[43] Other critics, however, have seen documentary film as giving voice to those who have been silenced due to differences in gender, race, class, ethnicity, or sexuality, and this is where Dinata and her filmmakers stand.

Pertaruhan addresses these omissions by making Indonesian women the subject of an omnibus documentary made by Indonesians, exploring transnational Indonesian workers abroad in Hong Kong; female circumcision in Indonesia; the paucity of Pap smears in Indonesia due to social taboos; and female labor in the fields of stone breaking and illegal prostitution. Given the political climate, a film about women and sexuality would seem unlikely to get made. In fact, according to Dinata, the impetus for making *Pertaruhan* was precisely because Indonesian society was becoming less and less open, and more and more conservative, especially with the debate over and passage of the Pornography Law, which was enacted two months before the film opened. Dinata wanted to resist this kind of censorship. When I asked Dinata why *Pertaruhan* focuses on women, she explained, "There are many faces of Indonesian women. There are interesting multidimensional characters of Indonesian women, because we grew up in a very interesting and challenging society. I would always feel obliged to portray them in as complex a manner as possible, because we are not that simple. We are not one-faceted human beings. We are very unique."[44] And when I asked her why she focused on sexuality, Dinata replied, "Because that's the basis for anything. . . . Sexuality deals with more than the actions itself—it deals with health, it deals with your rights, it deals with so many things." It's clear that Dinata also hoped to expose Indonesian audiences to societal restrictions that were increasing the risk of early illness or death: "Because most women in Indonesia don't even know their basic rights, that your body is your decision. Health issues are your own decision."[45]

As I have explained, the filmmakers, collaborators, and crew of these omnibus films made in Indonesia and produced by Dinata often step in front of the camera or are part of the community filmed. Dinata replaces traditional documentary's one auteur with many collaborators. *Pertaruhan* had five directors. Ani Ema Susanti, who directed the first segment on overseas workers, titled *Mengusahakan Cinta* (*Effort for Love*), was herself a former overseas Indonesian worker in Hong Kong. Ani Emi Susanti follows two Indonesian overseas workers in Hong Kong: the middle-aged and college-educated Ruwati, who is engaged to marry a widower back in Java, and who must decide whether or not to allow herself to be medically examined for a tumor and thus vaginally penetrated (by a gynecological instrument, which is against the wishes of her fiancé, who insists that she must remain a "virgin" before the wedding), and the brash young lesbian Ryantini, a married woman with a daughter back home in the village to support, who has found love with another Indonesian woman worker in Hong Kong.

The taboo subject of female circumcision (*khitan*) constitutes the second story, *Untuk Apa?* (*What's the Point?*), directed by two television journalists, Iwan Setiawan and Muhammad Ichsan. Although the practice was banned by the Indonesian government in 2006, it appears that support for it is growing in rural areas. As friends, the two male filmmakers proposed this subject for the workshop Project Change!, because Iwan Setiawan, who is Christian, was shocked to find out from Muhammad Ichsan, who is Muslim, that there was female circumcision in Indonesia. Since the practice is so rarely discussed, and is confined to certain groups in certain areas in Indonesia, many Indonesians have not even heard of it. But with fundamentalism on the rise, the practice of khitan or female circumcision persists. The filmmakers interview several young women who are trying to come to terms with their own experience of being circumcised, as well as religious leaders who support the practice. The women are honest and vulnerable in speaking out against circumcision, which is often performed against their will. But there is no outside foreign auteur that leads the Indonesian audience to the truth, as is often the case in US ethnographic or documentary films about Indonesia.

The third film, directed by Lucky Kuswandi, takes as its theme the appalling medical care that women get in Indonesia, especially unmarried women. Like the first two short films, the title for *Nona Nyonya?* (*Miss or Mrs?*) appears only at the end of the film. Instead of a title, we first see an intertitle stating that there are only seven thousand OB/GYNs for a population of 230 million. We also hear a doctor explain that the biggest cause of death in women is cervical cancer. The film is set mainly in the cosmopolitan capital city of Jakarta. Several young unmarried women explain their difficulty in obtaining a Pap smear. For the most part, they are condemned by nurses and doctors for seeking such medical attention without a husband's approval. Line producer Cinzia Puspita Rini smuggles in a hidden camera to get a Pap smear. However, the doctor refuses to give her a Pap smear and, when he learns that she is sexually active, he actually intones the Lord's Prayer (to ward off Satan) when finally giving her the examination. Another longtime Kalyana Shira associate, Ade Kusumaningrum, an "antipenetration lesbian," is shown going to an appointment for her first Pap smear and has her vagina penetrated for the first time. Vaginal penetration, unless married to a man, is such a societal taboo due to strict definitions of virginity that even when a woman needs gynecological medical observation or treatment for her health, she cannot be offered such care, no matter her class or ethnicity, without her parents' or husband's permission. Thus, the crew collaborated to an extent that is atypical for a documentary film, and their own bodies were penetrated as subjects of the film. The stakes are higher when one is working not just below the line, to use the Hollywood industrial term, but in front of the camera, and above the line, as a writer.

The final segment, *Ragat'e Anak* (*For the Sake of the Kids*), was directed by Ucu Agustin, a journalist and documentary filmmaker who was also the director of *Perempuan Kisah Dalam Guntingan* (*Women behind the Cut*, 2008), a documentary that focused on the censorship of *Perempuan Punya Cerita*, and *Konspiracy Hening* (*Conspiracy of Silence*, 2010), a documentary that exposed the inequalities in the health care system in Indonesia. *Ragat'e Anak* is an extremely powerful portrait of two mothers, Nur and Mira, who work as stone breakers by day and prostitutes in a Chinese graveyard by night, in Gunung Bolo, in the area of Tulungagung in East Java. Originally Ucu Agustin began her research with the question of why so many Indonesian transnational workers were HIV positive. She had assumed that they contracted the disease from their foreign employers. In fact, men married to TKW (overseas female workers) had contracted HIV from prostitutes while their wives were abroad working, and the wives subsequently contracted it from their husbands. Although *Pertaruhan* has four different stories and different directors, it depicts three different economies of working women: the Chinese women in Hong Kong who need to work (like Ruwati's employer in the first story), the Indonesian women who leave their husbands to go work abroad (like Ryantini in the first story), and the Indonesian women who work as prostitutes and service the husbands of the workers sent abroad (like Mira and Nur in the final story).

With the opening title of the film *Pertaruhan*, one is already aware that something new is being shown:

> Bekerja sama dengan Kalyana Shira Foundation
> Mempersembahkan
> Pertaruhan
> Sebuah Karya Kokektif dari Workshop Project Change 2008
> [In conjunction with Kalyana Shira Foundation
> We offer you
> Pertaruhan
> A Collective Work from the Workshop Project Change 2008]

Pertaruhan explores the different uses of subjectivity not just in the content of the film but in its actual production and exhibition. A film like *The Act of Killing* is sent around the world to prestigious film festivals and then gets distribution in major cities in the United States and Europe, and the filmmaker auteur goes on a press junket, interviewed by major newspapers, journals, and magazines, with endorsements by other major male documentary auteurs like Werner Herzog, and culminating in an Oscar nomination. The omnibus films made by Dinata get major theatrical distribution in every major Indonesian city and are also directly roadshowed or brought to various communities for at least a year afterward, but get little film festival exposure and are difficult to access abroad. Often the films will be uploaded on YouTube for a while with no English subtitles. The term "roadshow" was originally used in 1960s Hollywood to signify the heavy marketing for epic films like *Camelot* (1967) or *The Sound of Music* (1965) as prestigious cultural events. For the Kalyana Shira Foundation, roadshowing *Pertaruhan* refers to the year after the premiere of a film that Dinata, coproducer Vivian Idris, and several of the directors spent taking the film to the people, traveling to cities in Java, Sumatra, Bali, Kalimantan, and Sulawesi to provide special free screenings to women's groups, activists, students, and local government offices dealing with women's issues. These showings often provoked heated discussions. Director Lucky Kuswandi explained that sometimes the reactions were quite defensive, as in Lampung, Sumatra, where invited officials claimed that they had already done a lot for women.[46] Another director, Ani Ema Susanti, who wears a headscarf or hijab, was asked by audience members in Bandung: "Aren't you ashamed wearing a *krudung* [hijab] and talking about lesbians?"[47] The point of the roadshow for Dinata's films (also done for *Berbagi Suami* and *Perempuan Punya Cerita*) is to raise consciousness and promote social change by creating a dialogue around taboo issues like female circumcision, lesbianism, women's health, and definitions of purity, prostitution, and HIV/ AIDS. Unlike the original Hollywood roadshow, which was designed to drum up great profit and demand for an expensive epic film, Dinata roadshows un-censored versions of censored films, ensuring that the women's stories that she produces are still seen and heard.

What these filmmakers are doing with *Pertaruhan* is transformative: they are changing the genre of documentary into something daring, intimate, and collective. Although this is a Kalyana Shira production led by Dinata—head of a production house that has made over ten feature films, including sex comedies and dramas, musicals, animations, and many commercials, public service announcements, television shows, online content, and music videos— *Pertaruhan* was marketed as an omnibus film intended to showcase the work of emerging documentary filmmakers. But it also showcases real women's lives, of various ages and classes and ethnicities, even abroad.

The representation of Nur is a deconstruction of the model wife/mother of Kartini and that of the oversexualized Gerwani that I discussed earlier: she is the mother who sacrifices herself through her labor for her children. The same could be said for the representation of the lesbian Ryantini and the sexually active Cinzia, who demands a Pap smear, as was true in the fiction omnibus film characters of Sumantri, Wulan, Safina, Esi, and Lakshmi. The deconstruction of the virgin standard shows the health dangers for women, in terms of not getting treated for cancer or other illnesses (the overseas worker Ruwati, the café waitress Kelly), and the face of women who had undergone female circumcision (Darol Mahmada the activist who confronts her kyai father, as well as other women).

Ragat'e Anak is the most gut-wrenching and riveting of four very brave and challenging films, because we are brought intimately into the lives of Mira and Nur, and see how their labor, for the sake of their children, takes a toll on their own health and well-being. The first scene opens with Nur sitting under the blazing hot sun, breaking stones in a bright red T-shirt, providing a contrast to the black-and-white infrared filming of her work at night in the Chinese graveyard. Because this footage is infrared, the men and women's eyes become like shiny points, their expressions eerily visible to us viewers. The world of illegal prostitution has been transformed into a society of ghosts or walking dead. We recognize Nur and yet we don't recognize her, as she clucks at potential clients. Like an X-ray, these images are the inverse of the representation of the national ideology of what it means to be a perfect mother.

The exotic sexual availability of the figure of the Indonesian woman, so typified in Paul Gauguin's figure of Annah la Javanaise, along with the nineteenth-century romanticism of Gustave Courbet's *The Stone Breakers* (1849–50), a work of social realism that scandalized Salon visitors of Paris, are collapsed, deconstructed, and detonated in the final fourth film of *Pertaruhan* in the person of Nur of *Ragat'e Anak*, a stout, hard-working woman, who sits on the ground breaking stones with her bare hands while her toddler daughter plays nearby (figure 4.7). Nur explains that she can make forty dollars a month breaking stones into pebbles, and the rest of the money that she needs to feed her children and send them to school comes from prostitution, which comes to a dollar a client.

Another stone breaker/prostitute, the slender, younger Mira, talks about the man that she lives with, her companion or *kiwir*, a gangster who extorts prostitutes for money. The women's proximity to death—they literally are selling sex on graves—creates a visual death world in which they are threatened by police raids that force them to run away in the dark, violent clients, and diseases, including HIV/AIDS. Near the end Mira has lost hope, and Nur consoles her: "Think of your parents and kid. It's sinful to think that way. Dying is human. We can't decide our lives. God does." The women are matter-of-fact and honest about their lives. We see Nur coming home after midnight and picking up her daughter from the babysitter. "Of course, I'm tired. I collect and break pebbles during the day. And I work in the graveyard at night. But what else am I going to do? I do this for my kids. To get them through school. I don't want my kids to drop out of school. I don't want my kids to have the kind of life I'm having." Then we return to Nur sitting on the ground, breaking stone in her bright red shirt. It echoes the opening shot of this final film of the omnibus, and we hear her voice-over again: "I want my children to be educated and useful human beings. I hope they have a better life."

For the premiere of the movie in Jakarta, Mira and Nur took a break from their usual daily routine of breaking stones and working the graveyard to attend. This meant that they would have to make the long trip by train to Jakarta and stay in a hotel. After the end of the premiere screening, the Jakarta audience applauded Mira and Nur during the question-and-answer time.

FIGURE 4.7 Nur breaks stones in *Ragat'e Anak* (*For the Sake of the Kids*), directed by Ucu Agustin, from the omnibus film *Pertaruhan* (*At Stake*, 2008), produced by Nia Dinata.

Having seen themselves on the screen, Mira and Nur's reaction was that they had never realized how hard their lives were, or had the time to reflect on their own individual female experience. Happiness was not a right, or something to be expected, and neither was self-reflection.

Although it is not uncommon for a documentary to be a collaboration of different voices, *Pertaruhan* was intended to be a commercial feature film, exhibited in major theaters all across Indonesia, but the filmmakers did the further work of enabling a more collective viewing and interpreting environment in the form of the roadshow. In the United States, commercial documentary films are marketed in theaters as the work of a (usually) male genius. In the classic history of documentary, historian Erik Barnouw divided documentary directors into implicitly male character types, including explorer, reporter, advocate, bugler, prosecutor, chronicler, promoter, observer, catalyst, guerrilla, and discoverer.[48] The antithesis of this would be a working collective, an omnibus film with four stories by five different filmmakers whose names only appear at the end of the film. Like the filmmaker who films the scene of herself getting a Pap smear, while being scolded by the censorious patriarchal prayer-intoning doctor who would deny her medical care, in the omnibus films produced by Dinata, the object of visual biopolitics is also the subject of resistance.

Michel Foucault states that it is racism that provides the norm, the necessary prerequisite that allows for the taking of another's life, that may just be due to exposure or vulnerability to death, or political demise and exclusion.[49] We have seen that since 1965 anyone labeled leftist in Indonesia could be imprisoned, murdered, raped, tortured, or otherwise exposed to death, but we can also see biopolitics at work in more mundane, daily examples, like how Indonesian women's sexuality is constricted in a way that does not allow them to determine their own health, as the Dinata-produced films *Berbagi Suami, Perempuan Punya Cerita,* and *Pertaruhan* all reveal. The violence of visual biopolitics can be very clearly, outwardly violent, but violence can also be implicit in the mundane effects of visual biopolitics.

One point where the body and the state meet as a matter for discipline and a matter for regularization is sexuality. Dinata's films explore the cultural and state use of biopolitics to contain, survey, study, and control the body, and as a means to manage life and death. These films reveal the tensions and the hypocrisies behind the regularization and the discipline of sexuality. In *Berbagi Suami* we see how polygamy can affect the health of the family differently in rich families versus poor families, in the story of the shared sexually transmitted disease that infects all four wives in the family that lives in the slum. Polygamy affects the physical health of the wives but also their children. In the story of Ruwati in *Pertaruhan* we see how mores against any kind of penetration of a woman's vagina by anyone other than her husband could mean that her health is affected, in this instance because a tumor in the uterus cannot be monitored, because a woman's virginity needs to be kept intact if she is still unmarried. Unmarried women, rich and poor, are denied Pap smears, to the point where a woman is afraid to get physically checked if she is not married, and we even follow a woman, who is a lesbian and anti-penetration, to her first appointment for a Pap smear. Transnational female work is revealed to break up families and keeps mothers from children. A girl vulnerable to sexual assault is also vulnerable to sex trafficking in *Perempuan Punya Cerita,* and the wife of a drug addict who has died of AIDS and infected her is rejected by the family and the community and denied her own child, due to mores around shame, and has also become vulnerable to early death. *Pertaruhan* uncovers the secrecy of female circumcision, and all the possible health and political issues involved. Finally the figure of the stonebreaker/ prostitute/mother in *Pertaruhan* belies the myth of the sexually available good-time girl, la Javanaise. Many women leave the village, creating a market for illegal prostitution and thus spreading HIV from the husbands left behind to the transnational female workers when they return to Indonesia. In so many ways, these films produced by Nia Dinata resist visual biopolitics.

In this sense Dinata's films uncover the three aspects of visual biopolitics that I have described before: (1) how visual biopolitics is used by the state and by religion to discipline and regularize sexuality; (2) how the norm is visualized by culture and the state, from the point of view of the person doing the scanning (think, for example, of the disapproving doctor intoning the Lord's Prayer as he takes a Pap smear) as well as the filmmakers (it is Cinzia, after all, who is part of the filmmaking team, getting the Pap smear done, and who films with a hidden camera); and (3) how the shards of an identity that is labeled evil, such as female sexuality, are pieced back together into a collective, agentive "we."

In this book I have delineated how Gauguin's painting turned the pain of a young girl without parents into a sexualized myth; how documentary can be used to reenact genocide for the titillation of Western viewers unaware of their own complicity; how the archive of colonial footage could be unsettled and put to work in a different way in *Mother Dao*; and finally, how the collective approach to filmmaking and storytelling in the omnibus film can interrogate women's sexuality and thus women's health in resistance to governmental, cultural, and religious expectations and regulation.

Nia Dinata was part of an efflorescence of independent film production after the Reformasi in Indonesia, a period in which protestors demanded the overthrow of Suharto and his crony New Order generals, free general elections, and an end to corruption in the form of cartels and monopolies. Under the guidance of Dinata and with the support of her production company, the omnibus film became a place for a collective coming together of filmmakers.

Film independan mirrored the collective activism that led to the Reformasi era. New film festivals were founded all around the country. The promise of this filmmaking is how it can provide a different model than auteur filmmaking that promotes homo economicus. Movies coming out of the film independan movement, especially Dinata's work, involve the network—particularly the producer as part of a network that incorporates and encourages other voices, not just those of other directors, but below the line and the very subjects of the films.

Thus, from *Berbagi Suami* to *Perempuan Punya Cerita* and *Pertaruhan*, Dinata's filmmaking is not about heroes or auteur geniuses, but about collectives. Dinata herself lauds the idea of how the early founders of Indonesia put forward not an ideology built on one particular religion, but the idea of unity in diversity. The moderate generation of Nia Dinata believes in a new Indonesia, one that they helped usher in with the election of President Joko Widodo in 2015 and again in 2019.

Another key aspect of Dinata's films is how she remakes the idea of documentary, in terms of how it is understood, both in Indonesia and more generally in regard to the genre itself. Thus, in the Reformasi period, Dinata's work contributed to an overhaul of how documentary was produced and treated. The divide between fiction and documentary becomes fluid in Dinata's collaborative producing: she shows how fiction film can include and address real people's experiences through innovative research and collaboration in the production process. Research is essential. For the first film, Dinata researched polygamy across different classes, from the elite Jakartans, to the slums of Jakarta, and among the ethnic Chinese. *Perempuan Punya Cerita* gathered together the producers and directors to conduct research, visiting clinics, talking to teenagers in Yogyakarta about teenage sex, and posing as potential buyers of children in the city of Indramayu. In a kind of reaction to the overthrow of the New Order, Indonesian filmmakers wanted to try all kinds of genres, as long as they could raise sufficient funds to produce the films. Karen Strassler elegantly uses the term "refraction" to talk about how ordinary Javanese people use and look at photographs. In this process, "everyday encounters with photographs entangle widely shared visions with affectively charged personal narratives and memories."[50] In a sense, then, Dinata is using film to refract the history that is normally told and to allow different voices to gain access to expression. It is a kind of active refraction about politics, history, sexuality, and a means of resisting visual biopolitics.

To conclude, the method of storytelling and filmmaking Dinata has promoted provides only one model for resisting visual biopolitics: differing forms of subjectivity are explored, not just in the content of the films but also in their actual production, distribution, and exhibition. As I have explained, in Indonesian, there are many ways of saying "I." One common way, which is rooted in a cultural humility that eschews arrogance and egoism, is to use the inclusive "we," or "kami," which means "I the speaker and the others who stand with me." In Dinata's approach to filmmaking we have a continuation of this diffusion of subjectivity: many authors, depicting many classes, ethnicities, and sexualities, and using many types of venues to bring the film to diverse audiences who pay in movie theaters or who are nonpaying in community centers and schools.

Project Change! workshops continue to be held every two years, and have produced not just the omnibus features *Pertaruhan* and *Working Girls* but also short documentary films that tend to be shown together in film festivals and in roadshows at universities and community centers. One such film is *Emak dari Jambi* (2015), directed by Anggun Pradesha and Rikki M. Fajar, which follows Ibu Kurtini, a mother from Jambi, Sumatra, as she reunites with her firstborn child, Anggun (and also the director), who is *waria* (transgender) and lives in Jakarta (figure 4.8). Anggun is vain, vulnerable, loving, and fierce toward her naive and uncomprehending mama; both learn to create a different kind of mother-daughter relationship. Well-crafted and visually exciting, the works coming out of Project Change! span the gap between realism and documentary; the first-time filmmakers are honest, funny, flamboyant, and unafraid to shed light on the chasms of class, gender, labor, sexuality, and health. These are films that smash down norms by exploring tales of souls seeking authenticity and acceptance. Near the end of *Emak dari Jambi*, we see Anggun and her mother along with Anggun's friends laughing and standing by the sign for Taman Lawang, an infamous nocturnal pickup location for transgender prostitutes in Jakarta (figure 4.9). The suffering and oppression of these waria, a familiar representation, is undeniable, but so is the way that they protect each other and nourish each other, as a chosen family.

EPILOGUE: NIGHT SONG

In 2009, I was invited to join Nia Dinata and her team for a roadshow to Bali for *Pertaruhan*. The film was screened at night in Den Pasar to a packed audience, and the directors and producers patiently spoke to and debated with the women's groups and government organizations in Bali that came to the screening and to the workshop held the day after the screening. Such roadshows of the film are as important to Kalyana Shira as getting theatrical distribution or taking it to the Berlin Film Festival.

After the last event was over, we took a night flight back to Jakarta. As we drove back from the airport packed in a van, we were still excited from the trip and from the encounters we had had, even though our flight had been delayed, the traffic was congested, and we were late coming home. All of a sudden we remembered that it was going to be August 17 the next day, Independence Day, and, as if on cue, all of us broke out into song, as if we were giddy children coming home from a school outing: national songs like the anthem "Hallo Bandung," and regional songs that had once been taught in school in languages like Batak and Padang. These were the songs that children had learned during Suharto's regime, when education was only

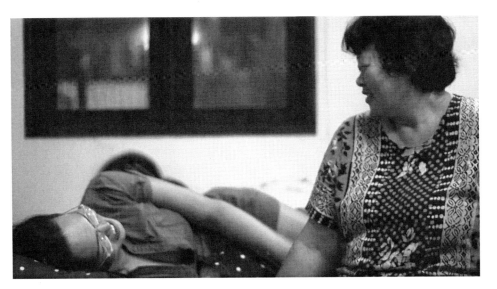

FIGURE 4.8 Anggun and her mother Kurtini in a scene from the documentary short *Emak dari Jambi* (*Mother from Jambi*, 2015), directed by Anggun Pradesha and Rikki M. Fajar, produced by Nia Dinata.

FIGURE 4.9 Anggun, her mother Kurtini, and her friends hang out at the sign for Taman Lawang in Jakarta in a scene from the documentary short *Emak dari Jambi* (*Mother from Jambi*, 2015), directed by Anggun Pradesha and Rikki M. Fajar, produced by Nia Dinata.

in Indonesian. (On the other hand, we also sang Queen's "Bohemian Rhapsody." Freddie Mercury has long been a major icon in Indonesia.)

That excitement and that giddiness tap into a vein—call it faith—that runs deep in these endeavors to make collective documentary feature films. Even as the filmmakers are critical of the medical system and a growing conservatism in Indonesia, even stronger is a deep and abiding concern for a country and a people wracked with the traumas and scars of decades of colonialism, occupation, and military autocracy. The desire to make such films does not stem from a drive for fame or notoriety, and certainly not for riches, but is instead a desire to take a stand and call out the complexity of what it means to be Indonesian and a woman in the twenty-first century. Like Bonnie's joy in driving Ade home after her first Pap smear, crowing that it feels like Nationalist Awakening Day, there is a joy in the making of collective films like *Pertaruhan* that is revelatory and transformative, something which, at the end of the day, causes one to break into song with gratitude, and with something akin to love.

The Fourth Eye

I began this book by talking about the fourth eye, exemplified by the impossibly knowing gaze of the African American girl Dae'anna watching her mother confront the police officer who killed her mother's boyfriend, Philando Castile, in 2016. The fourth eye witnesses how one's family and self must constantly negotiate being, possession, and vulnerability to rape and death, as a person of color who is vilified as other by the dominant society.

When the mother sees herself and her boyfriend Philando being seen by the police officer as black, and therefore vulnerable to violence and death, she is seeing her situation with a third eye.

The fourth eye witnesses that constitution of the third eye. The fourth eye not only sees that the emperor has no clothes, she sees that everyone is pretending that the emperor does have clothes. The fourth eye is profoundly collective: an inclusive "we," a communal "I," a black daughter comforting—and observing—her mother and how she constitutes herself in the face of police violence and a nation's visual biopolitics. The fourth eye requires us to be both the patient and the doctor: the patient who has to constantly explain

FIGURE C1 View of studio. Still from *Annah la Javanaise* (2020), directed by Fatimah Tobing Rony, visual and animation direction by Ariel Victor, sound design and score by Aghi Narottama.

FIGURE C2 Annah escapes. Still from *Annah la Javanaise* (2020), directed by Fatimah Tobing Rony, visual and animation direction by Ariel Victor, sound design and score by Aghi Narottama.

to the doctor what that psychic trauma is and what is required to heal from that.

The fourth eye is found in a still Javanese dancer whose trembling middle finger references the beating hearts of the revenants of dancers mysteriously killed in order to bolster official history; in a filmmaker whose collective films expose the visual biopolitics used against Indonesian women's sexuality; and in a thirteen-year-old girl, a putative Javanese model and maid—a being, a spirit—whose gaze beckons one across the centuries to become a witness to what happened to her, and whose pose is in itself a protection against visual biopolitics.

This book is also the fourth eye. As a writer and as a filmmaker, I yearn to be done with seeing future and past and present selves caught in a visuality (of display, painting, photography, and film) that is inextricably linked to biopolitics, colonialism, globalization, and neoliberalism, even as I know that one book is not going to change all that, overnight.

And yet let us continue the reckoning.

How do we look?

We look back. We resist. We reclaim.

And we create.

Notes

INTRODUCTION

1 Fauser, *Musical Encounters at the 1889 Paris Worlds Fair*, 168.
2 Sylvia Wynter refers to Man2 or homo economicus as a global phenomenon. The ravaging of the Earth, which has led to climate change, was not accomplished by North America and Europe alone. See McKittrick and Wynter, "Unparalleled Catastrophe for Our Species?," 20.
3 Baldwin, "My Dungeon Shook," 9.
4 I am inspired by an interview of Ava DuVernay, who said this about her series *When They See Us* on the boys who were unjustly accused in the 1989 Central Park Jogger case, "What kinds of boys truly get to be young and carefree, and what others are indicted on sight?" Kahn, "Let the Record Show," 74.
5 I thank Patricia White for her clarification and insight on this point.
6 Lepore, "The Public Historian."
7 Foucault, *The History of Sexuality*, vol. 1, 138–39. Foucault writes, "One might say that the ancient right to *take* life or *let* live was replaced by a power to *foster* life or *disallow* it to the point of death" (138).
8 Here Foucault alludes to the diffuse nature of killing of biopolitics: "Sovereignty took life and let live. And now we have the emergence of a power that I would call the power of regularization, and it, in contrast consists in making live and letting die." Foucault, "Society Must Be Defended," 67.

9   Foucault, "Society Must Be Defended," 256. The norm that goes into effect is racialization. Foucault declares that racism is a basic mechanism of power: "If you are functioning in the biopower mode, how can you justify the need to kill people, to kill populations, and to kill civilizations? By using the themes of evolutionism, by appealing to a racism" (257).

10 US examples of states of exception would include the incarceration of Japanese Americans in US camps during World War II, and the Patriot Act enacted by George W. Bush in 2001, which allowed the attorney general to take aliens into custody and suspend all their rights. See Agamben, *State of Exception*, 3, 22.

11 McKittrick and Wynter, "Unparalleled Catastrophe for Our Species?," 11.

12 Rony, *The Third Eye*, 7.

13 Ironically, the limit to Foucault's and subsequent theories of biopolitics is that of race. Alexander Weheliye brilliantly points out that the conceptualization of biopower takes the Holocaust as the exceptional limit. See Weheliye, *Habeas Viscus*, 53–73.

14 Sylvia Wynter in McKittrick, and Wynter, "Unparalleled Catastrophe for Our Species?," 31. Political scientist Wendy Brown describes how life and death are inextricably linked to homo economicus, the new neoliberal subject, as a formation in which market values are extended to all aspects of social life in Brown, *Undoing the Demos*.

15 Wynter, in McKittrick and Wynter, "Unparalleled Catastrophe for Our Species?," 20 (emphasis in original).

16 Mbembe, "Necropolitics," 28.

17 Gilmore, *Golden Gulag*, 261.

18 Daulatzai, *Fifty Years of the Battle of Algiers*.

19 Larasati, *The Dance That Makes You Vanish*, 99.

20 Pandolfo, "The Thin Line of Modernity."

21 Rony, *The Third Eye*.

22 Taub, "We Have No Choice," 47.

23 Hartman, "Venus in Two Acts," 11.

24 As Marcia Chatelain argues, the fact that black girls (or Indonesian girls) are undertheorized in history does not mean that they should be ignored. Chatelain, *South Side Girls*, 6.

25 Alexander, *The New Jim Crow*; DuVernay, *13th*.

26 Baldwin and Mead, *A Rap on Race*, 189.

27 The film *No Más Bebés* (dir. Renee Tajima-Peña, 2015) follows Maria Hurtado and others more than forty years later as they visit the place where their lives were ruined: the deserted skeleton of a maternity ward where they were sterilized against their will. What determined that the Latinas in *No Más Bebés* should be sterilized was not just the hospital, the doctors, the administrators, or a government policy, but a whole US culture that was obsessed with population control and saw the Mexican as less than human. African American women, Puerto Rican women, and poor white women in other parts of

the United States were also sterilized against their will, based on the belief that their fertility must be terminated. This is what Foucault describes as both a disciplining of bodies and a focus on the species body, the regulation of populations through intervention and regulatory controls.

28 Another example of the consequences of visual biopolitics is the response of law enforcement to the murders along the Highway of Tears, a section of Highway 16 in British Columbia, where a disproportionate number of indigenous Canadian women have gone missing every year since 1969. The area lacks public transportation, so many locals rely on hitchhiking. Over the decades, many indigenous women have been murdered or disappeared, their bodies found many months or years later, abandoned in the thick forest bordering this highway. Police response has been lackadaisical at best, and for over forty years the cases have gone uninvestigated and the women's deaths officially attributed to accident, suicide, or drug overdose. As the survivors explain, when an Indian woman goes missing, the police refuse to investigate (she remains unseen; no poster is made, no search begun, and she remains unnamed, invisible), but when a white woman goes missing, signs are immediately posted with the woman's name and photo, asking for information (her face is seen, her name made known; she is made visible, a search ensues). See Levin, "Dozens of Women Vanish." The brutal murder of Savanna LaFontaine-Greywind in 2017 sparked protests in indigenous communities in the United States and Canada, leading to the fight for new legislation protecting Native American women. See Monet, "A Native American Woman's Brutal Murder"; Dunne, "No More Stolen Sisters."

29 I thank Kristen Hatch for this insight.

30 Mulvey, "Visual Pleasure and Narrative Cinema," 837–48.

31 Foucault, *Manet and the Object of Painting*.

32 Michele Wallace decries the invisibility of black female creativity and black female critical thought, and interrogates the notion that the black hole represents the dense accumulation, without explanation or inventory, of black feminist creativity. Wallace, "Variations on Negation," 214–18.

33 Baldwin, "My Dungeon Shook." I thank Gonzalo Lamana for his insight on the letter to James Baldwin's nephew and for bringing my attention to this point.

34 Lim, "Serial Time."

35 The continuation of the Orientalizing myths of Java, Bali, and Sumatra found in nineteenth-century universal exposition pavilions informs Indonesian nationalism as well as contemporary documentaries by US auteurs. For example, the notion of the good mother, extolled under the Suharto regime and a continuing ideal in the present day, was exemplified by nineteenth-century Javanese writer Kartini, known as Ibu Kartini (or Mother Kartini). Ibu Kartini's goodness is the counterpart of the wickedness of the Gerwani sexual dancer; this dyad ultimately upholds and bolsters the state's version of Indonesian history, and it had repercussions for Jumilah. The myth of Java as atemporal, courtly, refined kingdom is key to both anthropological discourse and to the

creation of the Indonesian government post-Sukarno, who borrowed the symbols of Javanese power that were perfected under Dutch colonialism and used them for his own regime. Java was key to the nineteenth century, evidenced by the Javanese village of dancers displayed at the 1889 World's Fair, which was connected to the colonial South Sea adventures necessary for the myth of Paul Gauguin. Another key role is that of the myth of Bali, as the source of modernist European painting (the Russian-born painter Walter Spies, the Mexican painter Miguel Covarrubias) and film (André Roosevelt's *Goona-Goona* and Mead and Bateson's *Trance and Dance in Bali*) and the cover-up of the massacres in Bali during the 1965 killings. I trace the Indonesian woman from the Dutch exoticizing of the colonial image that led to the 1889 Exposition Universelle that eventually named Annah, to the dancer in Mead's and Oppenheimer's films and discussed by Rachmi Diyah Larasati, to the women and men recontextualized in found-footage film of the early twentieth century, to the twenty-first-century omnibus films produced by Nia Dinata.

36 McKittrick and Wynter, "Unparalleled Catastrophe for Our Species?," 23.

CHAPTER ONE: ANNAH LA JAVANAISE

1 Brettell, "The Return to France," 306–7. I am indebted to Kathleen McHugh, Grace Hong, and Jenny Sharpe for their comments on a paper I gave at UCLA in 2010 on the topic of Annah la Javanaise, as well as to Kellie Jones, Carol Ockman, Angela Dalle Vacche, Bliss Cua Lim, and Kristen Hatch.

2 Baudelaire, "The Painter of Modern Life," 13.

3 Frèches-Thory, "The Exhibition at Durand-Ruel," 85.

4 Sweetman, *Paul Gauguin*, 372.

5 Frèches-Thory, "The Exhibition at Durand-Ruel," 87.

6 Vollard, *Recollections of a Picture Dealer*, 173.

7 Slavery was abolished in 1848, so there was no legal slavery in France in the 1890s, but the term "négresse" had the connotation of "female slave." In fact, an example of the use of "négresse" was written by Gauguin's grandmother, Flora Tristan: "It is established that all women can go out alone; most of them followed by a female slave [une négresse], but it isn't obligatory." Tristan, "Les Femmes de Lima" (my translation). The word is currently considered derogatory. When Dominique Strauss-Kahn went to trial for taking part in parties with prostitutes, the women were referred to as "négresses," "material," and "dossiers," by the Lille businessman who had secured the women for his parties, such that "négresses" become indistinguishable from the goods. See Day, "Strauss-Kahn in the Dock."

8 Vollard, *Recollections of a Picture Dealer*, 173.

9 Compare the United Kingdom, which raised the age of consent from thirteen to sixteen in 1885. Hatch, *Shirley Temple and the Performance of Girlhood*, 14.

10 Solnit, *A Field Guide to Getting Lost*, 59.

11 On the serial equalization of women, see Lim, "Serial Time."

12 Heath, "Narrative Space," 36.

13 Heath, "Narrative Space," 35.

14 Kluver and Martin, *Kiki's Paris*, 189.

15 Teilhet-Fisk, *Paradise Reviewed*, 99.

16 Gauguin, *My Father, Paul Gauguin*, 203.

17 Cited in Field, "Gauguin's Noa Noa Suite," 503.

18 J. Mucha, *Alphonse Mucha: His Life and Art*, 122–23.

19 Julien Tiersot, *Le Ménestrel* 55 (1889): 165–66, at 165, translated by Annegret Fauser, in Fauser, *Musical Encounters at the 1889 Paris World's Fair*, 146. Fauser's book convincingly delineates how racial theory became engaged with theories of music.

20 Fauser, *Musical Encounters at the 1889 Paris World's Fair*, 10.

21 Jonnes, *Eiffel's Tower*, 119.

22 Fauser, *Musical Encounters at the 1889 Paris World's Fair*, 168.

23 "Échos de Paris," *L'Événement*, August 27, 1889, 1, as quoted and translated by Fauser, *Musical Encounters at the 1889 Paris World's Fair*, 171.

24 Jonnes, *Eiffel's Tower*, 119.

25 Judith Gautier, *Les Musiques Bizarres à l'Exposition de 1900*, 5, in Fauser, *Musical Encounters at the 1889 Paris World's Fair*, 171.

26 Jean-Pierre Chazal, "'Grand Succès pour les Exotiques': Retour sur les spectacles javanais de l'Exposition Universelle de Paris en 1889," *Archipel* 63 (2002): 134–36, in Fauser, *Musical Encounters at the 1889 Paris World's Fair*, 166.

27 Fauser, *Musical Encounters at the 1889 Paris World's Fair*, 174.

28 Danielsson, *Gauguin in the South Seas*, 154. Danielsson refers to Annah as "a young half-caste girl, Indian and Malay." He writes, "Anna's [sic] false certificate of origin must have called forth pleasant memories of the Universal Exhibition in 1889, when Gauguin had paid frequent visits to the Javanese village there."

29 From Gauguin, *Letters to His Wife and Friends*, 118. The letter in French can be found in Letter to Émile Bernard undated (Paris, March 1889) in Gauguin, *Lettres de Gauguin à sa Femme et à Ses Amis*, 157.

30 And he was not the only one to have a dalliance with a native villager. At least one Frenchwoman ran off with one of the Wild West Indians of the Buffalo Bill show. Jonnes, *Eiffel's Tower*, 132.

31 Elizabeth Childs sees Gauguin's use of photography as a control over time, a control over "collapse in the wake of Western imperialism." She argues that he prefers photography to the real. Childs, "The Colonial Lens," 52, 60, 64.

32 Rony, *The Third Eye*, 6, 24. Seeing anthropology is how the exotic is already known when we see a life group at a museum, or watch an early ethnographic film, but it also refers to the gaze of performers in an ethnographic film or at a museum or world's fair, seeing themselves being seen.

33 Foucault, *The History of Sexuality*, vol. 1, 146.

34 Foucault, *The History of Sexuality*, vol. 1, 147.

35 My translation.

36 Foucault, *The History of Sexuality*, vol. 1, 136.

37 Stoler, *Race and the Education of Desire*, 194. Stoler argues that the Stratz pornographic racial taxonomy, *Women in Java*, "was a discourse and a domain of knowledge that was productive of, and responsive to, taxonomies of power and a range of desires that articulated unevenly with the multiple hierarchies of nation, gender, race, and class" (188).

38 See Clark, "Preliminaries to a Possible Treatment of 'Olympia'"; Clark, *The Painting of Modern Life*; and O'Grady, "Olympia's Maid."

39 Foucault, *Manet and the Object of Painting*, 44. For more on Victorine Meurent, see Lipton, *Alias Olympia*.

40 O'Grady, "Olympia's Maid," 15.

41 Grigsby, "Thinking about Olympia's Maid." Grigsby details the pervasive hostility that the French held toward the "négresse": "A dictionary of argot or slang informs us that 'ugly' could be signified by the phrase 'wet nursed by a monkey.' In nineteenth-century Paris, a bottle of red wine could be called an eggplant, a beet, a peony, or a Negress. To drink a bottle of red wine was to stifle, suffocate, or strangle a choirboy or a Negress.... This was another aspect of life in Paris for the free black woman negotiating hatred, indifference, desirability, dehumanization, fashionability, desexualization, and violence, and all for a wage" (447–48).

42 The history of the term "négresse" is usually assumed only to be women of African descent, but the term was used to refer to any female who was not white or East Asian. Huey Copeland's essay, "In the Wake of the Negress," explores the term's genealogy and the representation of the "négresse" in order to conceive of a way to include African American producers whose work is excluded from the art world of the West. Without the "négresse" there is no modernism, and yet her work in the museum is barely exhibited.

43 Brettell, "The Return to France," *Art of Paul Gauguin*, 306–7.

44 Rony, *The Third Eye*, 21–44.

45 Childs, "The Colonial Lens," 57.

46 Childs, "The Colonial Lens," 58–65.

47 Childs, "The Colonial Lens," 52.

48 Childs, "The Colonial Lens," 64.

49 Childs, "The Colonial Lens," 60.

50 Achille Mbembe argues that savage life is seen as animal life, "a horrifying experience, something alien beyond imagination or comprehension. In fact, according to Arendt, what makes the savages different from other human beings is less the color of their skin than the fear that they behave like a part of nature, that they treat nature as their undisputed master." Mbembe, "Necropolitics," 23.

51 The verso has a *Study for Aita tamari vahine Judith te parari* that art historian Richard Brettell discusses, in which we see the naked figure of Annah in the painting, reclining on a chair, yet with her head cut off, which leads Brettell to date *Reclining Nude* as after the *Study for Aita tamari vahine Judith te parari*. Brettell, "The Return to France," catalog number 161, 308.

52 Brettell, "The Return to France," catalog number 162, 308–9. I agree with Brettell that it is likely a study of Annah la Javanaise, who wore earrings like

that (his Tahitian models tended to be painted less androgynously, and with flowers in their hair, rather than earrings). Her features are also very different, not too dissimilar from photographs of Annah la Javanaise.

53 This watercolor monotype, *Reclining Tahitian*, was shown at the Museum of Modern Art exhibition *Metamorphoses*, and the curator, Starr Figura, informed me that she believes it is a counterproof made from the pastel, *Reclining Nude*, so it would be the same model, probably Annah la Javanaise. In correspondence Ms. Figura wrote, "The title, like a lot of Gauguin's titles, was probably applied by a dealer or gallery at some point and then handed down from there, so not a title from Gauguin himself. There are other works on paper that have such generic titles and include the word 'Tahitian' despite the fact that the work itself does not actually depict a Tahitian" (Starr Figura, email to the author, May 9, 2014).

54 Scholars such as Peter Brooks and Rod Edmond have commented on the homosexual tension in *Noa Noa*, noting both Gauguin's own attraction to a young male in *Noa Noa* and the fact that Gauguin may have been taken for a *mahu*, or male transvestite. Edmond, *Representing the South Pacific*, 252; and Brooks, "Gauguin's Tahitian Body." Stephen Eisenman in *Gauguin's Skirt* theorizes that Gauguin embraced the idea of the "mahu," as a liminal androgynous subjectivity.

55 Discussed in Sweetman, *Paul Gauguin*, 312; and Charles F. Stuckey with Peter Zegers, catalog number 8 in Brettell, "The Return to France," 28–29.

56 Brettell, "The Return to France," *Art of Paul Gauguin*, 309. Brettell argues that the model in *Manao Tupapao* has a stronger sexual identity than the more androgynous model of *Reclining Nude*.

57 Jarry and Pollock, *Avant-Garde Gambits*, 20–21.

58 Paul Gauguin, *Noa Noa par Gauguin*, ed. Jean Loize (Paris, 1966), 24.

59 Paul Gauguin, *Noa Noa*, Louvre MS, 109–10, as quoted by Richard Brettell, catalog number 154, in Brettell, *The Art of Paul Gauguin*, 280.

60 O'Brien, *The Pacific Muse*, 221.

61 O'Brien, *The Pacific Muse*, 221.

62 Claire Fréches-Thory in Brettell, *The Art of Paul Gauguin*, 195–97.

63 Sweetman, *Paul Gauguin*, 261.

64 Sweetman, *Paul Gauguin*, 359.

65 Brettell, *The Art of Paul Gauguin*, 492–94. The man is identified as Belgian painter Meyer de Haan.

66 Lim, "Serial Time."

67 Solomon-Godeau, "Going Native: Paul Gauguin and the Invention of Primitivist Modernism."

68 Bongie, *Exotic Memories*, 77. See also Matthews, *Paul Gauguin: An Erotic Life*; Eisenman, *Gauguin's Skirt*; and Edmond, *Representing the South Pacific*.

69 Trachtenberg, *Reading American Photographs*, 56.

70 Essays of identification in film theory abound. One example is Wollen, "Godard and Counter Cinema," 79–91.

71 S. Mucha, *Alphonse Mucha*, 155.

72 Mucha, known for his Art Nouveau paintings, made several series of photographs in the late 1890s, in particular of female models who posed for him in his studio at the rue du Val-du-Grâce, but these photographs appear to have been taken before his move to that larger studio. Many artists at that time used photographs as preliminary studies. Art historians including Petr Wittlich have seen in his photographs works that show the spirit of the studio at the time, which was also apparently the site of the first cinematic projection by the Lumière brothers. Petr Wittlich, "Photographs in the Studio," in S. Mucha, *Alphonse Mucha*. See also Jan Mleoch, "The Legacy of Mucha's Photographs," in S. Mucha, *Alphonse Mucha*, 119.

73 J. Mucha, *Alphonse Mucha*, 54–55. Both Mucha and Wittlich identify the sitter as Gauguin. Wittlich, "Photographs in the Studio," 116.

74 Kluver and Martin, *Kiki's Paris*, 189.

75 J. Mucha, *Alphonse Mucha*, 54–55.

76 Thank you to Tomoko Sato, the curator at the Mucha Museum, for sharing with me information on these photographs by Mucha.

77 Frèches-Thory, "The Exhibition at Durand-Ruel," 87.

78 Sweetman, *Paul Gauguin*, 377.

79 Sweetman, *Paul Gauguin*, 378.

80 Sweetman, *Paul Gauguin*, has the plate after 440, "Judith around 1896," Collection Thomas Millroth, Stockholm.

81 Sweetman, *Paul Gauguin*, 379.

82 Cited in Sweetman, *Paul Gauguin*, 379.

83 Judith Gérard, *Mémoires*, MS in the possession of Dr. Gerda Kjellberg, Stockholm, as quoted in Danielsson, *Gauguin in the South Seas*, 150–51.

84 I thank Bliss Cua Lim for this insight.

85 *Noa Noa*, 16, as quoted in Edmond, Rod. *Representing the South Pacific: Colonial Discourse from Cook to Gauguin*. Cambridge: Cambridge University Press, 1997, 249.

86 Gauguin, *Noa Noa*, Louvre MS, 23, as quoted in Edmond, *Representing the South Pacific*, 250.

87 Similar to the colonial officer in the George Orwell short story, "Shooting an Elephant," the colonizer is intimidated by being gazed at by the natives. But the inversion also deflects the colonialist desire to rape the girls. Rony, *The Third Eye*, 42.

88 Gauguin, *Noa Noa*, 34–35.

89 Danielsson, *Gauguin in the South Seas*, 190–91.

90 Solomon-Godeau, "Going Native," 316–17, 323.

91 Solomon-Godeau, "Going Native," 323.

92 I thank Kristen Hatch for this insight.

93 Asad, *On Suicide Bombing*, 14.

94 Even Gayatri Spivak cannot end her tale without tracing the story of the non-menstruating body of the suicidal "hapless" Bhubanesari in her famed essay, "Can the Subaltern Speak?"

95 Patty O'Brien discusses how these girls were Gauguin's "muses" who were also expected to "meet all his needs: sexual, aesthetic, and domestic—while remaining pliant and undemanding of him." She calls Gauguin the "epitome of the enviable 'sexual tourist,' who openly lived out the sexual fantasy of his artistic images." O'Brien, *The Pacific Muse*, 220–21.

96 Frèches-Thory, "The Exhibition at Durand-Ruel," 86.

97 Gilmore, *Golden Gulag*, 261.

98 In a social media post, writer Joyce Maynard declared that she was not writer J. D. Salinger's mistress. She was already eighteen and a freshman at Yale in 1972 when J. D. Salinger saw her article in the *New York Times* and invited her to visit him in New Hampshire. She left college to live with him. A year later he pushed her out the door with two fifty-dollar bills in her hand and told her never to come back. Like Gauguin, Salinger had a predilection for short liaisons with teenage girls. But Maynard was a writer, and many years later, she decried how historians called her "Salinger's mistress." Stoeffel, "Joyce Maynard."

99 "What I want, in short, is that my (mobile) image, buffeted among a thousand shifting photographs, altering with situation and age, should always coincide with my (profound) 'self'; but it is the contrary that must be said: 'myself' never coincides with my image; for it is the image which is heavy, motionless, stubborn (which is why society sustains it), and 'myself' which is light, divided, dispersed." Barthes, *Camera Lucida*, 12.

100 Sweetman, *Paul Gauguin*, 377.

101 Sweetman, *Paul Gauguin*, 377.

102 Danielsson, *Gauguin in the South Seas*, 155.

103 Danielsson, *Gauguin in the South Seas*, 163.

104 Danielsson, *Gauguin in the South Seas*, 163.

105 Vollard, *Recollections of a Picture Dealer*, 173.

106 Gauguin, *Letters to His Wife and Friends*, 295–96.

107 Danielsson, *Gauguin in the South Seas*, 165.

108 Brettell, "The Return to France," 307.

109 Sweetman, *Paul Gauguin*, 408.

110 Sweetman, *Paul Gauguin*, 408.

111 Dowd, "A Goddess, a Mogul and a Mad Genius," SR1.

CHAPTER TWO: THE STILL DANCER

An earlier version of a section of chapter 2 originally appeared in "The Photogenic Cannot Be Tamed: Margaret Mead and Gregory Bateson's 'Trance and Dance in Bali,'" *Discourse* 28, no. 1 (Winter 2006): 5–27.

1 Rachmi Diyah Larasati reports that students in elementary school, middle school, and high school were required to watch the film on September 30 until at least 1999. Only in 2017 was there a change in law that prohibited elementary and middle school children from watching the film, due to its adult content (violence and sex).

2 In East Java where Rachmi Diyah Larasati was born, the torture, imprisoning, and killings of anyone labeled leftist continued well past 1965 into 1972. Most of the prisoners there were women.

3 Rony, *The Third Eye*, 21.

4 See Rony, *The Third Eye*, 106–7, 157, 178, 189, 213.

5 Rony, *The Third Eye*, 7–8.

6 This film helped to establish Mead's persona as a motherly ideal, writing columns for *Redbook* magazine, head of the American Museum of Natural History, and director of *Bathing Babies in Three Cultures* (1951), her next film. In this film, babies in Bali and New Guinea are shown being washed by their brisk, impersonal mothers, filmed in extreme long shot, outdoors, in stark contrast to the American babies (shown in close-up in their bathtubs), who in voice-over description and in mise-en-scène are allied with the Civilized.

7 Kate R. Pourshariati, email correspondence with author, from an unpublished manuscript dated July 17, 2015, now published: Kate R. Pourshariati, "Trance and Dance in Bali," National Film Registry Essay, National Film Preservation Board, Library of Congress, 2020, https://www.loc.gov/static/programs/national-film-preservation-board/documents/Trance-and-Dance-in-Bali.pdf.

8 "The obsessive consumption of images of a racialized Other known as the Primitive is usefully labeled fascinating cannibalism. By 'fascinating cannibalism' I mean to draw attention to the mixture of fascination and horror that the 'ethnographic' occasions: the 'cannibalism' is not that of the people who are labeled Savages, but that of the consumers of the images of the bodies—as well as actual bodies on display—of native peoples offered up by the popular media and science" (Rony, *The Third Eye*, 10).

9 It appears that Mead purposefully played up the medical/pathological appeal of the film. In a letter from Mead to Bateson on September 29, 1950, Mead states that she titled the film *Trance and Dance in Bali* because it "would attract both literary and psychological audiences." In a letter dated October 27, 1961, to Mr. Daniel Lesser, administrative assistant for the New York University Film Library, Mead asked why her films were not included in their catalog of psychology and mental health films. The films that Mead produced from Bateson and Mead's Bali footage of 1936–39 and from their New Guinea footage were quite lucrative. Many of the renters and buyers of the films were not universities but hospitals, medical associations, institutes for psychotherapy, museums, high schools, clinics, mental health organizations, nursing schools, libraries, and churches. See folder M20, Margaret Mead Archives, Manuscript Division, Library of Congress. I am grateful to the late Mary Margaret Wolfskill, whose knowledge and generosity as librarian of the Margaret Mead Collection at the Library of Congress made my research possible.

10 Rony, *The Third Eye*, 67.

11 Belo explained that they had records of trances of Pagoetan from November 1936 to January 1938 (Belo, *Trance in Bali*, 125). In a letter, Mead describes her frustration at the Balinese refusal to take psychological tests and calls them "schizy"

(Mead, Bajoeng Gede, Kintamini, S. Bali, letter to Tao, August 13, 1936, in box N23, Margaret Mead Archives, Manuscript Division, Library of Congress).

12 Belo, *Trance in Bali*, 129. As liberalizing as Belo's discourse is, like Mead and Bateson, she had an explanation for trance, which anthropologized it as a kind of false consciousness. Belo argued that trance responded to a fascination with the feeling of lowness: "Behavior that would be a degradation—animal-like behavior which the Balinese were careful to avoid in their current manners, and which was even institutionalized as a punishment for incest—becomes in the trance state pleasurable and delightful" (223).

13 Mead, *Blackberry Winter*, 231. Here Mead alludes to Rawa, the intermediary, as having made this decision, although she does not directly name him.

14 Pollmann, "Margaret Mead's Balinese," 10.

15 Pollman, "Margaret Mead's Balinese," 18.

16 What André Roosevelt called the goona goona (black magic). Rony, *The Third Eye*, 148.

17 Ironically now due to the cheapness of travel and a very popular Green School founded by North American jewelers John and Cynthia Hardy, the area near Ubud, known for its court dancing, music, and arts, is many months out of the year majority white, with Europeans on holiday and "digital nomads" from North America and other parts of the West.

18 Rony, *The Third Eye*, 21.

19 Chakrabarty, *Provincializing Europe*, 105. Anthropologist Margaret Wiener argues that differing notions of what was visible and what was invisible are actually "tropes that refer to competing epistemologies and constructions of the real" between the Dutch and the Balinese. Like scholars Chakrabarty on history or Akhil Gupta on reincarnation narratives, Wiener writes extensively about the problems of anthropologizing as either a dismissal of "indigenous discourses as false consciousness" or a reinterpretation "to show they are 'really' about something we already know." Wiener, *Visible and Invisible Realms*, 12. Gupta writes about competing notions of time in "The Reincarnation of Souls and the Rebirth of Commodities."

20 Mead, *Coming of Age in Samoa*.

21 Boasian anthropology explained many problems as being of a social, not a biological, origin, which implied that societies and cultures could be changed. Pollmann, "Margaret Mead's Balinese," 7.

22 In 1934, Mead's mentor and lover, anthropologist Ruth Benedict, explained that those who went into trance or experienced seizures were respected and prized as community members. Benedict, "Anthropology and the Abnormal." Historian Lois Banner suggests that Bateson and Mead's description of the Balinese as schizophrenic stems from their view of the frequent practice of trance: "Mead was to see young men in trance walking on coals and biting off the heads of chickens. It added up to what seemed to Mead and Bateson a 'schizophrenic' pattern, in line with current definitions of that mental condition as involving hearing voices and being removed from personal and social

interaction." Banner, *Intertwined Lives*, 367. In fact, Banner points out, Bateson had been interested in schizophrenic patients as early as 1932, and had written Mead in 1934 about his interest in studying "incipient schizophrenics" (368). After conducting research in Bali, Mead and Bateson continued to forward the notion that Balinese culture was schizophrenic. Using psychoanalysis (although they were not trained in that field), Mead and Bateson laid the blame for the schizophrenia of Balinese culture on the mother, whom they saw as frigid and cruel. A child's fear of his mother gets repressed, only to emerge when engaged in theater. Mead and Bateson wrote, "In real life, the European is often at a loss to tell when two Balinese are quarreling, but on the stage, emotions are so accurately delineated that no mistake is possible." Mead and Bateson explained the importance of studying the Balinese "in which the ordinary adjustment of one individual approximates in form the sort of maladjustment" that Americans refer to as "schizoid" in order to understand and ameliorate what they referred to as the growing "toll of dementia praecox" in the United States (Bateson and Mead, *Balinese Character*, xvi. It was a conclusion about mothering that, Lois Banner explains, was part of a trend in the United States to criticize women for the neuroses of their sons (*Intertwined Lives*, 372).

23 Mead, *Blackberry Winter*, 231.

24 Belo, *Trance in Bali*, 125. In a letter to Mead, Belo wrote, "Stop by when you can—we'll talk about ordering the show. I'm not so *very* keen for Pagoetan as that place plays altogether too often (. . . the rumor is they play sometimes several times a week). There's something horrible about it." Jane Belo, letter to Mead, Sajan, Bali, November 29, 1937, folder N26, Margaret Mead Archives, Manuscript Division, Library of Congress. In a letter a few days earlier from Bateson to Belo, November 26, 1937, Bangli, Bateson explains how to shoot with the exposure meter and asks how much Pagoetan would cost. Mead records that they paid 15 Dutch guilders (Mead Notes, Kris Dance in Pagoetan, December 16, 1937, folder N26, Margaret Mead Archives, Manuscript Division, Library of Congress). She writes that Bateson's film ran out as they were filming the trance, so that it was actually Belo who filmed most of the actual kris trance, and Bateson did most of the coming out of trance action.

25 Belo, *Trance in Bali*, 125.

26 Belo, *Trance in Bali*, 154–55. Jane Belo also describes Ni Ngales in trance in her notes: "I go back to watch Ni Ngales awhile—she cries, then is quiet, cries again. At one point she arches her body upwards from her sitting position on the ground, on her face an expression of painful ecstasy, very sexual. She is so terribly ugly, she may well be unsatisfied. She took this chance to have her orgy (was not 'supposed to' go in trance)" (Jane Belo, notes, December 16, 1937, folder N26, Margaret Mead Archive, Manuscript Division, Library of Congress).

27 Belo, *Trance in Bali*, 11. Belo continues, "When people went in trance, they would behave like children. They would cry, call out to father and mother, express urgent and unpredictable desires, and would not be quieted until these desires were satisfied. Being like gods, they would behave like children. In

some way the gods themselves were children" (12). This last sentence is so curious. Belo suggests the reality and subjectivity of the gods, and yet her overall discourse focuses on real versus fake.

28 Belo, *Trance in Bali*, 152.

29 "Though we admit that some are faking when they appear to fall unconscious we would like to know if they are genuinely entranced, for if that is the case, how could they rise in unison and proceed with the dance?" Belo, *Trance in Bali*, 153.

30 Belo, *Trance in Bali*, 156.

31 Pandolfo, "The Thin Line of Modernity," 118.

32 Pandolfo, "The Thin Line of Modernity," 121.

33 In killing others one is killing oneself, in the example of the suicide bomber. Pandolfo, "'The Burning.'"; Asad, *On Suicide Bombing*; Asad, *Formations of the Secular*; Mbembe, "Necropolitics."

34 Belo, *Trance in Bali*, 157.

35 Belo, *Trance in Bali*, 158.

36 In her notes, Mead also describes Soekoen as *nakal* (naughty) (Kris Dance in Pagoetan, December 16, 1937, Margaret Mead Archives, Manuscript Division, Library of Congress).

37 Belo, *Trance in Bali*, 159.

38 Belo, *Trance in Bali*.

39 Belo, *Trance in Bali*, 158.

40 Pollman, 15. Krista Thompson describes the ways that colonial photography pictured the colonial gaze as "tropicalization," defined as "the complex visual systems through which the islands were imaged for tourist consumption and the social and political implications of these representations on actual physical space on the islands and their inhabitants." Thompson, *An Eye for the Tropics*, 5. She writes, "Significantly, one aspect of the islands' picturesque image that promoters had to maintain was precisely the colonies' reputations as disciplined societies. The medium of photography itself became central in the perpetuation and maintenance of this disciplined image; it served as a form of discipline. The very process of representing and deeming parts of the landscape and inhabitants as picturesque marked their incorporation into a disciplinary society" (17). See also my discussion of the photogenic in Rony, "The Photogenic Cannot Be Tamed."

41 Thompson, *An Eye for the Tropics*, 17.

42 Belo, *Trance in Bali*, 159.

43 Schneider, "Performance Remains," 103. For more see Schneider, *Performing Remains*.

44 See Robinson, *The Dark Side of Paradise*.

45 "This is accompanied by the anthropological construction of Mead and Bateson who saw the Balinese themselves as a people who were 'characteristically refined and elegant,' 'emotion without climax,' and who 'prioritize community harmony.'" Santikarma, "Pecalangan di Bali," my translation.

46 Likewise, after the 2002 bombing in Bali, the governor stated that although it was a terrible tragedy, Bali had not changed: "Bali doesn't change. The beaches are still there. Our culture is still there. The friendliness of the Balinese people isn't gone. What is gone is the image. Recovery of the image is the first step to bringing back tourists to Bali" (Santikarma, "Pecalangan di Bali").

47 The word "amok" comes from the Malay *amuk*, or the verb *mengamuk*. "Amok," *Merriam-Webster*, https://www.merriam-webster.com/dictionary/amok, n.d., accessed December 17, 2018). Merriam-Webster defines it as: 1. an episode of sudden mass assault against people or objects usually by a single individual following a period of brooding that has traditionally been regarded as occurring especially in Malaysian culture but is now increasingly viewed as psychopathological behavior occurring worldwide in numerous countries and cultures; 2. in a violently raging, wild, or uncontrolled manner—used in the phrase run amok; 3. in a murderously frenzied state.

48 Leslie Dwyer and Degung Santikarma, "When the World Turned to Chaos," 291, as quoted in Larasati, *The Dance That Makes You Vanish*, 39. For a comprehensive history and study of political violence in Bali, see Robinson, *The Dark Side of Paradise*. See also Santikarma, "Monument, Document and Mass Grave."

49 Van Heeren, *Contemporary Indonesian Film*, 109.

50 Robinson, *The Killing Season*, 6.

51 Beta, Latifa, and Utami, "A Critical Perspective on Visual Imagery."

52 Larasati, *The Dance That Makes You Vanish*, 35.

53 Paramaditha, "Contesting Indonesian Nationalism."

54 Sharpe, *In the Wake*, 96–97.

55 Sharpe, *In the Wake*, 97.

56 Larasati, *The Dance That Makes You Vanish*, 28.

57 Robinson, *The Killing Season*, 10.

58 Robinson, *The Killing Season*, 15.

59 Rapold, "Interview."

60 Brad Simpson, Megan Streit, Mark Reyes, Susan O'Hara, Andrew Conroe, eds., "US Promoted Close Ties to Indonesian Military as Suharto's Rule Came to an End in Spring, 1998," Briefing Book no. 633, National Security Archive, July 24, 2018, https://nsarchive.gwu.edu/briefing-book/indonesia/2018-07-24/us-promoted-close-ties-indonesian-military-suhartos-rule-came-end.

61 Lusztig, "The Fever Dream of Documentary," 53.

62 I thank Sylvia Tiwon for this insight. See Tiwon, "Lust of the Eye," 200.

63 Rachmi Diyah Larasati in discussion at panel, "The Suppressed Archive: Tracing Histories in Southeast Asian Cinema and Dance," at "Making Southeast Asian Culture: From Region to World," University of California, Berkeley, April 22, 2016.

64 Fraser, "We Love Impunity," 21–22.

65 Lusztig, "The Fever Dream of Documentary," 55.

66 Cribb, "'The Act of Killing,'" 147.

67 "Joshua's position is established by his voice—obviously that of a foreigner, albeit quite skilled in Indonesian—combined with the way the characters

often speak when they answer his questions directly: slowly and with lots of hand gestures, as if concerned he will not understand the combination of language and context-based meanings. This effectively blocks the identification of Indonesian viewers with the figure of the altruistic political actor behind the camera, making it linguistically and culturally foreign. (Some Indonesian viewers, however, will undoubtedly identify themselves with Oppenheimer's position anyway.) For foreign, and particularly, liberal Western, festival-going audiences, the effect is reversed: we can more easily place ourselves in the position of consumers of well-packaged information about how the distant, yet fascinating, Third World has yet to become fully 'developed.' We often feel emotionally drawn in, sympathetic with and disturbed by the plight of Others, yet simultaneously, if not consciously, comforted by the moral satisfaction that there is still a 'need' for us to lead the world in the process of becoming more civilized." Yngvesson, "Film Review," 215.

68 Yngvesson, "Film Review," 214–15.

69 Hoskins and Lasmana, "The Act of Killing," 264.

70 Oppenheimer's prodigious talents could be used to explore the savagery present in his own country of the United States, in which violent historical and continuous atrocities against Native Americans, African Americans, and other marginalized people have been occurring for centuries. The violences and injustices that occurred involved much more than just a few bad evil men of Sumatra, as his documentaries would seem to posit. The killings served a globalized system of power that upheld the economic and political neoliberal engine of the United States.

71 See Tiwon, "Failure of the Imaginary"; Tiwon, "Models and Maniacs."

72 Larasati, *The Dance That Makes You Vanish*, 15.

73 Larasati, *The Dance That Makes You Vanish*, xvi.

74 Larasati, *The Dance That Makes You Vanish*, 124–25.

75 Larasati, *The Dance That Makes You Vanish*, 126.

76 Larasati, *The Dance That Makes You Vanish*, 127.

77 Larasati, *The Dance That Makes You Vanish*, 133.

78 Larasati, *The Dance That Makes You Vanish*, 159.

CHAPTER THREE: MOTHER DAO

An earlier version of a section of chapter 3 originally appeared in "The Quick and the Dead: Surrealism and the Found Ethnographic Footage Films of *Bontoc Eulogy* and *Mother Dao: The Turtlelike*," *Camera Obscura* 18, no. 1 (2003): 128–35.

1 "Genjer-Genjer—Lilis Suryani [PKI-Song]," posted with the pseudonym Mister Gaje, YouTube, November 20, 2012, https://www.youtube.com/watch?v=9ECW_Xlsu2A.

2 Lilis Suryani's album *Gang Kelinci* (1965) is often seen as a criticism of then President Sukarno's turn from a more liberal democracy to "Guided Democracy."

3 Clifford, "On Ethnographic Surrealism," 117–18. Critiques of Clifford's idea of ethnographic surrealism include that of Michael Richardson, "An Encounter of Wise Men and Cyclops Women," who also states that surrealism was not an art movement but "an attitude, a way of living, seeing and relating to the world," not an avant-garde movement since they denied they were artists, "neither an ideology nor a vocation but a praxis" (58). Richardson accuses Clifford of seeing surrealism through postmodernist eyes and asserts the need to see surrealism and anthropology as two separate things, claiming that there were no connections between surrealism and relativist ethnography (61–64).

4 Clifford, "On Ethnographic Surrealism," 118.

5 Clifford, "On Ethnographic Surrealism," 117.

6 Rosen, "Document and Documentary."

7 Bazin, "The Ontology of the Photographic Image," 15–16.

8 Bazin, "The Ontology of the Photographic Image," 9.

9 Bazin, "The Ontology of the Photographic Image," 14.

10 Strassler, *Refracted Visions*, 23.

11 "Attending to memory-work does not mean abandoning entirely the project of speaking back to colonialist histories and nostalgia. It does mean letting go of some received wisdoms and cherished assumptions—that the colonial is ever present in postcolonial lives; that postcolonial subjectivity by definition pivots on the transition from the colonial to the postcolonial; that there are subaltern circuits in which colonial critiques are lodged; that there is resistance in the smallest of gestures and the very lack of gesture at all; and that telling of the colonial past is a therapeutic act." Stoler and Strassler, "Memory-Work in Java," 202.

12 Stoler and Strassler, "Memory-Work in Java," 201.

13 See for example Pinney, *Photography and Anthropology*; Edwards, *Anthropology and Photography*.

14 Sontag, "Melancholy Objects," 52–53.

15 Sontag, "Melancholy Objects," 54.

16 This section was first presented as a paper on February 24, 2008, at the Max Planck Institute in Berlin, Germany, for a workshop titled "The Educated Eye." I am grateful to the organizers of the workshop, Gregg Mitman, Kelly Wilder, and Sara Stukenbrock, and the Max Planck Institute for inviting me to participate, as well as to Faye Ginsburg and the many other participants who provided much feedback on the paper.

17 Causey, *Hard Bargaining in Sumatra*, 79.

18 Causey, *Hard Bargaining in Sumatra*, 242.

19 Pfeiffer, *Lady's Second Journey Round the World*.

20 Anderson, *Mission to the East Coast of Sumatra in 1823*.

21 Anderson, *Mission to the East Coast of Sumatra in 1823*, 223.

22 Some examples where scholars argue that cannibalism is a Western myth, or at least an exaggeration, are Barker, Hulme, and Iversen, *Cannibalism and the Colonial World*; Causey, *Hard Bargaining in Sumatra*; and Arens, *The Man-Eating Myth*.

23 Viswanathan, *Outside the Fold*, 40.

24 Rafael, *Contracting Colonialism*, 21.

25 DeWaard, *Pioneer in Sumatra*, 25.

26 DeWaard, *Pioneer in Sumatra*, 36.

27 de Certeau, *The Practice of Everyday Life*, 32.

28 Even *New York Times* art reviewer Holland Carter remarked on the fact that Batak art was not seen to be as classical as Javanese art, and thus became lumped under the category of tribal or primitive art (July 15, 1994).

29 Ompung Sinambela, interview with author, August 1994.

30 Chakrabarty, *Provincializing Europe*, 109–12.

31 Chakrabarty, *Provincializing Europe*, 112.

32 Creese, "A Puputan Tale," 3–4.

33 Desnos, *Cinéma*, 15.

34 Niogret, "Regards d'autrefois et d'aujourd'hui," 86–87.

35 Wees, *Recycled Images*, 54–55. Wees has a very interesting taxonomy for found-footage films, which are the compilation, the collage, and the appropriation film, all of which have different ideological purposes.

36 Wees, *Recycled Images*, 11.

37 Lautréamont, *Maldoror*, 26.

38 Michel Foucault, "Right of Death and Power over Life," in *The History of Sexuality*, vol. 1, 1990, 139–40.

39 Baldwin and Mead, *A Rap on Race*, 203.

40 Please see chapters 1, "Seeing Anthropology: Félix-Louis Regnault, the Narrative of Race, and the Ethnographic Exposition," and 2, "The Writing of Race in Film: Félix-Louis Regnault and the Ideology of the Ethnographic Film Archive," for detailed discussion on inscription in Rony, *The Third Eye*.

41 Vincent Monnikendam, dir., *Mother Dao, the Turtlelike* (*Moeder Dao de Schildpadge liikende*), Yamagata International Documentary Film, 1995, http://www.yidff.jp/97/cat045/97c048-e.html.

42 Fabian, *Time and the Other*, 77.

43 Fabian, *Time and the Other*, 92.

44 Griffiths, *Wondrous Difference*; Peterson, *Education in the School of Dreams*.

45 Foucault, "Society Must Be Defended," 74.

46 Barthes, *Camera Lucida*, 115–19.

47 Barthes, *Camera Lucida*, 115–19.

48 Foucault, "Right of Death and Power over Life," in *The History of Sexuality*, vol. 1, 1990, 140–41.

49 Pat Ward Williams, *Accused/Blowtorch/Padlock*, 1986, in the Whitney Museum, New York.

50 Mbembe, "Necropolitics," 23.

51 Mbembe, "Necropolitics," 24.

52 Arendt, *Origins of Totalitarianism*, 192.

53 Paul Gilroy, *The Black Atlantic*, 63, as quoted in Mbembe, "Necropolitics," 39.

54 Barthes, *Camera Lucida*, 95–96.

55 Niogret, "Regards d'autrefois et d'aujourd'hui," 87.
56 Franklin, "Tracy K. Smith, America's Poet Laureate."

CHAPTER FOUR: NIA DINATA

An earlier version of a section of chapter 4 originally appeared in "Transforming Documentary: Indonesian Women and Sexuality in the Film *Pertaruhan* (*At Stake*) (2008)," in *Women and Media in Asia: Exploring the Precarious Self*, ed. Youna Kim, 159–76 (London: Palgrave Macmillan, 2012).

1 Abu-Lughod, *Do Muslim Women Need Saving?*
2 In Indonesia, since 1998 women have dominated independent feature films as producers and as directors. Until recently in the United States, women have rarely directed top-grossing Hollywood films. In other countries, including Indonesia and Iran, more women fill these directing and producing roles than in the United States. This is not an insignificant fact. Most people assume that predominantly Muslim countries would have fewer opportunities for women than the United States. Yet the Hollywood film industry consistently churns out the content that visualizes the norms of society and supports the subjectivity of homo economicus while hiring a minuscule percentage of women, both illustrating and furthering visual biopolitics. See Martha M. Lauzen, "The Celluloid Ceiling: Behind-the-Scenes Employment of Women on the Top 100, 250, and 500 Films of 2018," https://womenintvfilm.sdsu.edu/wp-content/uploads/2019/01/2018_Celluloid_Ceiling_Report.pdf, a 2019 report on a study sponsored by the Center for the Study of Women in Television and Film, San Diego State University. This study has been tracking the number of women in the film and television industry for twenty-one years.
3 In 2006, Nia Dinata got funding from Lux Soap to produce four short films by four women directors, and she chose first-time directors, including Cinzia Puspita Rini, who directed one of the films, *The Matchmaker*, about a young man and woman who fall in love in a Jakarta bookstore. Puspita went on to be assistant director on *Perempuan Punya Cerita* and *Pertaruhan* (she is on camera as well, as the unmarried woman requesting a Pap smear, over whom the doctor intones the Lord's Prayer) and also an assistant director on *Chants of Lotus*. The four short films were marketed as *Lux, 4 Kisah Wanita, Karya 4 Sineas Wanita*, and *Beauty Gives You Superpowers*. They were quickly shot, beautifully produced, light romantic comedy films that fit the rubric of a soap that gives women superpowers. These films were not nationally exhibited or released, but *The Matchmaker* did get screened in film festivals. Besides Lux Soap, Kao Indonesia, another company known for selling face cleansers and household cleaners, was one of just a few of the investors who have funded films by Dinata. Kao Indonesia funded her short documentary from 2011, *Batik Our Love Story*. Fascinated with the Chinese Indonesian batik producers in the town of Lasem, Java, where she shot *Ca-bau-kan*, Dinata returned to make a documentary about them, and traveled to other places in Java and Madura as well. But almost

all of her films have been financed by independent investors: as her husband, Constantin Papadimitriou (Kiki), executive producer for all of the films that Dinata directs, joked at one fund-raising meeting I went to in 2007, "the women make the films and I raise the money so they can make them."

4   For more on Indonesian cinema during the New Order regime, see Sen, *Indonesian Cinema*.

5   In 2019, the chains were Cinema XXI, CGV, Cinemax, and Flix.

6   Sen, "Indonesia: Screening a Nation in the Post-New Order," 102.

7   Sunindyo, "Murder, Gender, and the Media," 125. Other informative articles on the construction of the woman as ideal wife/mother can be found in Sen, "Indonesian Women at Work"; and Kuswandini, "The Rise and Fall of Indonesia's Women's Movement," *Jakarta Post*, April 21, 2010.

8   Tiwon, "Models and Maniacs," 69.

9   Thompson, "Indonesia Passes Tough New Anti-porn Laws."

10   Nia Dinata, interview with author, December 22, 2008, Jakarta, Indonesia.

11   Nia Dinata, email message to author, March 22, 2021. Dinata's quote originally appeared in a 2008 Berlinale press release.

12   Van Heeren, *Contemporary Indonesian Film*, 184.

13   Terence N. Hull and Ninuk Widyantoro, "The Right to Choose: Indonesian Activists Keep Fighting to Have Abortion Decriminalized," *Inside Indonesia* 97, September 27, 2009, https://www.insideindonesia.org/the-right-to-choose?highlight=WyJodWxsIiwiaHVsbCdzIlo%3D. For more on the discriminatory effects of recent laws, see "Indonesia: Barriers Preventing Women Achieving Reproductive Health," Amnesty International Press Release, November 4, 2010, https://web.archive.org/web/20101107003031/http://www.amnesty.org/en/news-and-updates/report/Indonesia-left-without-choice-barriers-reproductive-health-Indonesia-2010-11; and *Jakarta Post*, "154 Bylaws Haunt Women," *Jakarta Post*, January 30, 2010, https://www.thejakartapost.com/news/2010/01/30/154-bylaws-haunt-women-15-more-come.html; and Prodita Sabarini, "Indonesia: Discrimination over Access to Reproductive Health," *Jakarta Post*, July 25, 2009, International Planned Parenthood Federation, https://web.archive.org/web/20090814152105/http://www.ippf.org/en/News/Intl+news/Indonesia+Discrimination+over+access+to+reproductive+health.htm.

14   Dian Kuswandini, "The Rise and Fall of Indonesia's Women's Movement," *Jakarta Post*, April 21, 2010, http://www.europe-solidaire.org/spip.php?article17226; and Julia Suryakusuma, "From Both Sides Now: Shari'ah Morality, "Pornography," and Women in Indonesia," Ed. David K. Linnan, *Legitimacy, Legal Development, and Change: Law and Modernization Reconsidered* (Routledge, 2012) 193–212.

15   *Straits Times*, "West Java Cracks Down on 'Adult' Foreign Pop"; Paddock, "Professor Sings at Indonesia Rally."

16   Joko Anwar went on to create the HBO Asia television series *Halfworlds* of 2015 and 2017 and is a successful director of several thrillers like *Pengabdi Setan* of

2017. Lucky Kuswandi went on to direct *Selamat Pagi Malam* (2014) and *Galih dan Ratna* (2017).

17 Dewi, "Nia Dinata."

18 Mulvey, "Visual Pleasure and Narrative Cinema."

19 Bordwell, "Film Futures."

20 White, *Women's Cinema, World Cinema*, 133.

21 White, *Women's Cinema, World Cinema*, 134.

22 Deshpande, "The Future Is Now."

23 Indeed, it was because she was at the Cannes Film Market in 2006 that she happened to see the omnibus film *Paris, je t'aime*, which inspired her to make an omnibus film.

24 Beyond Dinata's mission to develop screenwriting talent is her goal to develop acting talent. Many of the stars of the film got their first acting roles from Dinata: Sarah Sechan was a known television personality; Shanty (a star of *Berbagi Suami*) was previously a singing star; Rieke Diah Pitaloka (who also appeared in *Berbagi Suami*) was a comedian; and Susan Bachtiar was a media personality and an English teacher.

25 But as directors we also made suggestions about other scripts. For Melissa Karim's script about Lakshmi, a woman who is HIV positive on the run with her daughter, I asked, "Wouldn't Lakshmi go to her relatives first? What if we see that they reject her because of her HIV status and so thus she really has nowhere to go?" This change was also incorporated into the script. The writers and producers were very open to our feedback as directors.

26 Of all the jobs that the crew filled, perhaps the one that seems the least likely to be found in the United States is the rainstopper. This is the person brought in to pray that the shoot will go well and that there will be no rain. Or, if there is rain, he's charged with stopping it. The rainstopper, Sukanta, was the uncle of our unit production manager, Ferry Ardyan. Whether or not you believed in his ability, it was great for morale to have someone on board to watch over the spiritual health of the shoot. Another interesting job description is that of the fixer, like the fixers on our film, Reni Septiani and Syaiful. These were locals who would help us with the shoot and make sure the production went smoothly. Of the two fixers on our film, one, Syaiful, played the role of Ahmad Rokim's friend Pak Ipul.

27 Van Heeren, *Contemporary Indonesian Film*, 168.

28 Van Heeren, *Contemporary Indonesian Film*, 140.

29 Nia Dinata, interview with author, December 22, 2008.

30 See Van Heeren, *Contemporary Indonesian Film*, chapter 6 and conclusion, 157–202, for in-depth discussion on Islam, politics, and film.

31 Diani, "Wanted."

32 Van Heeren, *Contemporary Indonesian Film*, 186.

33 Intan Paramaditha, "Protectors and Provocateurs; Reading the New Film Law as Cultural Performance," paper presented at Southeast Asian Cinemas Conference, Saigon, July 1–4, 2010, 4, 7, as quoted in Van Heeren, *Contemporary Indonesian Film*, 188.

34 Van Heeren, *Contemporary Indonesian Film*, 187–90.

35 Van Heeren, *Contemporary Indonesian Film*, 188.

36 Diani, "Wanted"; and Nia Dinata, interview with the author, March 25, 2019.

37 Van Heeren, *Contemporary Indonesian Film*, 89.

38 Van Heeren, *Contemporary Indonesian Film*, 88.

39 Van Heeren, *Contemporary Indonesian Film*, 110.

40 Nia Dinata, interview with author, December 22, 2008.

41 For more on how indigenous peoples are made ethnographic, see Rony, *The Third Eye*, 7–8.

42 Historians of documentary like to cite John Grierson as being the first to coin the term "documentary" in 1926, but actually he only writes of *Moana* having "documentary value." See Grierson, "Flaherty's Poetic *Moana*," 25. In 1930, Paul Rotha used the term "documentary" to describe the genre in his book *The Film Till Now: A Survey of the Cinema*, when he wrote "The Documentary or Interest Film, including the Scientific, Cultural and Sociological Film."

43 Winston, "The Tradition of the Victim in the Griersonian Documentary."

44 Nia Dinata, interview with author, December 22, 2008.

45 Nia Dinata, interview with author, December 22, 2008.

46 Lucky Kuswandi, interview with author, August 5, 2009, Jakarta.

47 Ani Ema Susanti, interview with author, December 20, 2008, Jakarta.

48 Barnouw, *Documentary*.

49 "17 March 1976," in Foucault, "Society Must Be Defended," 75.

50 Strassler, *Refracted Visions*, 23.

Bibliography

Abu-Lughod, Lila. *Do Muslim Women Need Saving?* Cambridge, MA: Harvard
 University Press, 2013.
Agamben, Giorgio. *Homo Sacer: Sovereign Power and Bare Life.* Translated by Daniel
 Heller-Roazen. Palo Alto, CA: Stanford University Press, 1995.
Agamben, Giorgio. *State of Exception.* Chicago: University of Chicago Press, 2005.
Alexander, Michelle. *The New Jim Crow: Mass Incarceration in the Age of Colorblind-
 ness.* New York: New Press, 2010.
Anderson, John. *Mission to the East Coast of Sumatra in 1823.* Edinburgh: William
 Blackwood. Reprint, Kuala Lumpur: Oxford University Press, (1826) 1971.
Arendt, Hannah. "Selections from *The Human Condition.*" In *Biopolitics: A Reader,*
 edited by Timothy Campbell and Adam Sitze, 98–133. Durham, NC: Duke
 University Press, 2013.
Arendt, Hannah. *Origins of Totalitarianism.* New York: Schocken Books, 2004.
Arens, W. *The Man-Eating Myth: Anthropology and Anthropophagy.* New York:
 Oxford University Press, 1979.
Asad, Talal. *Formations of the Secular: Christianity, Islam, Modernity.* Palo Alto, CA:
 Stanford University Press, 2003.
Asad, Talal. *On Suicide Bombing.* New York: Columbia University Press, 2007.

Baldwin, James. "My Dungeon Shook: Letter to My Nephew on the One Hundredth Anniversary of the Emancipation." In *The Fire Next Time*. New York: First Vintage International, 1993. First published in *The Progressive*, December 1962.

Baldwin, James, and Margaret Mead. *A Rap on Race*. New York: Dell, 1971.

Banner, Lois W. *Intertwined Lives: Margaret Mead, Ruth Benedict, and Their Circle*. New York: Alfred A. Knopf, 2003.

Barker, Francis, Peter Hulme, and Margaret Iversen. *Cannibalism and the Colonial World*. Cambridge: Cambridge University Press, 1998.

Barnouw, Erik. *Documentary: A History of the Non-fiction Film*. 2nd revised ed. New York: Oxford University Press, 1993.

Barthes, Roland. *Camera Lucida: Reflections on Photography*. Translated by Richard Howard. New York: Hill and Wang, 1981.

Bateson, Gregory, and Margaret Mead. *Balinese Character*. New York: New York Academy of Sciences, 1942.

Baudelaire, Charles. "The Painter of Modern Life." In *The Painter of Modern Life and Other Essays*, edited by Jonathan Mayne. London: Phaidon, 1983.

Bayle-Ottenheim, Jacques, and Salon international du livre insulaire. *Paul Gauguin vers L'île Voisine: Suivi d'une Sélection Bibliographique [Sur] Paul Gauguin et Les Îles*. Quimper, France: Bibliographie de Bretagne, 2001.

Bazin, André. "The Ontology of the Photographic Image." In *What Is Cinema?*, vol. 1, translated by Hugh Gray, 9–16. Berkeley: University of California Press, 1967.

Belo, Jane. *Trance in Bali*. New York: Columbia University Press, 1960.

Benedict, Ruth. "Anthropology and the Abnormal." In *An Anthropologist at Work: Writings of Ruth Benedict*, edited by Margaret Mead. Boston: Houghton Mifflin, 1959. Original edition, 1934.

Benjamin, Walter. "The Task of the Translator." In *Illuminations: Essays and Reflections*, 69–82. Translated by Harry Zohn. New York: Schocken, 1969.

Bernard, Émile. *Souvenirs inédits sur l'artiste peintre Paul Gauguin et ses compagnons, lors de leur séjour à Pont-Aven et au Pouldu*. Lorient, France: Impremerie du Nouvelliste du Morbihan, 1941.

Beta, Annisa R., Inditian Latifa, and Nila Ayu Utami. "A Critical Perspective on Visual Imagery: Understanding the Mental Connection between Torture Scenes in the Film *Pengkhianatan G30S/PKI* and Indonesian Nationalism during the New Order Regime." Paper presented at Second Global Conference of Making Sense of Pain, Warsaw, Poland, May 22–24, 2011.

Bhabha, Homi K. "Of Mimicry and Man: The Ambivalence of Colonial Discourse." In *The Location of Culture*, 85–92. London: Routledge, 2004.

Bongie, Chris. *Exotic Memories: Literature, Colonialism, and the Fin de Siècle*. Cambridge: Cambridge University Press, 1991.

Bordwell, David. "Film Futures." *SubStance* 31, no. 1 (2002): 88–104.

Brettell, Richard. *Modern Art 1851–1929: Capitalism and Representation*. Oxford: Oxford University Press, 1999.

Brettell, Richard. "The Return to France." In *The Art of Paul Gauguin*, edited by Richard R. Brettell, 297–304. Washington, DC: National Gallery of Art, 1988.

Brettell, Richard, with Peter Zegers. "Catalogue Numbers 159–214." In *The Art of Paul Gauguin*, edited by Richard R. Brettell, 304–78. Washington, DC: National Gallery of Art, 1988.

Brooks, Peter. "Gauguin's Tahitian Body." In *Body Work: Objects of Desire in Modern Narrative*, 162–98. Cambridge, MA: Harvard University Press, 1993.

Brown, Wendy. *Undoing the Demos: Neoliberalism's Stealth Revolution*. New York: Near Futures, 2015.

Burns, Judy, and Jill MacDougall, with Catherine Benamou, Avanthi Meduri, Peggy Phelan, and Susan Slyomovics. "An Interview with Gayatri Spivak." Edited by Judy Burns. *Women and Performance* 5, no. 1 (1990): 80–92.

Butler, Judith. *Gender Trouble: Feminism and the Subversion of Identity*. New York: Routledge, 1990.

Caldwell, John Thornton. *Production Culture: Industrial Reflexivity and Critical Practice in Film and Television*. Durham, NC: Duke University Press, 2008.

Callimachi, Rukmini. "The Horror before the Beheadings." *New York Times*, October 25, 2014.

Carroll, Noel. *The Philosophy of Horror: Or Paradoxes of the Heart*. New York: Routledge, 1990.

Causey, Andrew. *Hard Bargaining in Sumatra: Western Travelers and Toba Bataks in the Marketplace of Souvenirs*. Honolulu: University of Hawaii Press, 2003.

Chakrabarty, Dipesh. *Provincializing Europe: Postcolonial Thought and Historical Difference*. Princeton, NJ: Princeton University Press, 2000.

Chatelain, Marcia. *South Side Girls: Growing Up in the Great Migration*. Durham, NC: Duke University Press, 2015.

Childs, Elizabeth C. "The Colonial Lens: Gauguin, Primitivism, and Photography in the Fin de Siècle." In *Antimodernism and Artistic Experience*, edited by Lynda Jessup, 50–70. Toronto: University of Toronto Press, 2001.

Clark, Timothy J. *The Painting of Modern Life: Paris in the Art of Manet and His Followers*. Princeton, NJ: Princeton University Press, 1984.

Clark, Timothy J. "Preliminaries to a Possible Treatment of 'Olympia' in 1865." *Screen* 21, no. 1 (Spring 1980), 18–42.

Clifford, James. "On Ethnographic Surrealism." In *The Predicament of Culture: Twentieth Century Ethnography, Literature, and Art*, 117–51. Cambridge, MA: Harvard University Press, 1988.

Cohen, Matthew Isaac. *Performing Otherness: Java and Bali on International Stages, 1905–1952*. Basingstoke, UK: Palgrave Macmillan, 2010.

Cooper, Melinda. *Life as Surplus: Biotechnology and Capitalism in the Neoliberal Era*. Seattle: University of Washington Press, 2008.

Copeland, Huey. "In the Wake of the Negress." In *Modern Women: Women Artists at the Museum of Modern Art*, edited by Cornelia H. Butler and Alexandra Schwartz, 481–97. New York: Museum of Modern Art, 2010.

Creese, Helen. "A Puputan Tale: 'The Story of a Pregnant Woman.'" *Indonesia*, no. 82 (October 2006): 3–4.

Cribb, Robert. "The Act of Killing." *Critical Asian Studies* 46, no. 1 (2014): 147–49.

Danielsson, Bengt. *Gauguin in the South Seas.* Translated by Reginald Spink. London: George Allen and Unwin, 1965.

Danielsson, Bengt. "Gauguin's Tahitian Titles." *Burlington Magazine* 109, no. 769 (1967): 228–33.

Dargis, Manohla. "She Shtups to Conquer: Why Is Hollywood So Full of Whores?" *LA Weekly*, April 18, 2001.

Daulatzai, Sohail. *Fifty Years of the Battle of Algiers: Past as Prologue.* Minneapolis: University of Minnesota Press, 2016.

Day, Elizabeth. "Strauss-Kahn in the Dock: A Ringside Seat at the Trial." *Observer*, February 22, 2015. http://www.theguardian.com/world/2015/feb/22/dominique-strauss-kahn-lille-pimping-trial.

de Certeau, Michel. *The Practice of Everyday Life.* Berkeley: University of California Press, 1984.

Deshpande, Shekhar. "The Future Is Now: Film Producer as Creative Director." *Wide Screen* 2, no. 2 (2010): 1–14.

Desnos, Robert. *Cinéma.* Paris: Gallimard, 1966.

DeWaard, Nellie. *Pioneer in Sumatra: The Story of Ludwig Nommensen.* London: China Inland Mission, 1962.

Dewi, Mariani. "Nia Dinata: All It Takes Is Courage." *Jakarta Post*, March 29, 2009. http://www.thejakartapost.com/news/2009/03/29/nia-dinata-all-it-takes-courage.html.

Diani, Hera. "Wanted: Film Classification Board, Not Censorship." *Magdalene*, March 31, 2019. https://magdalene.co/story/film-classification-board-not-cencorship.

Doane, Mary Ann. "Film and the Masquerade: Theorising the Female Spectator." In *Femmes Fatales: Feminism, Film Theory, Psychoanalysis*, 17–32. New York: Routledge, 1991. Original edition, 1982.

Dong, Ky [Nguyen Van Cam]. *Amours d'un vieux peintre aux îles Marquises [Những mối tình của người họa sĩ già trên quần đảo M'ackiz].* Hanoi: Ngoai Van, 1990.

Dowd, Maureen. "A Goddess, a Mogul and a Mad Genius." *New York Times*, February 3, 2018.

Dunne, Carey. "'No More Stolen Sisters': 12,000-Mile Ride to Highlight Missing Indigenous Women." *Guardian*, June 7, 2019. https://www.theguardian.com/us-news/2019/jun/07/indigenous-women-missing-murdered-activists-ride-north-america.

Dussel, Enrique. "The 'World-System': Europe as 'Center' and Its 'Periphery' beyond Eurocentrism." In *Latin America and Postmodernity: A Contemporary Reader*, edited by Eduardo Mendieta and Pedro Lange-Churión, 93–121. Atlantic Highlands, NJ: Humanities Press, 2001.

DuVernay, Ava, dir. *13th.* Los Angeles: Netflix, 2016.

Edmond, Rod. *Representing the South Pacific: Colonial Discourse from Cook to Gauguin.* Cambridge: Cambridge University Press, 1997.

Edwards, Elizabeth. *Anthropology and Photography: 1860–1920.* New Haven, CT: Yale University Press, 1992.

Eisenman, Stephen F. *Gauguin's Skirt*. New York: Thames and Hudson, 1997.

Fabian, Johannes. *Time and the Other: How Anthropology Makes Its Object*. New York: Columbia University Press, 2014.

Fauser, Annegret. *Musical Encounters at the 1889 Paris World's Fair*. Rochester, NY: University of Rochester Press, 2006.

Field, Richard S. "Gauguin's Noa Noa Suite." *Burlington Magazine* 110, no. 786 (1986): 500–511.

Foucault, Michel. *History of Sexuality*. Vol. 1, *An Introduction*. Translated by Richard Hurley. New York: Random House, 1978.

Foucault, Michel. *Manet and the Object of Painting*. New York: Abrams, 2013. Original edition, Editions de Seuil, 2009.

Foucault, Michel. "Society Must Be Defended." In *Lectures at the Collège de France, 1975–76*. Translated by David Macey. New York: Picador, 2003.

Franklin, Ruth. "Tracy K. Smith, America's Poet Laureate, Is a Woman with a Mission." *New York Times Magazine*, April 15, 2018.

Fraser, Nick. "We Love Impunity: The Case of *The Act of Killing*." *Film Quarterly* 67, no. 2 (2013): 21–24.

Frèches-Thory, Claire. "The Exhibition at Durand-Ruel." In *Gauguin Tahiti*, edited by George Shackelford and Claire Frèches-Thory, 83–89. Boston: MFA, 2004.

Gauguin, Paul. *Cahier pour Aline*. Paris: Ste des amis de la Bibliothèque d'Art et d'Archéologie de l'Université de Paris, 1963. Original edition, 1892.

Gauguin, Paul. *Lettres de Gauguin à sa femme et à ses amis*. Edited by Maurice Malingue. Paris: Bernard Grasset, 1946.

Gauguin, Paul. *Noa Noa par Gauguin*. Edited by Jean Loize. Paris: André Balland, 1966.

Gauguin, Paul. *Paul Gauguin: Letters to His Wife and Friends*. Translated by Henry J. Stenning. Cleveland: World, 1949.

Gauguin, Pola. *My Father, Paul Gauguin*. Translated by Arthur G. Chater. New York: Hacker Art Books, 1988.

Gauguin, Pola. *Paul Gauguin, mon père*. Paris: Ed. de France (microform), 1938.

Gilmore, Ruth Wilson. *Golden Gulag: Prisons, Surplus, Crisis, and Opposition in Globalizing California*. Berkeley: University of California Press, 2007.

Gledhill, Christine, and Linda Williams. *Melodrama Unbound: Across History, Media, and National Cultures*. New York: Columbia University Press, 2018.

Grierson, John. "Flaherty's Poetic *Moana*." In *The Documentary Tradition*, edited by Lewis Jacobs. New York: Norton, 1979.

Griffiths, Alison. *Wondrous Difference: Cinema, Anthropology, and Turn-of-the-Century Visual Culture*. New York: Columbia University Press, 2002.

Grigsby, Darcy Grimaldo. "Thinking about Olympia's Maid." *Art Bulletin* 97, no. 4 (2015): 430–51.

Gupta, Akhil. "The Reincarnation of Souls and the Rebirth of Commodities: Representations of Time in 'East' and 'West.'" In *Remapping Memory: The Politics of Time Space*, edited by Jonathan Boyarin, 161–84. Minneapolis: University of Minnesota Press, 1994.

Hall, Stuart. "New Ethnicities." In *Black Film British Cinema*, edited by Kobena Mercer, 27–30. London: Institute of Contemporary Arts, 1988.

Hartman, Saidiya. *Lose Your Mother: A Journey along the Atlantic Slave Route*. New York: Farrar, Straus and Giroux, 2006.

Hartman, Saidiya. "Venus in Two Acts." *small axe* 26 (June 2008): 1–14.

Hatch, Kristen. *Shirley Temple and the Performance of Girlhood*. New Brunswick, NJ: Rutgers University Press, 2015.

Heath, Stephen. "Narrative Space." In *Questions of Cinema*, 19–75. Bloomington: Indiana University Press, 1981.

Heryanto, Ariel. *Identity and Pleasure: The Politics of Indonesian Screen Culture*. Singapore: National University of Singapore Press, 2014.

Hoskins, Janet, and Viola Lasmana. "The Act of Killing." *Visual Anthropology* 28 (2015): 262–65.

Howard, Greg. "The Easiest Way to Get Rid of Racism? Just Redefine It." *New York Times*, August 16, 2016.

Jarry, Alfred, and Griselda Pollock. *Avant-Garde Gambits: Gender and the Colour of Art History*. London: Thames and Hudson, 1993.

Joannis-Deberne, Henri. *Danser en Société Bals et danses d'hier et d'aujourd'hui*. Paris: Bonneton, 1999.

Jonnes, Jill. *Eiffel's Tower: And the World's Fair Where Buffalo Bill Beguiled Paris, the Artists Quarreled, and Thomas Edison Became a Count*. New York: Viking, 2009.

Kahn, Mattie. "Let the Record Show." *Vogue*, June 2009.

Kluver, Billy, and Julie Martin. *Kiki's Paris: Artists and Lovers, 1900–1930*. New York: Harry N. Abrams, 1989.

Larasati, Rachmi Diyah. *The Dance That Makes You Vanish: Cultural Reconstruction in Post-Genocide Indonesia*. Minneapolis: University of Minnesota Press, 2012.

Lauretis, Teresa de. "Desire in Narrative." In *Alice Doesn't: Feminism, Semiotics, Cinema*, 103–57. Bloomington: Indiana University Press, 1984.

Lautréamont, Comte de. *Maldoror*. Translated by Guy Wernham. New York: New Directions, 1965.

Lepore, Jill. "The Public Historian: A Conversation with Jill Lepore." *Humanities* 30, no. 5 (2009). https://www.neh.gov/humanities/2009/septemberoctober/conversation/the-public-historian.

Levin, Dan. "Dozens of Women Vanish on Canada's Highway of Tears, and Most Cases Are Unsolved." *New York Times*, May 24, 2016.

Lim, Bliss Cua. "Serial Time: Bluebeard in Stepford." In *Film and Literature: A Reader*, edited by Robert Stam, 163–90. Oxford: Blackwell, 2005.

Lipton, Eunice. *Alias Olympia: A Woman's Search for Manet's Notorious Model and Her Own Desire*. Ithaca, NY: Cornell University Press, 1992.

Lusztig, Irene. "The Fever Dream of Documentary: A Conversation with Joshua Oppenheimer." *Film Quarterly* 67, no. 2 (2013): 50–56.

Mathews, Nancy Mowll. *Paul Gauguin: An Erotic Life*. New Haven, CT: Yale University Press, 2001.

Mbembe, Achille. "Necropolitics." *Public Culture* 15, no. 1 (2003): 11–40.

McKittrick, Katherine, and Sylvia Wynter. "Unparalleled Catastrophe for Our Species? Or, to Give Humanness a Different Future: Conversations." In *Sylvia

Wynter: On Being Human as Praxis, edited by Katherine McKittrick, 7–89. Durham, NC: Duke University Press, 2015.

Mead, Margaret. *Blackberry Winter: My Earlier Years.* New York: Morrow, 1972.

Mead, Margaret. *Coming of Age in Samoa: A Psychological Study of Primitive Youth for Western Civilization.* New York: William Morrow, 1928.

Melamed, Jodi. *Represent and Destroy: The New Racial Capitalism.* Minneapolis: University of Minnesota Press, 2011.

Minh-ha, Trinh. "Outside In Inside Out." In *Questions of Third Cinema*, edited by Jim Pines and Paul Willeman, 133–49. London: British Film Institute, 1989.

Monet, Jenni. "A Native American Woman's Brutal Murder Could Lead to a Life-Saving Law." *Guardian*, May 2, 2019. https://www.theguardian.com/us-news/2019/may/01/savanna-act-native-women-missing-murdered.

Mrazek, Rudolf. *A Certain Age: Colonial Jakarta through the Memories of Its Intellectuals.* Durham, NC: Duke University Press, 2010.

Mucha, Jiří. *Alphonse Mucha: His Life and Art.* London: Heinemann, 1966.

Mucha, Jiří. *Alphonse Mucha: The Master of Art Nouveau.* Translated by Geraldine Thomsen. Prague: Knihtisk, 1966.

Mucha, Sarah. *Alphonse Mucha.* London: Frances Lincoln, 2005.

Mulvey, Laura. "Visual Pleasure and Narrative Cinema." In *Film Theory and Criticism*, edited by Leo Braudy and Marshall Cohen, 837–48. New York: Oxford University Press, 2004. Original edition, 1975.

Niogret, Hubert. "Regards d'autrefois et d'aujourd'hui." *Positif*, no. 428 (October 1996): 86–87.

O'Brien, Patty. *The Pacific Muse: Exotic Femininity and the Colonial Pacific.* Seattle: University of Washington Press, 2006.

O'Grady, Lorraine L. "Olympia's Maid: Reclaiming Black Female Subjectivity." *Afterimage* 20 (1992): 14–15.

Paddock, Richard C. "Professor Sings at Indonesia Rally." *New York Times*, March 16, 2019. https://www.nytimes.com/2019/03/16/world/asia/indonesia-criminal-defamation.html.

Pandolfo, Stefania. "'The Burning': Finitude and the Politico-Theological Imagination of Illegal Migration." *Anthropological Theory* 7, no. 3 (2007): 329–63.

Pandolfo, Stefania. "The Thin Line of Modernity." In *Questions of Modernity*, edited by Timothy Mitchell. Minneapolis: University of Minneapolis Press, 2000.

Paramaditha, Intan. "Contesting Indonesian Nationalism and Masculinity on Cinema." *Asian Cinema* 18, no. 2 (2007): 41–61.

Paramaditha, Intan. "Tracing Frictions in *The Act of Killing.*" *Film Quarterly* 67, no. 2 (2013): 44–49.

Peck, Raoul, dir. *I Am Not Your Negro.* New York: Velvet Film, 2016.

Pemberton, John. *On the Subject of "Java."* Ithaca, NY: Cornell University Press, 1994.

Peterson, Jennifer Lynn. *Education in the School of Dreams: Travelogues and Early Nonfiction Film.* Durham, NC: Duke University Press, 2013.

Pfeiffer, Ida. *Lady's Second Journey Round the World.* New York: Harper and Bros., 1856.

Pinney, Christopher. *Photography and Anthropology*. London: Reaktion, 2011.

Pollmann, Tessel. "Margaret Mead's Balinese." *Indonesia* 49 (April 1990): 10–18.

Rafael, Vicente L. *Contracting Colonialism: Translation and Christian Conversion in Tagalog Society under Early Spanish Rule*. Durham, NC: Duke University Press, 1993.

Rangan, Pooja. "How Do We Look? An Interview with Fatimah Tobing Rony." *Film Quarterly* 67, no. 2 (2013): 62–68.

Rangan, Pooja. *Immediations: The Humanitarian Impulse in Documentary*. Durham, NC: Duke University Press, 2017.

Raoul, E. *Javanais et Javanaises à l'Exposition de 1889*. Paris: Quantin, 1889.

Rapold, Nicolas. "Interview: Joshua Oppenheimer." *Film Comment*, July 15, 2013. https://www.filmcomment.com/blog/interview-joshua-oppenheimer-the -act-of-killing/.

Reuters. "That's What I Don't Like: West Java Cracks Down on 'Adult' Foreign Pop." February 26, 2019. https://www.reuters.com/article/us-indonesia-music/thats-what-i-dont-like-west-java-cracks-down-on-adult-foreign-pop-idUSKCN1QF10D.

Richardson, Michael. "An Encounter of Wise Men and Cyclops Women: Considerations of Debates on Surrealism and Anthropology." *Critique of Anthropology* 13, no. 1 (1993): 57–75.

Robinson, Geoffrey. *The Dark Side of Paradise: Political Violence in Bali*. Ithaca, NY: Cornell University Press, 1998.

Robinson, Geoffrey. *The Killing Season: A History of the Indonesian Massacres, 1965–66*. Princeton, NJ: Princeton University Press, 2018.

Rony, Fatimah Tobing. "The Photogenic Cannot Be Tamed: Margaret Mead and Gregory Bateson's 'Trance and Dance in Bali.'" *Discourse* 28, no. 1 (Winter 2006): 5–27.

Rony, Fatimah Tobing. *The Third Eye: Race, Cinema, and Ethnographic Spectacle*. Durham, NC: Duke University Press, 1996.

Rosen, Phil. "Document and Documentary: On the Persistence of Historical Concepts." In *Change Mummified: Cinema, Historicity, Theory*, 225–63. Minneapolis: University of Minnesota Press, 2001.

Rotha, Paul. *The Film Till Now, a Survey of the Cinema*. London: J. Cape, 1930.

Santikarma, Degung. "Monument, Document and Mass Grave." In *Beginning to Remember: The Past in the Indonesian Present*, edited by Mary Zurbuchen. Seattle: University of Washington Press, 2004.

Santikarma, Degung. "Pecalangan di Bali: 'Siaga Budaya' atau Membudayakan Siaga?" *Kompas*, September 29, 2002.

Schneider, Rebecca. "Performance Remains." *Performance Research* 6, no. 2 (2001): 103.

Schneider, Rebecca. *Performing Remains: Art and War in Times of Theatrical Reenactment*. Abingdon, UK: Routledge, 2011.

Sears, Laurie J. *Situated Testimonies: Dread and Enchantment in an Indonesian Literary Archive*. Honolulu: University of Hawaii Press, 2013.

Sen, Krishna. "Indonesia: Screening a Nation in the Post-New Order." In *Contemporary Asian Cinema: Popular Culture in a Global Frame*, edited by Anne Tereska Ciecko, 96–107. Oxford: Berg, 2006.

Sen, Krishna. *Indonesian Cinema: Framing the New Order*. London: Zed, 1994.

Sen, Krishna. "Indonesian Women at Work." In *Gender and Power in Affluent Asia*, edited by Krishna Sen and Maila Stevens, 35–62. London: Routledge, 1998.

Sharpe, Christina. *In the Wake: On Blackness and Being*. Durham, NC: Duke University Press, 2016.

Sharpe, Jenny. *Ghosts of Slavery: A Literary Archaeology of Black Women's Lives*. Minneapolis: University of Minnesota Press, 2003.

Siddiquee, Imran. "Not Everyone's *Boyhood*." *Atlantic*, September 10, 2014.

Sitney, P. Adams. "The Cinematic Gaze of Joseph Cornell." In *Joseph Cornell*, edited by Kynaston McShine, 69–89. New York: Museum of Modern Art, 1980.

Solnit, Rebecca. *A Field Guide to Getting Lost*. New York: Penguin, 2005.

Solomon-Godeau, Abigail. "Going Native: Paul Gauguin and the Invention of Primitivist Modernism." In *The Expanding Discourse: Feminism and Art History*, edited by Norma Broude and Mary D. Garrard, 314–31. New York: HarperCollins, 1992. Original edition, *Art in America* 77 (July 1989): 118–29.

Sontag, Susan. *On Photography*. New York: Doubleday, 1977.

Spivak, Gayatri Chakravorty. "Can the Subaltern Speak?" *Wedge* 708 (Spring 1985): 122–31.

Spivak, Gayatri Chakravorty. *A Critique of Postcolonial Reason: Toward a History of the Vanishing Present*. Cambridge, MA: Harvard University Press, 1999.

Stoeffel, Kat. "Joyce Maynard: Don't Call Me a 'Mistress.'" *The Cut, New York Magazine*, February 3, 2014. https://www.thecut.com/2014/02/joyce-maynard -dont-call-me-a-mistress.html.

Stoler, Ann Laura. *Race and the Education of Desire: Foucault's History of Sexuality and the Colonial Order of Things*. Durham, NC: Duke University Press, 1995.

Stoler, Ann Laura, with Karen Strassler. "Memory-Work in Java: A Cautionary Tale." In *Carnal Knowledge and Imperial Power: Race and the Intimate in Colonial Rule*, 162–203. Berkeley: University of California Press, 2002.

Strassler, Karen. *Refracted Visions: Popular Photography and Natural Modernity in Java*. Durham, NC: Duke University Press, 2010.

Stuckey, Charles. "The First Tahitian Years." In *The Art of Paul Gauguin*, edited by Richard R. Brettell, 210–17. Washington, DC: National Gallery of Art, 1988.

Sunindyo, Saraswati. "Murder, Gender, and the Media: Sexualizing Politics and Violence." In *Fantasizing the Feminine in Indonesia*, edited by Laurie Sears. Durham, NC: Duke University Press, 1996.

Suryakusuma, Julia. "From Both Sides Now: Shari'ah Morality, 'Pornography,' and Women in Indonesia." In *Legitimacy, Legal Development, and Change: Law and Modernization Reconsidered*, edited by David K. Linnan, 193–212. London: Routledge, 2012

Sweetman, David. *Paul Gauguin: A Life*. New York: Simon and Schuster, 1993.

Taub, Ben. "We Have No Choice: A Nigerian Girl's Desperate Bid to Get to Europe." *New Yorker*, April 10, 2017.

Teilhet-Fisk, Jehanne. *Paradise Reviewed: An Interpretation of Gauguin's Polynesian Symbolism*. Ann Arbor: University of Michigan Research Press, 1983.

Thompson, Geoff. "Indonesia Passes Tough New Anti-porn Laws." ABC News, October 31, 2008. https://www.abc.net.au/news/2008-10-31/indonesia-passes-tough-new-anti-porn-laws/188804.

Thompson, Krista A. *An Eye for the Tropics: Tourism, Photography, and Framing the Caribbean Picturesque*. Durham, NC: Duke University Press, 2006.

Tiwon, Sylvia. "Failure of the Imaginary: Gendered Excess of the Indonesian Nation." In *Trans-Status Subjects: Gender in the Globalization of South and Southeast Asia*, edited by Sonita Sarker and Esha Niyogi De. Durham, NC: Duke University Press, 2002.

Tiwon, Sylvia. "Lust of the Eye: *The Act of Killing* and Aesthetic Sensibility." *Critical Asian Studies* 46, no. 1 (2014): 200–203.

Tiwon, Sylvia. "Models and Maniacs: Rearticulating the Female in Indonesia." In *Fantasizing the Feminine in Indonesia*, edited by Laurie Sears. Durham, NC: Duke University Press, 1996.

Trachtenberg, Alan. *Reading American Photographs: Images as History, Mathew Brady to Walker Evans*. New York: Hill and Wang, 1989.

Tristan, Flora. "Les Femmes de Lima." *Revue de Paris* 32 (1836). https://fr.wikisource.org/wiki/Les_Femmes_de_Lima.

van Heeren, Katinka. *Contemporary Indonesian Film: Spirits of Reform and Ghosts from the Past*. Leiden: Brill, 2012.

Viswanathan, Gauri. *Outside the Fold: Conversion, Modernity, and Belief*. Princeton, NJ: Princeton University Press, 1998.

Vollard, Ambroise. *Recollections of a Picture Dealer*. Translated by Violet M. MacDonald. London: Constable, 1936.

Vollard, Ambroise. *Souvenirs d'un marchand de tableaux*. Paris: Éditions Albin Michel, 1937.

Wallace, Michele. "Variations on Negation and the Heresy of Black Feminist Creativity." In *Invisibility Blues: From Pop to Theory*, 213–40. London: Verso, 1990.

Waugh, Thomas. "Acting to Play Oneself: Performance in Documentary." In *The Right to Play Oneself: Looking Back on Documentary Film*, 71–92. Minneapolis: University of Minnesota Press, 2011.

Wees, William C. *Recycled Images: The Art and Politics of Found Footage Films*. New York: Anthology Film Archives, 1993.

Weheliye, Alexander G. *Habeas Viscus: Racializing Assemblages, Biopolitics, and Black Feminist Theories of the Human*. Durham, NC: Duke University Press, 2014.

White, Patricia. *Women's Cinema, World Cinema: Projecting Contemporary Feminisms*. Durham, NC: Duke University Press, 2015.

Wiener, Margaret J. *Visible and Invisible Realms: Power, Magic, and Colonial Conquest in Bali*. Chicago: University of Chicago Press, 1995.

Williams, Linda. *Figures of Desire: A Theory and Analysis of Surrealist Film*. Urbana: University of Illinois Press, 1981.

Winston, Brian. "The Tradition of the Victim in the Griersonian Documentary." In *New Challenges for Documentary*, edited by Alan Rosenthal, 269–87. Berkeley: University of California Press, 1988.

Wollen, Peter. "Godard and Counter Cinema: Vent d'Est." In *Readings and Writings: Semiotic Counter-Strategies*. London: Verso, 1982.

Yngvesson, Dag. 2014. "Film Review, Joshua Oppenheimer et al., *Jagal/Act of Killing*." *Wacana* 15, no. 1 (2014): 212–17.

Index

Deren, Maya, 78
Deshpande, Shekhar, 159–60, 169
Desilina, Nina, 168
Desnos, Robert, 131
DeWaard, Nellie, 124
Dewan Gereja-Gereja di Indonesia (Council of Churches in Indonesia), 172
Dharma Pertiwi, 151
Dharma Wanita, 151
Diallo, Nafissatou, 67
Dinata, Nia: actors supported by, 210n24; *Berbagi Suami* by, 160–61; censorship and activism of, 169–72; *Cerita Dari Pulau*, 166–69; collaboration in work of, 162–65, 184–86; diversity in work of, 154–58; film career of, 14, 19, 22–23; Indonesian film industry and, 161; Kalyana Shira production company and, 153–54; omnibus films of, 158–60; *Perempuan Punya Cerita* production, 161–62; *Pertaruhan* documentary by, 148–50, 173–80; on Pornography Law (Indonesia), 152; Suharto regime and, 150–53; visual biopolitics and work of, 106, 181–84; women filmmakers supported by, 208n3
diversity: in Dinata's filmmaking, 153–58; in network narrative casting, 167–69
Divine Horsemen: The Living Gods of Haiti (film), 78
Diyose, Dominique Agisca, 156
Djayadiningrat, Dimas, 170–71
documentary film: anthropology and ethnography and, 21–22, 72–73, 77–82, 85–87; auteur directors and, 93; auteur effect in, 93; collaboration in, 175–80; Dinata's production of, 148–50, 173–80, 183–86; endangered humanity in, 92, 98–99; as ethnography, 21–22, 73, 78; hypervisibility in, 93–95; Indonesian production of, 101–2; Mead-Bateson production of, 72–73, 77–82, 92–93, 95; network narrative blurring of documentary and feature film, 102; *Pertaruhan* and transformation of, 178–80; poor and marginalized subjects in, 174; reflexive documentary, 90–95; representation in, 93–95; under Suharto regime, 88–90, 94–95, 100–102; visual biopolitics and, 90–100. *See also* specific films

double consciousness, Du Bois's theory of, 11, 16
Du Bois, W. E. B., 11–12, 14
dukun (wise man or healer), 139
Dutch Colonial Institute, 131
Dutch colonial regime, 87–90, 118–28, 130–34, 140–46
Dutch East Indies: in *Mother Dao*, 137–46, 138. *See* Indonesia
DuVernay, Ava, 5, 191n4
Dwyer, Leslie, 88

East of Borneo (film), 130–31
Edmond, Rod, 48, 56, 197n54
Edwards, Elizabeth, 113
Eisenman, Stephen, 48
Eliana, Eliana, 167
Emak dari Jambi (documentary), 184, 185
endangered humanity, in documentary film, 92, 98–99
Engage Media, 102
ethnography: *Act of Killing* as, 21–22, 73, 74, 78, 98–100; colonialism and, 77–82; documentary film as, 21–22, 72–73, 77–82, 85–87; exoticization of Bali and Java and, 77–87, 78; Other in, 76–82; schizophrenia and, 77–78, 82–87; surrealism and, 113–16; visual biopolitics and, 18–20, 84–87, 98–100
Eve Exotique (Gauguin), 45, 48
exoticism: ethnographic film and, 77–82, 78; Larsati's discussion of, 103–7; photography and, 116; visual biopolitics and, 58–59
Exposition Universelle (1889), 4, 33–36, 78, 130, 193n35

Fabian, Johannes, 135
Fajar, Rikki M., 184
Fanon, Frantz, 9; on Blackness, 16; third space theory of, 11–12
fascinating cannibalism: in *Act of Killing*, 92–95, 99–100; Indonesian woman and, 103–7
Fatata te miti (Near the sea) (Gauguin), 29
Fauser, Annegret, 33–36
female circumcision *(khitan)*, Dinata's documentary on, 148–50, 175–80
Figura, Starr, 197n53
Film independan, 182–86
Film Law no. 8/1992 (Indonesia), 171–72

Morice, Charles, 29
Mother Dao, the Turtlelike (found footage film): poetry in, 146; power structures in, 136–46; production of, 131–34; resistance in, 134–36, *137*; temporality in, 112–13, 137–46; visual biopolitics and, 8, 11, 22, 106, 134–36, *141*
Mowll Mathews, Nancy, 48
Mucha, Alphonse, 29, 50–54, *51, 53*, 64–65, 198n72
Mucha, Jiří, 33, 50
Muhammadiyah, 172
Mulvey, Laura, 18, 155–56
Munson, Samuel, 122
Murnau, F. W., 131
Muslims, Batak of Sumatra and, 120

Nahdlatul Ulama, 172
Narottama, Aghi, 168–69
Nasution, Arswendi, 167
necropolitics, colonialism and, 59–60, 142–43
"Necropolitics" (Mbembe), 142
"négresse," as French derogatory connotation of, 194n7, 196nn41–42
neoliberalism: in *Act of Killing*, 93–95; colonialism and, 10–11
network narratives: blurring of documentary and fiction in, 166–69; breakdown of hierarchy in, 168–69; in Dinata's films, 158–60
neuroscience, visual biopolitics and, 9
New Order (Orde Baru, Indonesia), 8–9, 22; in *Act of Killing*, 91–94; hypermasculinity of, 91–95; Kartini as icon in, 93, 151, 193n35; Larsati's discussion of, 103–7; visual biopolitics and, 87–90; women's role in, 103–7
Nias, Indonesian myth of, 144–45
Ni Ngales, 80, 82–83, 85–87
Noa Noa (Gauguin), 32, 44–45, 56–57, 59, 197n54
Noer, Arifin C., 73, 88–90
Noer, Jajang C., 154–55
Nolan, Christopher, 157–58
No Más Bebés (documentary), 17, 192n27
Nommensen, Ingwer Ludwig, 117–18, 120–28, *121*
Nona Nyonya? (Miss or Mrs?) (film), 176

nongovernmental organizations, documentary films by, 102
norms: biopolitics and, 8–9; racism and, 20–21
Nosferatu (film), 131
Nugroho, Garin, 102, 161

Obama, Barack, 92
O'Brien, Patty, 45, 199n95
O'Conor, Roderick, 63
O'Grady, Lorraine, 39
Oka, Putu, 101–2
Olympia (Manet), 27, 29, 38–39, *40*, 43–46, 56, 59
omnibus films: Dinata's production of, 158–60, 173–80; distribution of, 177–80; women directors of, 161–62
online media, Indonesian production of, 102
Oppenheimer, Joshua, 6, 8, 11, 21–22, 73; *Act of Killing* directed by, 90–95; as auteur director, 95–100, 204n67, 205n70; *The Look of Silence* (documentary) by, 100–102
Orientalism: in *Act of Killing*, 99; Indonesian culture and, 193n35

Pack, Nina, 3, 32, 61
Pakusudewo, Tio, 156
Pancasila Youth group, 93
Pandolfo, Stefania, 12, 84, 96–97, 111, 143–44
Papadimitriou, Constantin (Kiki), 153, 208n3
Pap smears, scarcity in Indonesia of, 174, 176, 181, 208n3
Paramaditha, Intan, 91, 172, 210n33
Paris, je t'aime (film), 159–60, 210n23
Parisada Hindu Dharma Indonesia (Hinduism Society), 172
Partai Komunis Indonesia (Communist Party of Indonesia, PKI), 4–5, 89–90, 103–7; "Genjer Genjer" as party song for, 110–11
Patrice, Isabelle, 167
Payne, Alexander, 160
Pelzer, Karl, 128
Pembinaan Kesejahteraan Keluarga (PKK) (Female Empowerment and Welfare Movement), 151–53
Pengkhianatan G30S/PKI (film), 73, 74, 88–91, 98–102, 110, 173, 199n1
Perempuan Kisah Dalam Guntingan (Women behind the Cut) (documentary), 176

replica, Larsati's discussion of, 12, 21–22, 31, 52, 95, 102, 104–6, 114, 131
representation: of Blackness, 14; in documentary film, 93–95; framing and, 23
Republic of Indonesia, creation of, 5
resistance: female creativity and embodiment and, 6; sound as, 138–39; visual politics and theory of, 11–12
Reynolds, Diamond (Lavish), 15–16, 20
Reza, Riri, 159, 167, 171
Rheinische Mission, 121
Richardson, Michael, 206n3
right to kill, biopolitics and, 8–9
Rippl-Rónai, József, 32
roadshows, Indonesian film distribution and, 177–78, 180, 184–86
Robinson, Geoffrey, 88, 94–95
Rockefeller, Michael, 125
Rony, Fatimah Tobing, as film director, 161–69
Roosevelt, André, 80
Rose Hobart (film), 116, 130–32, 145
Rosen, Phil, 131
Rouch, Jean, 78
Rowlands, Gena, 160
Rukun, Adi, 100–102
Run Lola Run (film), 158

Saleh, Fadillah Vamp, 101–2
Salim, Ferry, 154
Salinger, J. D., 199n98
Salon painting, nude women in, 38
Sana'ah, *168*, 168–69
Sang Penari (film), 101
Santikarma, Degung, 87–90
SARA censorship, 172
Sardi, Lukman, 156
savagery: in *Act of Killing*, 91–95; colonialism and trope of, 41, 43, 59, 196n50; missionaries' views of, 122–28; Parisian obsession with, 60–67; visual biopolitics and, 84–90
schizophrenia, Mead's ethnographic film and, 77–78, 82–87, 200n9, 200n11, 201n22
Schneider, Rebecca, 87
Schneklud, Fritz, 52, 54
Schoedsack, Ernest, 120
Sechan, Sarah, 164, *165*, 210n24
Séguin, Armand, 57, 63

Septa, Yoga, 167
Seriem (Javanese dancer), 4, 33–36, *34*, 41, 79, 145
Sérusier, Paul, 52, *54*
Setiawan, Iwan, 175
Setyastuti (dancer and choreographer), 106
sexuality: in Dinata's films, 161–62, 174–80; exoticization of Bali and Java, 34–36; in French culture, 36–38; in Gauguin's work, 47; state regulation of body and, 181–86; visibility and, 17
shame culture in Indonesia, 152–53
Sharpe, Christina, 92
Shoah (documentary), 100
Short Cuts (film), 158
Si Singamangaraja XII, Raja, 121, 126
silence, visual biopolitics and, 104–7
sinetron (Indonesian telenovela), 150
Sitomorang, Sitor, 139
Slamet, Bing, 110
slavery: contemporary impact of, 92; in France, 194n7; in *Mother Dao*, 142–44; photography of, 49–50
Smith, Tracy K., 146
Society Must Be Defended (Foucault), 8
Soekia (Javanese dancer), 4, 33–36, *34*, 41, 79, 145
Soekoen, 86–87
Solnit, Rebecca, 31
Solo (Surakarta) court, 4
Solomon-Godeau, Abigail, 47, 58
Sontag, Susan, 116, 133, 144
Sopha, Ira Maya, 156
sound, as resistance, in *Mother Dao*, 138–46
Spies, Walter, 80
Spillers, Hortense, 9
Spivak, Gayatri, 198n94
Srebnik, Simon, 100
state power, biopolitics as, 8
states of exception, 8–9, 142–43, 193n10
St. Louis World's Fair (1904), 135
Stoler, Ann, 38, 113–15, 196n37
The Stone Breakers (Courbet), 179
storytelling: photography and, 118–28; savagery in, 13; visual biopolitics and, 9–10
Strassler, Karen, 114–15
Stratz, C. H., 38, 196n37
Strauss-Kahn, Dominique, 67, 194n7
Strindberg, August, 29